MW00825230

China Urbanizing

THE CITY IN THE TWENTY-FIRST CENTURY

Eugenie L. Birch and Susan M. Wachter, Series Editors

A complete list of books in the series is available from the publisher.

CHINA URBANIZING

Impacts and Transitions

Edited by

Weiping Wu
and
Qin Gao

PENN

UNIVERSITY OF PENNSYLVANIA PRESS

PHILADELPHIA

Published by
University of Pennsylvania Press
Philadelphia, Pennsylvania 19104-4112
www.upenn.edu/pennpress

Printed in the United States of America on acid-free paper

10 9 8 7 6 5 4 3 2 1

Library of Congress Cataloging-in-Publication Data
Names: Wu, Weiping, author, editor. |
Gao, Qin, author, editor.
Title: China urbanizing : impacts and transitions /
edited by Weiping Wu and Qin Gao.
Other titles: City in the twenty-first century book series.
Description: 1st edition. | Philadelphia : University
of Pennsylvania Press, [2022] | Series: The city in
the twenty-first century | Includes bibliographical
references and index.
Identifiers: LCCN 2022011665 |
ISBN 9781512823011 (hardback)
Subjects: LCSH: Urbanization—China. | Urbanization—
Social aspects—China. | Urban policy—China.
Classification: LCC HT384.C6 C53 2022 |
DDC 307.760951—dc23/eng/20220322
LC record available at https://lccn.loc.gov/2022011665

ISBN 9781512823011 (hardback)
ISBN 9781512823028 (eBook)

CONTENTS

Introduction   1
  Weiping Wu and Qin Gao

1. Paying for Urbanization: Land Finance and Impacts   16
  Weiping Wu

2. Cities for Whom? The 2017 Beijing Demolitions in Context   38
  Shiqi Ma and Jeremy Wallace

3. Housing Markets, Residential Sorting, and Spatial Segregation   61
  Shin Bin Tan, Wenfei Xu, and Sarah Williams

4. Has the Economic Situation of Rural Migrant Workers in
Urban China Been Improving? An Updated Assessment   91
  Shi Li and Binbin Wu

5. Urban Poverty in China: Has *Dibao* Been an Effective
Policy Response?   115
  Qin Gao

6. Implementing the National New-Type Urbanization Plan:
Regional Variations   131
  Juan Chen, Pierre F. Landry, and Deborah Davis

7. Dementia or Anomie: What Explains the Missing Older
Adults Phenomenon in China?   149
  Guibin Xiong

8. Environmental Impact of Urbanization in Post-Reform China   165
  Peilei Fan

9. Shifting Exposures in China's Urbanization Experience:
Implications for Health   188
       Justin Remais

10. Prospects and Social Impact of Big Data–Driven Urban
Governance in China: Provincializing Smart City Research   205
       Alan Smart and Dean Curran

List of Contributors   229

Index   233

China Urbanizing

Introduction

Weiping Wu and Qin Gao

t is only in the recent decade that China turned majority urban, a marked leap given that less than 20 percent of its population lived in cities around 1979. With the onset of economic reforms since then, the scope and magnitude of change occurring through urbanization are unprecedented, impacting nearly all facets of society. Over 700 million people live in cities now, with another 200–300 million more expected to urbanize in the next decade or so. The number of cities has increased from 213 in 1979 to 681 in 2020, according to China's National Bureau of Statistics.

Shaping China's urbanization since 1979 is a set of largely internal forces. Market reforms have led to fundamental and structural changes in the economic system and brought about genuine competition. In particular, after 1983 these changes have propelled manufacturing to the forefront (and later services), leading to nothing short of an industrial revolution and making cities the engine of growth. Guiding urban development is a market-enabled institutional fix, in the form of increased autonomy for local governments in terms of resource allocation and investment decisions. In addition, fueling the urban economies is the largest tide of migration in human history, with millions of farmers leaving the countryside for cities. But such human mobility intersects with the household registration system (or *hukou*)—a legacy of state socialism that excludes most migrants from enjoying the full benefits of urbanization and limits their social protection and upward mobility (World Bank and Development Research Center of the State Council 2014).

As a subject of inquiry, urbanization provides a conceptual container for the study of populations and the natural and built environments within spatial concentrations of human habitation and exchange. This book captures the impact of China's sweeping urbanization on the country's socioeconomic welfare, environment and resources, urban form and lifestyle, and population and health. It is also a book about China, in which we provide new perspectives to understand the transitions underway and the gravity of that progress, particularly in the context of demographic shifts and climate change. Given the breadth of urbanization research, we acknowledge the multidisciplinary nature of the discourse and bring together scholars through a collaborative forum of dialogue. By so doing, chapters in this volume engage inquiries that cross geographic, temporal, and disciplinary boundaries.

Situating Chinese Urbanization

Collectively, the contributions to this book achieve three interconnected aims. The first is to explore, empirically and historically, how the process of urbanization has shaped and been influenced by the social, economic, and physical interactions that take place in and beyond cities, as well as the state interventions intended to regulate such interactions. Various policies have endured from China's planned economy, largely as an intentional means of providing gradual marketization, and they often complicate the process of urbanization with outcomes both favorable and unfavorable to the state and society at large (W. Wu 2018b). Most challenging, among others, is the incomplete path to urban citizenship by millions of migrants (Solinger 1999), as well as farmers affected by the increasing encroachment of urban development into rural areas (the so-called in situ urbanization). Together with the unemployed, they constitute the bulk of the growing urban poor. Sharply diverging from the legacy of socialist cities, urban neighborhoods are now home to increasingly disparate populations in varying housing conditions. The socioeconomic realities on the ground point to a landscape more stratified by indicators of wealth, privilege, and life opportunities than in the past, when state socialism was in place. These conditions have been precipitating a recent policy dialogue, particularly at the national level, to shift from land-based urbanization to a more human-centered trajectory.

The second aim of the book is to examine the shifts and transitions emerging in urban China. As economic growth slowed down nationally following the 2008 global recession, the urban sector began showing signs of maturity and in some cases contraction, with mounting building vacancies in interior cities and local debt across the nation. Compounding this new economic and fiscal geography is the dramatic demographic transition that has been underway. Before China has gotten rich, it has gotten old, with an unprecedented proportion of an aging population, particularly in cities, where the country's prior one-child policy was enforced most effectively. On a more positive note, China's rising role in the global discourse on climate change has generated marked progress in how cities interact with the environment and planet. In no small way, this progress benefits from the multiplying applications of new technologies and data science. But demographic and environmental transitions point to an urgency for progress in that some of the gains Chinese cities are making will be wiped away by the consequences of climate change, as well as by unsustainable practices of municipal authorities. One such practice is the proliferation of land leases, which has accelerated the sprawling and fragmented urban spatial expansion (World Bank 2015).

Our third aim is to explore new sources of information for conducting research on urban China, as official data are known to be inconsistent and problematic in regard to population, as well as in other dimensions of society (Chan 2007). Scholars have long recognized the need to establish metrics and scales of inquiry that can appropriately accommodate the contemporary context (W. Wu 2018a). Particularly noteworthy are satellite and street-level imagery data drawn from technology companies such as Baidu and Google, as they provide more accurate and updated depictions of the built environment. Google Maps updates its satellite imagery on a roughly monthly basis, while other independent satellite operators may have more frequent imagery updates. A number of chapters in the book demonstrate the promise as well as the challenges in improved data collection methodologies and emerging sources of information, in our effort to account for the complexity and heterogeneity that characterize contemporary Chinese urbanization. An uncanny benefit of these new data sources has become even more pertinent amid the COVID-19 global pandemic and consequential barriers in conducting field research.

Notwithstanding the book's strong empirical contributions that are very much about China, we situate urbanization in the interconnected forces of historical legacies, contemporary state interventions, and human and environmental conditions. This conception is essential for capturing the complexity of the phenomenon in its historical and regional variations. Embracing this notion, the chapters in the book, some more explicitly than others, question the conventional imagination centering cities in the West. Theoretical touchstones have emerged as a result. First, as argued in the chapter by Smart and Curran, we recognize the need to "provincialize" smart city research. For urban governance powered by data analytics, China is probably setting the path, rendering efforts in the West comparatively lacking in ambition. To provincialize is to decenter perspectives that have allowed theories situated in the context and tradition of a particular world region to be seen as universal. Eurocentric ideas may be drawn from particular intellectual histories so as not to hold universal validity; by recognizing this, we are to provincialize Europe. Also related to the notion of provincializing is the narrative that the widening use of market instruments in China serves a rather different purpose from capital accumulation in the traditional sense. We see manifestation of this narrative in the practice of land finance, discussed in the chapter by Wu. This "planning centrality, market instruments" framing (F. Wu 2018) is one step closer to transporting China from being provincialized to charting a competing pathway, especially within the discourse of neoliberalism.

Parallel to our work, other China scholars have noted the necessity to add "new narratives to the urban imagination" (F. Wu 2020, 460), as highlighted in a special issue of the journal *Urban Studies*. The value of empirical studies, one of the special issue editors argues, is not always for general theorization but rather to present new ideas to enrich our understanding of cities (F. Wu 2020). On this point, however, there are divergent views. Within the special issue, Hamnett (2020) juxtaposes the uniqueness of Chinese urbanization with the historical notion of American exceptionalism that has been disputed in recent decades. His tentative conclusion makes the case for "a specific school of Chinese urban theory trying to theorize the peculiarities and particularities" (697), as the nature of Chinese urbanization is fundamentally different, particularly in regard to the "role of party and state and state ownership of land and financing of development" (693). Our position, however, is more nuanced, in that we recognize the critical role of domestic politics and power dynamics—as aptly captured in a recent edited volume by Eggleston, Oi, and Wang (2017)—while we look to advance a notion of "China in the World and the World in China" (Wu and Frazier 2018, xl). This is an attempt to move beyond "an exclusively state-centric framework" (xli), as growing connections and flows in ideas and practices between China and the rest of the world in both directions have fundamentally complicated a plausible imagination of Chinese exceptionalism.

To wit, adding to the fluid and uneven landscape of urbanization is a rank of shrinking cities, consequential of state sector and industrial restructuring. While the fundamental logic may differ, the dire outcome resembles the long-standing phenomenon of manufacturing rust belts in the West. This is the subject of a compilation of studies by Chinese scholars (Long and Gao 2019), and their insights echo ours. The so-called new normal in the twenty-first century further compounds the dynamism that we have frequently associated with a rising China. Economic slowdowns, coupled with the COVID-19 pandemic, have led to conundrums throughout the urban sector. The reshaping of economic, social, and environmental geography in cities is at the center of another collection that takes a similarly multidisciplinary approach and focuses on exploring a new development model at this historical inflection point (Huang 2020).

Together, these studies of urban China remind us that urbanization is far from a monolithic and nationwide phenomenon, a narrative echoed in yet another recent collection that traces mobility and marginality as it relates to urbanization in modern China (Clothey and Dilworth 2020). Any notion of a monolithic "Chinese school" of urban studies is also problematic in spite of recurring challenges on the ground and inveterate perspectives in academia. The last pertinent compilation addresses just this (Forrest, Ren, and Wissink 2019). It cautions that "the entwined issues of Chinese exceptionalism and methodological nationalism can restrict urban research, its interpretations, and broader applications" (J. Ren 2019, 231), and advocates that "by positioning the Chinese city in a comparative perspective" we can better understand urban China (X. Ren 2019, 14). This book is an important addition to the recent canon of urban China studies that marks the commencement of renewed attention to empirically grounded theorization in a global context.

Urbanization and Its Impacts

A market-enabled institutional fix, in which central and local governments use freer movements of labor and exchange of capital to propel economic development, has produced policies and patterns of urbanization somewhat unique to contemporary China (W. Wu 2018b). Without fundamentally altering the country's political and governance structure, this approach has produced spectacular results, at least if judging from the physicality of transformation. The Chinese city today looks different and develops in a drastically different fashion from the once egalitarian, low-profile, and walking-scale socialist city. Spaces of exclusivity that insulate privileged groups now juxtapose with settlements for the growing underclass in the cityscape. Pooling online real estate listing data, the chapter by Tan, Xu, and Williams provides evidence that Chinese cities—whether economically booming like Shanghai and Chengdu, or experiencing declines like Shenyang—are undergoing an increase in spatial differentiation of their market housing over time. The former, with larger population sizes and a more affluent, educated population, experiences more intensive residential sorting and high-end housing segregation.

At the center of urban processes during market reforms is the question of land. In the face of an increasing disparity between local fiscal revenue and expenditure responsibilities, the leasing of land use rights has become a critical source of income to offset the gap, and also serves as collateral for securing bank loans (the so-called land financialization). This imperative underscores the kind of incentive that municipal authorities have to engage in "land-infrastructure leverage" to help pay for urbanization. The chapter by Wu outlines the spatial manifestation of land finance (and financialization): the steady growth of the urban footprint, often in sprawling and fragmented fashion. Lateral expansion encroaches on scarce agricultural land while rendering future infill development more costly and reducing the agglomeration benefits of compact urban cores. This has been a key contributor to the reduction in urban population densities in thirty-five major cities across the country at a much faster annual rate of decline than cities in Europe, the United States, India, and sub-Saharan Africa from 2000 to 2014 (Xu et al. 2019). Of course, the first two regions are not entirely comparable given the much lower initial densities, but the latter two are. Not only is the downward trend in China outstanding, but it also points to how land-based urbanization exacerbates an already fragile human-environment relationship.

Additional environmental impacts are in the form of air pollution and heat-island effect, as shown in the chapter by Fan. The former is particularly challenging: more than half of the world's five hundred polluted cities are in China. While economic development helps to alleviate environmental problems such as air pollution and leads to more provision of urban green space, the dynamics can vary for different pollutants. For instance, in some cities, NO_2 (mostly from industrial pollution) has declined continuously, whereas $PM_{2.5}$ (whose source composition is much more complex and diverse) shows a nonlinear trend. The chapter by Remais further points out that the profound overhaul of transportation and energy use in China's cities has slowed progress on ambient air pollution reductions, including for particulate matter, ozone, nitrogen oxides, and mixtures of these and other pollutants.

These and other environmental challenges bring with them health consequences, though the impact of urbanization on human and social conditions are more wide-ranging. A positive effect on overall human health, measured in improved physical and mental outcomes, can be attributed to better infrastructure, particularly in the form of a sewerage system (Hou et al. 2019). On the other hand, the chapter by Remais shows that short- and long-term exposures to air pollutants across urban centers in China are associated with increased total, cardiovascular, and respiratory mortality, adverse pregnancy outcomes, and other significant health effects. Yet while the mechanisms by which urbanization influences health involve density-dependent processes (such as close contact) or socio-environmental phenomena (such as traffic accidents and injuries), establishing the health effects will require more nuanced and complex measures of urbanization that reflect urban features and characteristics, the number and configuration of cities, and urban activities that contribute to environmental and social stressors. There is still no consensus on the suitability of particular urbanization measures for epidemiologic analysis, nor for the surrounding health-relevant exposures that dominate, yielding major challenges for the estimation of the causal effects of urbanization on health in China. Hence, Remais's chapter also makes an important theoretical contribution through its critique of the often linear framework for understanding the dynamics of water quality, air pollution, and infectious diseases in China.

Nonetheless, we are fully cognizant of how urbanization affects human conditions at a more visceral level. A number of chapters in this volume hone in on this pressing issue, particularly as related to the millions of rural migrants now living in cities. The chapter by Ma and Wallace poses a critical question: cities for whom? While redevelopment changes the trajectory for the urbanization of land, its ground-zero demolition process in recent sweeps has severely affected migrants and threatened their already weak bonds to cities—yet another sign that migrant labor is more desired than migrant presence. Until recently, policy responses toward rural migrants had slowly moved in a more humane direction. As a result, their experience in the urban labor markets—the subject of study in the chapter by Li and Wu—improved: more choices in urban employment, more opportunities to enter high-end service industries, and more potential to choose white-collar occupations. Their wages increased rapidly as well, although the wage growth of well-educated rural migrant workers or higher-income groups exceeded that of less-educated ones or lower-income groups.

The sweeps of migrant residences profiled in the chapter by Ma and Wallace illustrate the contradictory impact of urbanization. They argue that the migrants who are able to remain in cities are likely to be thriving in part because many of those who are not doing well are being actively pushed out. The legacies of *hukou*, combined with state ownership of land, have created conditions of informality in "urban villages," where many migrants rent private housing and are more vulnerable to local government sweeps. Migrants now make up the bulk of the rising urban poor and present a long-term challenge that requires more sustainable and effective policies to address, as pointed out in Gao's chapter focusing on urban poverty and its policy responses. For instance, while the participation rate of rural migrant workers in urban social security programs has increased, a large number remain excluded because of barriers related to system design. *Dibao*, the primary safety net program to support the livelihood of the urban poor, is inaccessible to nearly all rural migrants in cities.

Urbanization touches not only the lives of migrants but also their families left behind in the countryside. These were estimated at fifty-eight million children, forty-seven million women, and forty-five million older adults in 2015 (Li et al. 2018). In Xiong's chapter, we witness the wrenching rise of rural older adults missing from their homes, reported at about half a million in 2015 alone. While declining health and mental capacity help explain this figure, there are social factors at work. Given the lack of a sufficient social security system in rural areas, older people traditionally rely on their adult children for care and financial support. Now with younger family members more likely to be away working in cities, a social breakdown in rural areas has accompanied large population outflows. Local governments have limited resources to attend to the problem of missing older adults, aggravating the situation.

Rapid urbanization has also challenged the system of governance, particularly as related to central-local relations. Cities have become the focal point in the administrative hierarchy, since they take on the role of growth engines nationwide and across different regions. For a long time, central and local government officials had divergent interests on questions of urban land requisition and demolition, with local officials pushing for more land grabs and the central government curbing this tendency in order to balance economic growth and political stability. The chapters by Wu and by Ma and

Wallace illustrate the central role of land in greasing the urban (re)development machines. But changing urban realities can prompt the realignment of bureaucratic incentives, as we have witnessed recently. The reassertion of the central government under the current political leadership in (re)directing urban trajectories is the subject of study in the chapter by Chen, Landry, and Davis. In response to some of the negative consequences of urbanization, the central government has launched the National New Comprehensive Urbanization Pilot Program on the heels of the National New-Type Urbanization Plan (2014–2020). There is evidence pointing to particular preferences in the selection of the pilot areas, and the authors' analysis shows that county-level economic development is the driving force behind further urbanization. This tendency may cause even greater disparities in China's already uneven urbanization process.

Transitions in Urbanization

Urbanization is by no means a linear process. Its course reflects as well as responds to transitions in the larger society. For instance, market transition has been the main driving force of urban expansion in the four decades since 1979. But as the growth of the national economy slowed after the 2008 global recession, signs of maturity appeared across the urban sector. Stagnating export markets have necessitated a new model of development based on domestic consumption and homegrown innovation. A confluence of these forces is reshaping urban socioeconomic and human geography. A number of chapters in the volume interrogate the major shifts and transitions emerging in China. Taken together, these transitions accentuate the urgent need for progress, as some of the gains Chinese cities are making may be offset by costs associated with additional investment and efforts.

The first is demographic transition: a shift from a high rate of natural population growth (a result of a high fertility rate) to a low rate of natural population growth. Policy efforts to promote later marriage and fewer children—most importantly the one-child policy that commenced in 1980 and lasted until 2015—have precipitated an earlier onset of demographic transition than in countries with a comparable level of wealth. Thus, China is getting old. As the relative size of the working-age population shrinks, the dependency ratio (dependent population divided by working-age population) is set to climb (Naughton 2018). The large influx of rural migrants has filled the gap in urban labor markets and fueled economic expansion. This comes with a high cost to the well-being of migrants' immediate and left-behind families, as shown in the chapters by Ma and Wallace and by Xiong.

The second is environmental transition. Generally, poor cities, primarily in the Global South, tend to create immediate and localized environmental problems. In contrast, cities of wealth are more likely to generate long-lasting and global environmental burdens, such as carbon emissions. While many Chinese cities have low levels of emissions on a per capita basis, the rapid pace and enormous scale of industrialization as well as the heavy reliance on fossil fuel have pushed the country to become the world's largest source of carbon. The chapter by Fan shows that more developed cities in China generally have lower levels of CO_2 emissions per capita than the national average, likely the result of the relocation of heavy industry to less developed neighboring regions. In contrast, cities with higher CO_2 emissions per capita mostly are those that are less developed and developing. Although some of these cities may have experienced economic growth (as measured by GDP per capita), they tend to have higher CO_2 emissions per capita than the developed cities.

The third can be termed the technological transition, detailed in the chapter by Smart and Curran. Articulating the interaction between urbanization and new technologies of governance, the chapter highlights how the scale of growth of the urban population both calls for and enables new management technologies based on the collection, analysis, and dissemination of big data. This transition is also predicated on substantial public investment in both technologies and infrastructural support systems. While it is too early to discuss in any depth, the heavy use of smart technologies, such as facial recognition and tracking with smartphones, in response to COVID-19 illustrates an emerging trend in urban China toward new forms of governance of biosecurity risks. Additional questions about privacy protection and state surveillance will become focal points in accounts of Chinese cities. Equally important, the technological transition is not neutral, as it has the potential to intensify risk inequalities in powerful ways (such as displacement of "backward" populations and informal inhabitants).

The final transition is a phenomenon that can be described as development delays. Considering health outcomes in his chapter, Remais refers to this as the length of time required to "reduce disease burden in a rapid, unplanned urbanization scenario to the level projected in a more controlled, planned urbanization scenario." It is an indication of additional years of continued investment in the infrastructure and human resources necessary to achieve the benefits that would have accrued earlier had health-protective policies been pursued. Climate change is inducing an analogous development delay by heightening the transmission of water-, sanitation-, and hygiene-related diseases. As the urbanization experience continues, such delays in otherwise expected health gains may confound the means of evaluating progress in health, limiting our ability to discern between policies that achieve population health and those that do not. The concepts of developmental progress and delays, while valuable for characterizing urban environmental health trends in broad strokes, fail to address key features of China's urbanization experience, including aspects that exhibit marked dynamism, sharp state changes, and important multiscale and cross-boundary characteristics. Clearly there are key areas where China's health and social progress have outpaced those of the global population, but with respect to most migrants as well as the urban poor, the risks associated with air and water pollution and the challenges of endemic and emerging infectious diseases remain enormous threats that undermine the age-old public health goal of achieving health before wealth.

Exploring New Sources of Information for Urban Research in China

Aside from enriching the conceptual and empirical grounds of studying urban China, this book makes a distinct methodological contribution. Until recently, scholars relied on official Chinese sources, including statistical yearbooks, census data, and official documents, as well as field research that typically focused on a limited scale. The accuracy and reliability of official data were questionable, but there were no good alternatives. Detailed statistics for individual cities were and remain limited in scope, even though provincial-level units publish their own statistics in addition to the national yearbooks of cities. Statistical data at a finer resolution, say at the neighborhood or block level, have generally been unavailable.

The Internet of things, however, has proved to be fruitful for urban scholars in search of alternative sources of information. The lack of more traditional infrastructure, such as landlines, has opened up opportunities for exchanges based on mobile and digital platforms. Infrastructural spending by the public and private sectors has facilitated the development of

information and communication technologies. Together, these developments underscore the rapid rise of so-called big data, including satellite imagery. For instance, Urban Data Party, a service provider dedicated to
urban big data, contains spatial data of all subway routes and stations in
Shanghai. Data based on Baidu Maps (the Chinese counterpart of Google
Maps) include the names of retail stores, addresses, coordinates, and business codes that are all geo-referenced.

Three chapters in this volume have tapped into emerging alternative
sources of information. Ma and Wallace use satellite imagery and digitalized
street views, courtesy of Google Maps, Planet, and Baidu Maps, to substantially supplement information from migrants and news reports. This allows
for a systematic measurement of the scale and scope of demolition in Beijing. High-resolution, high-frequency satellite images allow the authors to
identify the location of urban villages and trace the changes in their spatial
and temporal patterns. Using a quantitative approach in her chapter, Fan
has extracted for nine Chinese cities the spatial mean values of surface air
pollution by $PM_{2.5}$ (1999–2013) and NO_2 (1998–2011) from global satellite
and remote sensing imageries, both at 0.01×0.01 degrees spatial resolution.
The use of traditional air quality monitoring methods to collect similar data
would have been far more costly and time-consuming. The work in these
two chapters showcases the potential of combining different types of evidence, conducting analysis of big data, and discovering new theories with
the adoption of satellite imagery. While cross-checking for validity and reliability remains essential, the deployment of these data offers novel ways of
reading cities and generating urban epistemologies.

The chapter by Tan, Xu, and Williams draws entirely from another novel
source of data—online residential listings—that was unavailable before the
Internet age. By doing so, they overcome two critical limitations faced by
scholars studying residential segregation in the past. Traditionally, such studies relied on aggregated and aspatial census data defined by administrative
boundaries. Confronted with no access to official fine-grained, small-area
estimates, traditional studies also tended to lead to underestimation, given
the high population and building density in Chinese cities. In contrast, Tan,
Xu, and Williams use real estate listings from Fang.com ("Fang" is the pro-
nunciation of the Chinese word meaning "housing") for comparison across
multiple cities. Each unit listing includes the locational coordinates of the
residential complex, in addition to price, size, and time of construction,

making the data spatially situated. As a result, the authors are able to identify more localized, neighborhood-level patterns of segregation in ways that
using aggregated census data cannot. Clearly, the increasing proliferation
and popularity of online real estate websites in China have generated a new,
constantly updated, easily obtainable source of housing data that could be
used for research.

Organization of the Book

Following this introductory chapter, there are ten chapters in this volume.
To reflect the key themes of our collective contribution, we have organized
them into two sections. The five chapters in section 1 center around the first
aim: to explore how the process of urbanization has shaped and been influenced by the social, economic, and physical interactions that take place in
and beyond cities. Section 2, also with five chapters, emphasizes the shifts
and transitions emerging in urban China. For obvious reasons, it is not possible, nor is it desirable, to isolate the perspectives related to either aim.
Thus, the themes of impact and transition flow across the two sections. In a
similar fashion, our third aim of methodological exploration is captured by
a number of chapters in both sections.

While various contributors turn to conventions in different disciplinary
traditions, the overarching conceptual framing of this book remains consistent, with a sensitivity to the fluid state of development that China is undergoing and to its preexisting legacies. To wit, its cities generate environmental
and health impacts that resemble both more developed countries and less
developed counterparts. The demographic transition and social stratification taking place most intensely in urban areas present additional dilemmas
that challenge the prevailing theories of modernization and development.
Forms of urban governance arising in China before and during the CO-
VID-19 global pandemic put the country on the cutting edge of using smart
technologies. These are some of the key theoretical contributions that we
hope readers will take away. The sweeping pace and scope of urbanization
are bringing to the fore astonishing but unsustainable consequences for
human well-being and health and for the environment and climate. Understanding these impacts empirically through multidisciplinary perspectives
is another highlight of our undertaking in this book.

Acknowledgments

We are grateful for funding support by the Weatherhead East Asian Institute; Graduate School of Architecture, Planning and Preservation; China Center for Social Policy; and School of Social Work, all at Columbia University; as well as research assistance by Lanier Hagerty and Rui Yin.

Note

Throughout the book, illustrations without sources are based on the authors' own data or sources specified in the relevant chapter text.

References

Chan, Kam Wing. 2007. "Misconceptions and Complexities in the Study of China's Cities: Definitions, Statistics, and Implications." *Eurasian Geography and Economics* 48 (4): 383–412.

Clothey, Rebecca, and Richardson Dilworth, eds. 2020. *China's Urban Future and the Quest for Stability.* Montreal: McGill-Queen's University Press.

Eggleston, Karen, Jean C. Oi, and Yiming Wang, eds. 2017. *Challenges in the Process of China's Urbanization.* Stanford, CA: Walter H. Shorenstein Asia-Pacific Research Center.

Forrest, Ray, Julie Ren, and Bart Wissink, eds. 2019. *The City in China: New Perspectives on Contemporary Urbanism.* Bristol, UK: Bristol University Press.

Hamnett, Chris. 2020. "Is Chinese Urbanism Unique?" In "New Directions of Urban Studies in China," edited by Fulong Wu and Fangzhu Zhang, special issue, *Urban Studies* 57 (3): 690–700.

Hou, Bo, James Nazroo, James Banks, and Alan Marshall. 2019. "Are Cities Good for Health? A Study of the Impacts of Planned Urbanization in China." *International Journal of Epidemiology* 48 (4): 1083–90.

Huang, Youqin, ed. 2020. *Chinese Cities in the 21st Century.* New York: Palgrave Macmillan.

Li, Yuheng, Linrui Jia, Wenhao Wu, Jiayu Yan, and Yansui Liu. 2018. "Urbanization for Rural Sustainability—Rethinking China's Urbanization Strategy." *Journal of Cleaner Production* 178 (March): 580–86.

Long, Ying and Shuqi Gao, eds. 2019. *Shrinking Cities in China: The Other Facet of Urbanization.* Singapore: Springer Nature Singapore.

Naughton, Barry. 2018. *The Chinese Economy: Adaptation and Growth.* 2nd ed. Cambridge, MA: MIT Press.

Ren, Julie. 2019. "Conclusion: Everyday Cities, Exceptional Cases." In Forrest, Ren, and Wissink, *The City in China*, 231–46. Bristol, UK: Bristol University Press.

Ren, Xuefei. 2019. "Robert Park in China: From the Chicago School to Urban China Studies." In Forrest, Ren, and Wissink, *The City in China*, 1–16. Bristol, UK: Bristol University Press.

Solinger, Dorothy. 1999. *Contesting Citizenship in Urban China: Peasant Migrants, the State, and the Logic of the Market.* Berkeley: University of California Press.

World Bank. 2015. *East Asia's Changing Urban Landscape: Measuring a Decade of Spatial Growth.* Urban Development Series. Washington, DC: World Bank Group.

World Bank and Development Research Center of the State Council. 2014. *Urban China: Toward Efficient, Inclusive, and Sustainable Urbanization*. Washington, DC: World Bank Group.

Wu, Fulong. 2018. "Planning Centrality, Market Instruments: Governing Chinese Urban Transformation Under State Entrepreneurialism." *Urban Studies* 55 (7): 1383–99.

———. 2020. "Adding New Narratives to the Urban Imagination: An Introduction to 'New Directions of Urban Studies in China.'" In "New Directions of Urban Studies in China," edited by Fulong Wu and Fangzhu Zhang, special issue, *Urban Studies* 57 (3): 459–72.

Wu, Weiping. 2018a. "Poverty and Inequality: Introduction." In Wu and Frazier, *The SAGE Handbook of Contemporary China*, 941–46. London: SAGE.

———. 2018b. "Urbanization and Spatial Development: Introduction." In Wu and Frazier, *The SAGE Handbook of Contemporary China*, 821–26. London: SAGE.

Wu, Weiping, and Mark Frazier. 2018. Introduction to *The SAGE Handbook of Contemporary China*, edited by Weiping Wu and Mark Frazier, xxxvii–xlvii. London: SAGE.

Xu, Gang, Limin Jiao, Man Yuan, Ting Dong, Boen Zhang, and Chunmeng Du. 2019. "How Does Urban Population Density Decline over Time? An Exponential Model for Chinese Cities with International Comparisons." *Landscape and Urban Planning* 183 (March): 59–67.

CHAPTER 1

Paying for Urbanization: Land Finance and Impacts

Weiping Wu

Introduction

Under China's market transition, the process of urbanization has produced spectacular results, at least when judging from the physicality of transformation. This includes great strides in delivering basic infrastructure in ways that are more effective than most other developing countries with similar income levels, and building national networks of high-speed rail and roadway connecting cities that are the envy of even places in the industrialized world. Such progress has modernized the ways and conditions in which manufacturers produce goods, commerce and services provide for consumers, and people live and travel in and across locales. As a central theme of this volume, the impact of urbanization is ubiquitous. This chapter addresses the economic and physical dimensions primarily through an analysis of how urban infrastructure is structured around land finance and how this mechanism shapes cityscapes.

On an aggregate level, China has made significant progress in meeting the rising demand for infrastructure. Urban infrastructure financing in China is fundamentally different from that of most other countries (W. Wu 2018). In industrialized countries, borrowing is widely used as a key method because of the capital-intensive nature of urban infrastructure, especially in terms of up-front costs. Most such borrowing is directly from a functioning capital market and relies on a system of municipal bond rating (in contrast to the dominance of bank lending in China). After borrowing, local taxes are the most important source, constituting on average a 40 percent share (Bird 2004; Chan 1998). Other sources of funding include grants, subsidies, and user charges. Although the situation in developing countries varies substantially, local property taxes dominate the revenue structure, and loan financing tends to be a small source.

Overall in China, bank loans are the major source of funding for infrastructure projects (as opposed to capital markets). Five major state-owned commercial banks dominate the credit market for large infrastructure projects: Agricultural Bank, Industrial and Commercial Bank, Bank of Communications, Construction Bank, and Bank of China. Additionally, a policy bank established in 1994, China Development Bank, provides long-term financing for key projects supported by the state (Walsh, Park, and Yu 2011). Borrowing from these banks occurs largely through local government financing vehicles (LGFVs) or urban development investment corporations, often backed by future land lease revenue (Wong 2013). The latter process has morphed into full-fledged land financialization—using land as collateral to secure bank loans—particularly since 2008, when fiscal stimuli by the central government required local matching funds. In 2014, about 75 percent of land mortgages were furnished by the major banks previously noted (F. Wu 2019). Other key sources of finance include taxes and fee revenue (though not in the form of property taxes commonly levied in the West), especially land lease/transfer fees (W. Wu 2010). During the period from 2007 to 2014, for instance, receipts from land lease/transfer accounted for an average of 52 percent of revenue for prefectural-level cities (Fu, Xu, and Zhang 2019).

Of concern to scholars is the use of land leasing as a primary means of finance for urban infrastructure. This has led to what has been referred to in the literature as a "land-infrastructure-leverage trap" (Tsui 2011), in which local governments—relying on a finite quantity of land as collateral for bank loans—become reliant on an unsustainable system for funding capital-intensive infrastructure projects that may not lead to a level of economic development necessary to pay off the debt. In light of this, there has been much consternation within and outside China with regard to the level of debt LGFVs have taken on. Other factors contributing to the accumulation of local debt include increased local expenditure on services (but reduced revenue) as a result of the 1994 tax reform, stimulus spending and loosened credit policies to ease the 2008 global financial crisis, and a complacent state-controlled banking system willing to accommodate the wishes of local governments (Lin 2009; Tsui 2011; F. Wu 2019).

Rather critically, land-infrastructure-leverage or land finance has spatial implications. The conversion and subsequent leasing of rural land as a method for urban expansion has produced sprawling built environments, coined as "urban sprawl" in the literature. For instance, between 1990 and 2003, the built area in Shanghai more than doubled and in Beijing almost tripled (Wu, Xu, and Yeh 2007). Recently, urban land expansion has significantly outpaced the growth of the urban population in the majority of Chinese cities. Compared to the rest of East Asia, where only 22 out of about 270 cities experienced such a growth pattern between 2000 and 2010, China had 316 cities (out of 600) whose land growth outpaced population growth (World Bank 2015).

This chapter will first discuss a confluence of factors underlying the "land-infrastructure-leverage" strategy of infrastructure and urban development. I will outline how LGFVs leverage land leases and other profitable businesses to mobilize investment in urban construction and infrastructure, drawing from profiles of such entities in Beijing and Shanghai. Given the rapid pace of urbanization, local governments have resorted to land finance to meet an increasing range of responsibilities, while having much less in terms of dedicated budgetary allocation under current central-local fiscal relations. I will then address the impact of land finance on the spatial forms of cities, as manifested in fragmented expansion and vacant development (or the so-called ghost cities).

Understanding Local Government Financing Vehicles in China's Fiscal Context

China's fiscal system remains in transition, and much like macroeconomic reforms, decentralization has been gradual and incremental, responding to immediate problems often with short-term fixes. Under state socialism (1949–79), the central government had direct control over local governments in three main areas: allocation of materials and resources, production planning for key industries, and budgetary control of revenue and expenditure. A number of measures significantly altered central-local fiscal relations in the 1980s. Most notably, the central government declared that each of the four provincial entities would be viewed as a "separate kitchen" for fiscal purposes, which meant that, among other things, many municipalities could retain more of the revenue raised in their jurisdictions and were given more discretion in how they spent that revenue (Wong 1997; Wu and Gaubatz 2020). Following the 1994 tax reform, local government expenditure exploded as a percentage of total government spending. Yet local revenue has not kept pace. To wit, local governments had 80 percent of total government expenditure but only 48 percent of revenue in 2009, and this ratio has remained more or less steady since (for instance, it was 85 and 52 percent, respectively, in 2012). The overall effect of the reforms can thus be considered a decentralization of investment responsibilities and a recentralization of tax collection (Lin and Yi 2011; Wei 2014). An additional problem for local governments is that they are not allowed to establish taxes or issue bonds—save the ten local government entities permitted to issue bonds under a pilot program initiated in 2014 that was subsequently expanded to include all provincial governments in 2015—and hence rely on transfers of tax revenue from the central government.

One response to this dilemma of local public finance has been the creation by local governments, often at the municipal or county level, of extra-budget or off-budget corporations, known as LGFVs, which have four main functions. LGFVs are (1) financing platforms, raising funds for infrastructure projects; (2) public sector investors, managing and operating local government assets; (3) land development agents; and (4) project sponsors or owners (World Bank 2010; Figure 1.1). Thousands of LGFVs have existed throughout China, with wide variation in number per province and municipality. Most are under the direct control of municipal governments, while others may report to the municipal department of construction, a local asset management department, or the local development and reform commission. Compared with public infrastructure development companies in other countries, China's LGFVs do not have a scope of work that is codified into law, nor do they have transparent governance systems or a direct linkage between revenue and expenditure (World Bank 2010).

While procuring funds from capital markets (for example, through the sale of stocks or bonds) is generally not allowed for local governments, it is for LGFVs, since they are formally corporate entities (Tao 2015; Ueda and Gomi 2013). The principal backing asset for LGFVs is municipal land, the main asset owned by local governments (Tao 2015; Wong 2013). These LGFVs have engaged in heavy borrowing through project bonds, bank loans, and loans from shadow banks such as trust, securitization, insurance, and

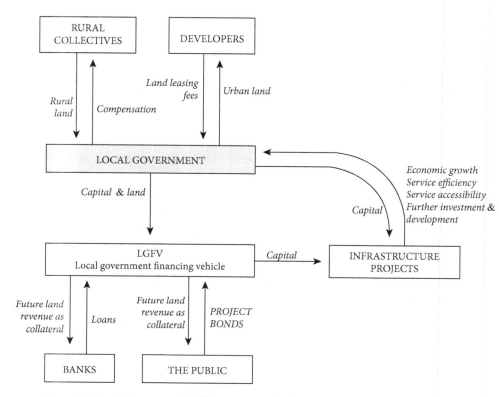

Figure 1.1. Land finance and LGFVs at center of urban infrastructure development. Source: Based on Lu and Sun 2013.

leasing companies. The debt of LGFVs is effectively guaranteed by local governments, despite such guarantees not being legally sanctioned (Lu and Sun 2013). It has been estimated that up to 76 percent of LGFV loans may be at risk of repayment problems because the infrastructure projects they are created to support do not generate sufficient cash flow (Garcia-Herrero and Santabarbara 2013). This situation was exacerbated by the global financial crisis of 2008, after which China's central government encouraged heavy borrowing by local governments as matching funds for national stimulus measures (Goodstadt 2012; F. Wu 2019). Even central government officials have warned about LGFV default risk (Weinland 2019).

Despite their ubiquity throughout China, limited data has been accumulated about LGFVs. Estimates about the number of LGFVs, as well as their debt and percentage of local government revenue, differ wildly even among central government agencies (Wong 2013). Based on data from the National Audit Office, LGFV debt accounted for 39 percent of total local government debt in 2013. The number of LGFVs was reported by the People's Bank of China as about ten thousand in 2010 (Cai et al. 2021). In order to provide a sense of the scope and function of LGFVs, I profile their experience in Beijing and Shanghai. These cities are unique in their size and the central government's direct control over them, yet the functions and mechanisms of their LGFVs are quite typical. There are two basic organizational models. The first, in the direction of Shanghai Chengtou, refers to an all-encompassing LGFV that is in charge of infrastructure financing and development in multiple sectors. This LGFV may have a number of subsidiaries or become a stakeholder in other relevant ventures. The second, as exemplified by Beijing and Chongqing, refers to LGFVs with sector-specific responsibilities and respective financial teams. Chongqing's initial eight LGFVs, all established in 2002 and under the oversight of the municipal government, are organized along sector and functional responsibilities, with separate financial accounts and management teams (World Bank 2010).

Shanghai

Shanghai was the first city to establish an LGFV, creating the General Corporation of Shanghai Municipal Property in 1992 with a mission to invest in urban infrastructure. The corporation was assigned a variety of fiscal resources from the municipal budget, including budgetary allocation for urban construction, the urban maintenance and construction tax revenue, and fees on public facilities (Wong 2013). It was a major developer of transport, water and sewage, and environmental infrastructure, in addition to being a real estate developer. Another of its mandates was to initiate new financing approaches, including bond issuance, concession management, bank borrowing, and capital market financing. By 2004, it had already mobilized US$16.8 billion of direct infrastructure investment (Gao 2007). Renamed as Shanghai Municipal Investment (Group) Corporation in 2014, it owns three specialized corporate groups, two listed companies, and multiple other subsidiaries.

Since its founding in 1992, as the dominating LGFV, Shanghai Chengtou has seen its financing mechanisms shift and expand. In the beginning, it relied on loans from such multilateral development banks as the World Bank and the Asian Development Bank, in addition to fiscal allocation from the Shanghai municipal government. Limited government investments were used to attract both international and domestic lending, including multiple public-private partnerships. The funds were then implemented for a wide variety of infrastructure projects, such as bridges, public transport, sewers, and ports. By the mid-1990s, its main source of finance was land lease and transfer fees, amounting to about RMB 100 billion (Zhou 2008). But with dwindling land availability and shrinking foreign investors to lease land to (as a result of the Asian economic crisis), Chengtou turned to the burgeoning domestic bond markets, taking advantage of high saving rates by the populace. In 1997, Shanghai Chengtou first issued bonds, setting the example that others would follow, and LGFV bonds are now generally referred to as "Chengtou bonds." In addition, some Chengtou subsidiaries also went public to issue stocks.

Furthermore, Shanghai Chengtou has begun to cede concession rights of operation for key infrastructure facilities, such as the Nanpu and Yangpu bridges after their completion, and used the capital to finance the construction of new infrastructure (in this case Xupu Bridge). Overall, at the turn of the twenty-first century, about half of Shanghai Chengtu's revenue came from bank loans (including multilateral development banks), about a quarter from government funding, about 10 percent from land lease/transfer, about 8 percent from bonds, and 3 percent from capital markets (Ji and Lv 2002). Government funding forms the capital base of Chengtou, averaging about RMB 3 billion annually. Land leasing has been the principal way Shanghai Chengtou raised funds outside of borrowing and budgetary allocation.

Today, Chengtou operates as a conglomerate with multiple subsidiaries, each operating in a particular sector on specific projects. It holds majority shares in seven subsidiaries (transport, waterworks, environment, solid waste, Shanghai Center development, asset management, and a holding company). In addition, it is a shareholder in four companies, in the areas of food production, real estate development, subway construction, and securities and stocks. One example is the Shanghai Pudong Water Corporation, now Shanghai Pudong Veolia Water Corporation, which in 2002 sold half its equity to French behemoth Veolia for RMB 2 billion (US$260 million), which was allocated as a credit to Shanghai Chengtou, thus enabling further infrastructure investment (Lorrain 2014). Since 2011, Chengtou has expanded beyond Shanghai, constructing ports in Qingdao (Shandong Province), Zhangzhou

(Fujian), and Taizhou (Zhejiang), and developing and operating industrial parks (for example, in Qidong, Jiangsu Province). The development of real estate projects has been a particularly profitable business (Jiang and Waley 2020).

Beijing

Representing a different operational model, Beijing has multiple LGFVs at the municipal level. Beijing Capital Group (BCG), one of the key LGFVs, was created in 1995 by the Beijing municipal government, which remains the largest shareholder (Lee 2010). Formed from the merger of seventeen state-owned enterprises, BCG has invested in a wide range of infrastructure projects, particularly in the water and sewer and transport sectors. The company also makes large investments in two other lines of business: real estate (particularly residential development and construction) and financial services (investment banking, private equity, loan guarantees, and mergers and acquisitions). It has three subsidiaries that are essentially real estate developers and another five that are financial service companies (Bai, Hsieh, and Song 2016). By 2012, BCG had invested over RMB 6 billion (US$900 million) in urban infrastructure, with returns on projects in the water sector generally in the 9–12 percent range (Owen 2012). While the water and sewage sector is a minority of the company's overall business, as of 2007 BCG had the second largest water and sewage treatment capacity in China behind only Veolia (Lee 2010).

In the water and wastewater sector, BCG has build-operate-transfer (BOT) contracts via companies in which it owns an equity stake, with its ownership of those companies ranging from 40 to 95 percent, though it also operates water contracts on its own (Owen 2012). A unique approach was developed in Hunan Province, where BCG signed an agreement to invest RMB 5 billion in wastewater treatment plants via BOT or transfer-operate-transfer (TOT) approaches (Pan, Zhong, and Chen 2011). In this framework, the Hunan Construction Bureau established a special office, with which the overall agreement was signed, while individual concession contracts were signed with municipal and county level governments for specific plants (Pan, Zhong, and Chen 2011).

On the transport side, BCG was a partner in the creation of Line 4 of the Beijing Metro, the first subway public-private partnership project in China.

The project was created via a special purpose vehicle (SPV) known as Beijing MTR Corporation, a joint venture between BCG, Hong Kong MTR Corporation, and Beijing Infrastructure Investment Company (BII). BCG had 49 percent of the investment—the total project was valued at more than US$2 billion—which included a thirty-year concession, with conditions to raise or lower fees charged to the SPV depending on revenue (Yuan et al. 2010). The estimated internal rate of return for the project was 7 to 8 percent, and a major motivation behind the creation of this SPV was for the public entities (BCG and Beijing Infrastructure Investment Company) to acquire knowledge from a private firm about innovation and efficient organizational structure (Liu and Wilkinson 2013).

BCG also acquired land development rights on behalf of Beijing Capital Land, a residential and commercial real estate development company in which BCG owned a 55.7 percent stake (Tian 2006). Beijing Capital Land's primary business was medium- to high-end residential development in Beijing, but it expanded into a wide variety of commercial developments, including hotels and shopping malls, and moved into geographic areas outside Beijing, including Tianjin, Taiyuan, Wuxi, and Chengdu. Moreover, Beijing Capital Land held abundant land as a means of competitive advantage, to the point of holding land beyond government-sanctioned time periods in terms of deadlines for development (Tian 2006). Of relevance to the discussion of land development, recent research has shown that in Beijing, land leases—particularly when done via tender process—are at times contracted at a rate below market value as the government pursues more public-oriented objectives, such as developing affordable housing (Yang et al. 2015).

Another key LGFV, BII, specializes in the construction, investment, financing, and operation of Beijing's subway system. The municipal government has close organizational links with BII, with the funding plan, governance practices, and business objectives all set by the city. In 2014, these links were an important factor for Moody's Investors Service issuing its first-time A1 rating to BII, which became the first of China's LGFVs to receive a score from a global rating agency. The municipal government also has strong incentives to provide support because of BII's strategic function in the city's public transport. Founded in 2003, BII receives fiscal budget allocations from the city, at about RMB 10 billion annually from 2008 to 2012, which will likely increase to 15.5 billion for 2013 to 2035 according to Moody's rating report. The municipal government also subsidizes BII to cover its operating loss, given the low subway fares set by the city in an effort to promote metro services to address severe problems of traffic congestion and air pollution.

Similar to other LGFVs in Beijing and beyond, BII engages in business complementary to rail operations, including train-related vehicle sales and property development. Its property business, further expanded in 2011, is primarily land development around planned rail construction sites as well as residential and commercial property development along BII rail lines. Following Hong Kong MTR's model of transit plus property, BII provides the capital expenditure to construct infrastructure around subway stations so that the land is ripe for development. The municipal government then leases the land through public auction and uses the proceeds to pay BII.

Land Finance and Infrastructure

Central to the operation of LGFVs, land is the primary asset used to secure loans (Lu and Sun 2013), and selling state assets, including land, is a primary means of raising funds for infrastructure construction. In 2009, for instance, the share of land revenue in the local budget ranged from 30 percent in Shanghai and 35 percent in Beijing to 43 percent in Chongqing and 48 percent in Tianjin (Goodstadt 2012). Furthermore, using future income of land leasing as collateral, local governments in aggregate secured almost twice as much in bank loans (also known as land mortgages) as in land revenue between 2008 and 2015 (F. Wu 2019).

Since land is the most valuable commodity under the control of municipal governments, generating revenue from leasing land use rights and obtaining land mortgages has become a popular local practice. Many local governments are dependent on leasing land for a considerable share of their revenue and have at the same time been increasingly involved in land and real estate development. This dependence becomes precarious as the value of land changes, especially given the risk of overdevelopment, itself a consequence of pro-growth policies from the center and competition among localities (Tsui 2011; Li 2012). Local governments and the banks that provide them with loans are consequently reliant on the real estate market to stay in good fiscal health.

There is a fundamental difference between industrial land leases on the one hand, and commercial and residential leases on the other. Reforms during the early 2000s encouraged new forms of infrastructure financing, including leasing land, leading to a massive surge in infrastructure investments designed to attract manufacturing (Tsui 2011). Private, one-on-one negotiations between the local government and developers are more often used for industry and generally bring in less revenue than do auctions. Auctions are more often used for commercial and residential transactions, and land for these types of development is artificially restricted in order to charge higher rents (Tao et al. 2010). Residential and commercial developments are perceived to be more "stuck in place" than industry, and they can generate more revenue. Yet industry is seen as a job-producing mechanism that lures apartment and commercial developers to come calling. Therefore, local governments use the revenue from commercial and residential land leases to subsidize industrial development. Between 2007 and 2014, residential and commercial land in prefectural-level cities constituted a relatively small share of converted (from rural to urban uses) and redeveloped land, yet it generated the bulk of land revenue (Fu, Xu, and Zhang 2019). One consequence of this practice was the rise in housing prices and subsequent lack of affordability (F. Wu 2019; Wu and Gaubatz 2020).

Under fiscal decentralization, development strategies that stimulate growth, typically involving significant investments in infrastructure (Zhang and Barnett 2014), are essential for local governments for at least two reasons. First, in order to maintain an upward career trajectory, local officials must satisfy top-down requirements in terms of increasing industrial development and economic growth. This results in competition among local officials as they maneuver for promotion as each five-year plan period comes to a close. Second, a somewhat different view posits that job evaluation measures are irrelevant for the vast majority of local officials, as they will be neither promoted nor demoted during their time in office (Gordon and Li 2011). In this scenario, maximizing fiscal "profits" is the primary concern, given that these profits are under the control of local officials and can be used for their personal benefit. In either case, the need to raise funds for capital expenditure while having limited revenue-generating options results in off-budget financing strategies, including leveraging land to raise funds for projects. In light of this, it is reasonable to place emphasis on personal motivations and decision-making as being at the heart of LGFV problems. Some scholars go so far as to use terms such as "frenzied enthusiasm," "unlawful autonomy," and "[elimination] of all personal responsibility" when describing flows of funds through LGFVs, leading in due course to "the LGFV's downfall" (Goodstadt 2012).

The land ownership milieu in China is a further motivating factor behind the use of land as leverage for infrastructure financing. As the sole owner of urban land, the local government is free to use the land for infrastructure, to enter into negotiations with interested parties, or to place the land up for auction or tender sale, ultimately keeping all the proceeds (Tao et al. 2010). What's more, local governments can appropriate rural land from collectives as they see fit and provide relatively small reimbursements in return. Collectives are left with little recourse, as they are unable to lease land to interested parties on their own, and they cannot prevent land requisition by local governments. It has been estimated that fifty-three million farmers lost their land in the process of urbanization in the two decades before the early 2010s (World Bank and Development Research Center of the State Council 2014). Both rural and urban land is therefore an easily acquired and relatively cheap asset for local officials to use in attempting to raise funds.

In a drastic attempt to correct distortions, the central Ministry of Land and Resources (which became part of the Ministry of Natural Resources as of March 2018) issued another regulation in April 2002, mandating that all land conveyance for commercial users be undertaken through transparent and competitive mechanisms: public tender, auction, or listing (so-called *zhao pai gua*). The goal was to reduce the dominance of negotiation in land leases. Official data show an increasing level of land lease transparency: between 2003 and 2016, an average of 74 percent of land leases were through conveyance; the share of land conveyance cases through negotiation—the least transparent, least competitive, and most easily manipulated format—declined from about 75 to 33 percent.

Impact of Land Finance on the Cityscape

The question of land is among the most critical in the study of the Chinese city and financing of urbanization. Amid increasing disparity between local fiscal income and expenditure responsibilities, land leasing has become a critical source of revenue to offset the gap. Such an imperative underscores the kind of incentive that municipal authorities have to keep land finance active. Research shows that economic competition across cities (as well as across city districts) and the scale of land finance are directly related to the extent of urban physical expansion (Qin, Liu, and Li 2016; Liu, Chen, and Lu 2018). There is evidence, however, that in more developed regions, land finance is becoming a less important impetus for urban expansion than in regions lagging behind (Wang and Zhang 2018). The spatial manifestation is at least twofold: the outward sprawl of built-up areas and the oversupply of land for new towns and districts; and the leapfrogging and fragmented spatial patterns of expansion at the urban fringes.

The rapidly expanding built-up area of cities results in excessive loss of precious arable land. According to official estimates, newly built urban areas in China grew by 50 percent from 2000 to 2010, which partially accounted for the loss of 8.3 million hectares of arable land (Chen 2011). Using nighttime stable light and other data, researchers show a similar trend: the total urban area increased from 31,076 square kilometers in 2001 to 80,887 square kilometers in 2013, growing annually around 13 percent. Such expansion consumed 33,080 square kilometers of agricultural land. During the same period, the rest of the world experienced urban expansion at the annual rate of about 3 percent (Shi et al. 2016). Moreover, the rate of urban land expansion has far outpaced that of population growth. From 1990 to 2011, the built-up land per capita in urban areas increased from 82.6 square meters to 132.9 square meters, growing at a rate of 54.2 percent (the population used in the calculation included migrants). By comparison, the built-up land per capita in rural areas increased from 148.6 square meters to 220.5 square meters, with a growth rate of 48.4 percent (Cai, Xiong, and Gao 2013).

Another visible indication of runaway land development is the ghost cities. These newly constructed but relatively uninhabited city districts, or in some cases whole cities, have come to serve as a reminder that there are limits to growth even in the context of contemporary China. Few cities better illustrate the excess of the ghost city than Ordos, a city in the semiautonomous region of Inner Mongolia. Exceptionally striking images of the city's district of Kangbashi—forests of vacant apartment towers, wide deserted and disheveled streets, and empty storefronts—have thrust Ordos into the international limelight. Once touted as a symbol of modernity, the new district is located twenty-five kilometers south of Dongsheng, the area's largest existing population center, home to just over half a million inhabitants. Vigorous construction began in 2006, with plans for the new district featuring a gamut of civic and cultural facilities, as well as tens of thousands of housing units and planted trees. In 2010, all urban construction was brought to an abrupt halt, resulting in throngs of suspended or abandoned residential projects (Woodworth 2015). Exaggerated as it may be, the current fate of

Ordos reflects broader flaws in the logic of urban expansion as adopted by cities throughout the country. These ghost cities, malls, and other developments demonstrate the limits of not only speculative real estate but "endless" growth and development more broadly (Sorace and Hurst 2016).

In addition to excessive land development, the fragmented pattern, especially at the urban fringes and in new districts, adds to the undue footprint of expansion. Surrounding the urban core is rural land owned by villages, many of which are in the form of "village corporations" that negotiate land sales individually with the municipal government. Complicating the matter are significant informal land sales that exist at multiple levels of exchange (Lin and Ho 2005). Moreover, the noncontiguous development pattern is related to quotas to protect basic farmland. Since there is no reliable distinction between farmland at different locations, some plots of agricultural land close to built-up areas are not permitted to be developed. In aggregate, the convoluted process of land ownership and land acquisition, as well as the unintended consequences of farmland protection, produce urban peripheries characterized by disjointed land use and piecemeal development. Approximately 95 percent of urban growth takes place in the form of leapfrogging around the urban peripheries (World Bank and China Development Research Center 2014). Figure 1.2 is an example of such lateral expansion of built-up areas, as seen in Nanjing over a period of twenty years. Rapid in pace, the expansion is accompanied by dispersion of residential population. Simultaneously, new economic functions become more concentrated on the outskirts, as well as substantial new housing construction in suburban areas. Commercial expansion has been driven by large hotels, a convention center, shopping malls, and wholesale markets. In addition, three new university towns have taken shape in the outskirts.

These fragmented developments are costly for future infill and reduce the benefits of the compact urban core. Infrastructure networks, including roads, sewers, and telecommunications, have to bypass the fragmentations and thus become more costly per unit of service area (World Bank 2008). Planners, constrained by existing institutional settings, are relatively powerless to apply long-term planning principals (Fang and Pal 2016). Land use efficiency and environmental impact are not fully taken into account in the process of land conversion. Coordinated management, perhaps at a regional level, is the first step to ensuring sustainable patterns of urban spatial growth (World Bank 2008; Fang and Pal 2016).

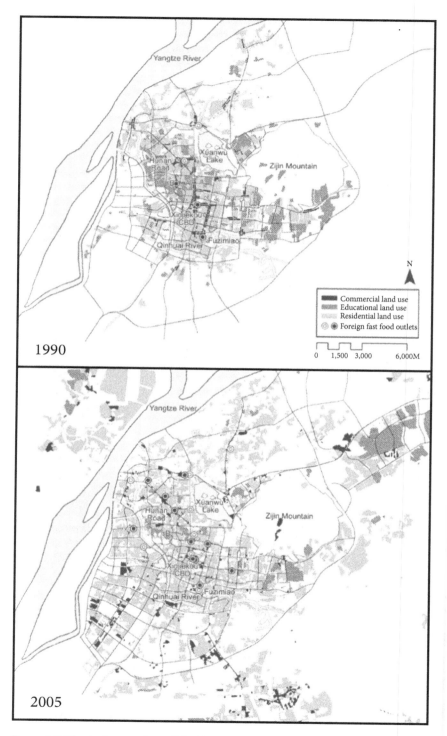

Figure 1.2. Physical expansion of Nanjing, 1990–2010. Source: Based on Zhang et al. 2014.

Conclusion

The reliance on land finance stems from a set of contradictions facing local governments. They have a powerful incentive to place local banks' excess liquidity into real estate, which would subsequently expand the local housing market and their bottom lines. They have a direct interest in seeing land and construction prices rise, which are significant parts of housing prices, to increase fiscal revenue. On the other hand, local governments have neither sufficient tax resources nor sufficient authority to leverage capital markets. In borrowing from domestic banks to finance infrastructure, local governments face virtually no limits and little accountability. State banks are also ill-equipped to provide the discipline expected from capital markets. However, it is unlikely for local governments to count on revenue from asset sales (mainly land) as a major lasting source of funding to expand infrastructure construction and maintenance.

The revenue generated through land leasing and the logic behind this strategy have become increasingly entangled with the production of local infrastructure. By expanding services to the urban fringes, local governments bolster the appeal of land within the municipality to developers and investors searching for inexpensive but serviced parcels. This in turn makes increasingly larger amounts of fringe area viable for urban use, which finances additional infrastructure construction, attracts even more developers, and propagates a cycle of land leasing and infrastructure investment. Given that the land finance strategy is driven by borrowing and causes localities to accumulate debt over time, it is little wonder that this practice has produced a staggering deficit at the local level, to such a magnitude that economists within China and abroad fear widespread economic instability from local government default.

There is a general agreement among scholars that this "land-infrastructure-leverage" strategy is unsustainable for local finance, particularly in the long run, for at least three reasons (W. Wu 2018). First, when land values rise, borrowing becomes easier, but falling land values will cause banks to be more conservative, meaning more land must be leased off. This raises land value volatility as an issue, with implications for the ability of local governments to maintain debt repayments and continue funding infrastructure, especially as real estate markets become overheated and the likelihood of a bubble rises (Tsui 2011; Li 2012). On the other hand, an economic downturn would likely force a fire sale of land into an already illiquid market, creating a cycle in which land values continue to plummet (Lu and Sun 2013). Second, sold land use rights represent foregone sources of income for local governments. Unlike property taxes used in many other countries, proceeds from land leases in no way guarantee a steady flow of funds from year to year. Also, there is evidence that land supply is constrained in the medium term, particularly for booming cities along the eastern seaboard (Lu and Sun 2013). Actual land transaction data show that more land has been converted for urban use in inland regions during 2007–14 even though less land revenue is generated there, an indication of the declining land supply in the coastal provinces (Fu, Xu, and Zhang 2019). Third, with in situ urbanization and expansion, there is increasing tension between the loss of arable land and cities' dependence on land leasing for revenue. This also represents a significant challenge to the already fragile human-environment relationship aggravated by rapid urbanization.

More importantly, the rules governing local government finance in China are changing. Stricter requirements for bank loans mortgaged on land were issued by the People's Bank of China in 2012 (Chen and Wu 2020). In October 2014, the State Council issued Rule No. 43, stating that as of 1 January 2016, LGFVs would no longer be allowed to issue LGFV bonds. This effectively shut down Chengtou bonds as a source of funds for local governments. In addition, the New Budget Law of 2015 ordered local governments to sever ties with LGFVs and allowed provincial governments to convert LGFV debt to municipal bonds through a three-year debt-bond swap program (Oi 2020). As a result, localities had to rely on alternative financing channels, such as issuing regular municipal bonds for public-interest projects fully backed by tax revenue, and forming public-private partnerships for infrastructure developments that do not carry a government guarantee (Ang, Bai, and Zhou 2015). The land-infrastructure-leverage strategy is just one of the unintended and uncontrollable consequences of urbanization. Contradictions like this problematize the environmental, social, and economic well-being of the contemporary Chinese city.

References

Ang, Andrew, Jennie Bai, and Hao Zhou. 2015. "The Great Wall of Debt: Corruption, Real Estate, and Chinese Local Government Credit Spreads." Georgetown McDonough School of Business Research Paper no. 2603022, PBCSF-NIFR Research Paper no. 15–02. SSRN Working Papers Series, May. http://papers.ssrn.com/sol3/papers.cfm?abstract_id=2603022.

Bai, Chong-En, Chang-Tao Hsieh, and Zheng Michael Song. 2016. "The Long Shadow of China's Fiscal Expansion." Brookings Papers on Economic Activity, Fall. www.brookings.edu/wp-content/uploads/2017/02/baitextfall16bpea.pdf.

Bird, Richard. M. 2004. "Getting It Right: Financing Urban Development in China." ITP paper 0413, International Tax Program, Institute for International Business, Rotman School of Management, University of Toronto, January.

Cai, Jiming, Chai Xiong, and Hong Gao. 2013. "Mismatch Between Urbanization of Population and Land in China." *Jingjixue dongtai* [Dynamic of economics] 6 (August): 15–22.

Cai, Meina, Jianyong Fan, Chunhui Ye, and Qi Zhang. 2021. "Government Debt, Land Financing and Distributive Justice in China." *Urban Studies* 58 (11): 2329–47. https://doi.org/10.1177/0042098020938523.

Chan, Kam Wing. 1998. "Infrastructure Services and Financing in Chinese Cities." *Pacific Rim Law and Policy Journal* 7 (3): 503–28.

Chen, Jie, and Fulong Wu. 2020. "Housing and Land Financialization under the State Ownership of Land in China." *Land Use Policy*. Published ahead of print, June. https://doi.org/10.1016/j.landusepol.2020.104844.

Chen, Xin. 2011. "Urbanization 'Threatens Food Security'." *China Daily*, 28 March. http://www.chinadaily.com.cn/business/2011-03/28/content_12237917.htm.

Fang, Yiping, and Anirban Pal. 2016. "Drivers of Urban Sprawl in Urbanizing China—a Political Ecology Analysis." *Environment and Urbanization* 28 (2): 599–616.

Fu, Shihe, Xiacong Xu, and Junfu Zhang. 2019. "Land Conversion and Misallocation across Cities in China." Working Paper WP19SF1, Lincoln Institute of Land Policy, June. www.lincolninst.edu/sites/default/files/pubfiles/fu_wp19sf1.pdf.

Gao, Guofu. 2007. "Urban Infrastructure Investment and Financing in Shanghai." In *Financing Cities: Fiscal Responsibility and Urban Infrastructure in Brazil, China, India, Poland, and South Africa*, edited by George E. Peterson and Patricia Clarke Annez, 220–28. Los Angeles: SAGE.

Garcia-Herrero, Alicia, and Daniel Santabarbara. 2013. "An Assessment of China's Banking System Reform." In *Who Will Provide the Next Financial Model?*, edited by Sahoko Kaji and Eiji Ogawa, 147–76. Tokyo, Japan: Springer.

Goodstadt, Leo F. 2012. "China's LGFV Crisis 2011: The Conflict Between Local Autonomy and Financial Reforms." Working Paper no. 3/2012, Hong Kong Institute for Monetary Research. https://ssrn.com/abstract=1988841.

Gordon, Roger H., and Wei Li. 2011. "Provincial and Local Governments in China: Fiscal Institutions and Government Behavior." Working Paper 16694, National Bureau of Economic Research. www.nber.org/papers/w16694.

Ji, Jincheng, and Huimin Lv. 2002. "Uncover the Secret of Shanghai's Drastic Transformation through Understanding Financing System Reform" [Cong tourongzi tizhi gaige jiedu shanghai jubia de aomi]. *Xinhuanet*, 28 June. http://finance.sina.com.cn/o/20020628/226855.html.

Jiang, Yanpeng, and Paul Waley. 2020. "Who Builds Cities in China? How Urban Investment and Development Companies Have Transformed Shanghai." *International Journal of Urban and Regional Research*. Published ahead of print, June. https://doi.org/10.1111/1468-2427.12918.

Lee, Seungho. 2010. "Development of Public Private Partnership (PPP) Projects in the Chinese Water Sector." *Water Resources Management* 24 (9): 1925–45.

Li, Meng. 2012. "China's Local Government Debt Crisis." *SERI Quarterly* 5 (April): 33–39.

Lin, George C. S. 2009. *Developing China: Land, Politics, and Social Conditions*. London: Routledge.

Lin, George C. S., and Samuel P. S. Ho. 2005. "The State, Land System, and Land Development Process in Contemporary China." *Annals of the Association of American Geographers* 95 (2): 411–35.

Lin, George C. S., and Fangxin Yi. 2011. "Urbanization of Capital or Capitalization of Land? Land Development and Local Public Finance in Urbanizing China." *Urban Geography* 21 (1): 50–79.

Liu, Ruichao, Dongjing Chen, and Lan Lu. 2018. "The Impact of Land Finance on Urban Sprawl." *Chengshi wenti* [Urban issues] 5:85–91.

Liu, Tingting, and Suzanne Wilkinson. 2013. "Can the Pilot Public-Private Partnerships Project Be Applied in Future Urban Rail Development? A Case Study of Beijing Metro Line 4 Project." *Built Environment Project and Asset Management* 3 (2): 250–63.

Lorrain, Dominique. 2014. *Governing Megacities in Emerging Countries*. Farnham, UK: Ashgate.

Lu, Yinqiu, and Tao Sun. 2013. *Local Government Financing Platforms in China: A Fortune or Misfortune*. Working Paper WP/13/243, International Monetary Fund, Washington, DC.

Oi, Jean C. 2020. "Future of Central-Local Relations." In *Fateful Decisions: Choices That Will Shape China's Future*, edited by Thomas Fingar and Jean C. Oi. Stanford, CA: Stanford University Press, 107–27.

Owen, David Lloyd. 2012. *Pinsent Masons Water Yearbook 2012–2013*. 14th ed. London: Pinsent Masons.

Pan, Wentang, Lijin Zhong, and Jining Chen. 2011. "Improving Performance of Wastewater Sector via Private Sector Participation." *Journal of Water Sustainability* 1 (2): 203–13.

Qin, Meng, Xiuyan Liu, and Songlin Li. 2016. "China's Urban Sprawl Puzzle: Panel Data and Analysis on Government Behavior." *Jingjixue dongtai* [Dynamic of economics] 7:21–33.

Shi, Kaifang, Yun Chen, Bailing Yu, Tingbao Xu, Linyi Li, Chang Huang, Rui Liu, Zuoqi Chen, and Jianping Wu. 2016. "Urban Expansion and Agricultural Land Loss in China: A Multiscale Perspective." *Sustainability* 8 (8): 790–806.

Sorace, Christian, and William Hurst. 2016. "China's Phantom Urbanisation and the Pathology of Ghost Cities." *Journal of Contemporary Asia* 46 (2): 304–22.

Tao, Kunyu. 2015. "Assessing Local Government Debt Risks in China: A Case Study of Local Government Financial Vehicles." *China and World Economy* 23 (5): 1–25.

Tao, Ran, Fubing Su, Mingxing Liu, and Guangzhong Cao. 2010. "Land Leasing and Local Public Finance in China's Regional Development: Evidence from Prefecture-Level Cities." *Urban Studies* 47 (10): 2217–36.

Tian, Yongchun. 2006. "The Application of Simulation to Project Evaluation for Real Estate Developers in China." Master's thesis, Department of Architecture, Massachusetts Institute of Technology. http://hdl.handle.net/1721.1/37447.

Tsui, Kai-yuen. 2011. "China's Infrastructure Investment Book and Local Debt Crisis." *Eurasian Geography and Economics* 52 (5): 686–711.

Ueda, Kenji, and Yuko Gomi. 2013. "Shadow Banking in China and Expanding Debts of Local Governments." Institute for International Monetary Affairs, Newsletter No. 23, 5 August.

Walsh, James P, Chanho Park, and Jiangyan Yu. 2011. "Financing Infrastructure in India: Macroeconomic Lessons and Emerging Markets—Case Studies." IMF Working Paper WP/11/181, International Monetary Fund, Washington, DC.

Wang, Yubo, and Ao Zhang. 2018. "Study on Regional Difference of Linkage Between Land Fiscal Components and Urban Land Use Scale." [In Chinese.] *Journal of Northeastern University (Social Science)* 20 (5): 498–504.

Wei, Shen. 2014. "The Logic (or Illogic) of China's Local Government Debts out of Control— Law, Governance or Other Perspectives." *Hong Kong Law Journal* 44 (3): 887–916.

Weinland, Don. 2019. "China Warned of Local Debt Vehicle Default Risk." *Financial Times*, 18 December. www.ft.com/content/be52259a-2163-11ea-92da-f0c92e957a96.

Wong, Christine. 1997. "Overview of Issues in Local Public Finance in the PRC." In *Financing Local Government in the People's Republic of China*, edited by Christine Wong, 27–60. Hong Kong: Oxford University Press for the Asian Development Bank.

———. 2013. "Paying for Urbanization in China: Challenges of Municipal Finance in the Twenty-First Century." In *Financing Metropolitan Governments in Developing Countries*, edited by Roy W. Bahl, Johannes F. Linn, and Deborah L. Wetzel, 273–308. Cambridge, MA: Lincoln Institute of Land Policy.

Wong, Christine, and Richard Bird. 2004. "China's Fiscal System: A Work in Progress." Paper presented at the Conference on China's Economic Transition, Pittsburgh, PA, November.

Woodworth, Max D. 2015. "Ordos Municipality: A Market-Era Resource Boomtown." *Cities* 43 (March): 115–32.

World Bank. 2008. "The Fragmented City: Issues in Urban Land Use in China." East Asian and Pacific Region Urban Development Sector Unit Background Paper, Washington, DC.

———. 2010. "The Urban Development Investment Corporations (UDICs) in Chongqing, China." Technical Assistance Report, Washington, DC.

———. 2015. *East Asia's Changing Urban Landscape: Measuring a Decade of Spatial Growth.* Urban Development Series. Washington, DC: World Bank.

World Bank and Development Research Center of the State Council. 2014. *Urban China: Toward Efficient, Inclusive, and Sustainable Urbanization.* Washington, DC: World Bank.

Wu, Fulong. 2019. "Land Financialisation and the Financing of Urban Development in China." *Land Use Policy*. Published ahead of print, December. https://doi.org/10.1016/j .landusepol.2019.104412.

Wu, Fulong, Jiang Xu, and Anthony Gar-On Yeh. 2007. *Urban Development in Post-Reform China: State, Market, and Space.* London: Routledge.

Wu, Weiping. 2010. "Urban Infrastructure Financing and Economic Performance in China." *Urban Geography* 31 (5): 648–67.

———. 2018. "Financing Urbanization and Infrastructure." In *The SAGE Handbook of Contemporary China*, edited by Weiping Wu and Mark Frazier, 878–97. London: SAGE.

Wu, Weiping, and Piper Gaubatz. 2020. *The Chinese City.* 2nd ed. London: Routledge.

Yang, Zan, Rongrong Ren, Hongyu Liu, and Huan Zhang. 2015. "Land Leasing and Local Government Behavior in China: Evidence from Beijing." *Urban Studies* 52 (5): 841–56.

Yuan, Jing-Feng, Mirosław J. Skibniewski, Qiming Li, and Jin Shan. 2010. "The Driving Factors of China's Public-Private Partnership Projects in Metropolitan Transportation

Systems: Public Sector's Viewpoint." *Journal of Civil Engineering and Management* 16 (1): 5–18.

Zhang, Min, Weiping Wu, Lei Yao, Ye Bai, and Guo Xiong. 2014. "Transnational Practices in Urban China: Spatiality and Localization of Western Fast Food Chains." *Habitat International* 43 (July): 22–31.

Zhang, Yuanyan Sophia, and Steven Barnett. 2014. "Fiscal Vulnerabilities and Risks from Local Government Finance in China." IMF Working Paper WP/14/4, International Monetary Fund, Washington, DC, January.

Zhou, Pei. 2008. "New Operation Models for Tianjin Urban Infrastructure Investment Corporation." Master's thesis, Tianjin University of Science and Technology.

CHAPTER 2

Cities for Whom? The 2017 Beijing Demolitions in Context

Shiqi Ma and Jeremy Wallace

Introduction

On 18 November 2017, a building in Beijing's Daxing District was engulfed in flames. The fire killed nineteen, including eight children. Two days later, Cai Qi, Beijing's mayor, launched a forty-day campaign to demolish "all illegal residential structures" in the city. Local officials and their agents acted with haste to participate in the campaign and used aggressive tactics: cutting off water, electricity, and heating supplies to targeted areas as well as sending police officers to intimidate tenants by smashing their property and dragging their belongings out of the structures and into the streets. Ultimately, thousands of migrants abandoned their homes, shops, and factories, which were then demolished into rubble.

Many studies have examined urban demolitions in China. While some see an underlying economic logic linking demolition with local states' desire to maximize capital accumulation (Ho and Lin 2003; Hsing 2010; Wu 2016), others find releasing demographic burdens (Duckett and Wang 2015; Song, Zenou, and Ding 2008; Wu and Frazier 2018; Zhu 2004) or embracing modernization and formality (Gilbert and Ward 1985; Shin and Li 2013; Smart and Lam 2009) as significant explanatory factors. Separate from parsing why these demolitions are happening is understanding the urban reality they leave behind in their wake. Many dislocated migrants disperse following a demolition episode, and those migrants who avoided demolition still face heightened stress when others like them are forcefully shoved aside.

The Beijing demolition wave's confrontational nature and vast scale point to the need to investigate the case in more depth to see if existing explanations continue to hold or if additional factors have come into play. How do we understand the Beijing 2017 demolitions? While fully answering this question would have required an on-the-ground presence during the demolitions and in the decision-making rooms of the officials who ordered them, a focus on examining the national and local political context leading up to and during the demolitions can shed additional light on them.

We argue that a political shift has occurred that contributed to the demolition wave's ferocity. Until very recently, central and local government officials have had divergent interests on questions of urban land requisition and demolition, with local officials pushing for more land grabs and the central government curbing this tendency with its more balanced focus on both economic growth and political stability. However, as Xi Jinping and his team took power, the central leadership changed tack and has repeatedly emphasized the need to accelerate the upgrading of housing in cities while de-emphasizing concerns about protecting residences of migrant workers. This move in the center's political priorities aligned the central and local government's perspectives in a way that allowed for the marginalizing of migrant workers in large cities in recent years.

In so doing, the analysis here fits neatly into the book's broader aims. We demonstrate the complex and mutual relationship between space, people, and their interactions under urbanization. On the one hand, the changing realities of Chinese cities influence the incentives of central and local governments. On the other hand, the outcomes of these interactions, namely demolitions, are ground zero for urban redevelopment—taking land being used by some people at one time and shifting its use and form for others in the future. Redevelopment can restrain sprawl and connect to efforts at environmental improvement, including fighting climate change; but while it certainly alters the trajectory for urbanization of land, it also threatens the already weak bonds of migrants to cities. The demolition data that we examine here comes from migrants, news reports, and, crucially, satellite imagery, which allows for the possibility of systematically measuring the scale and scope of demolition not only in Beijing during this wave but also in other Chinese cities at various times.

The rest of the chapter proceeds as follows. We present our argument on the shift in central government policy direction and how it amplifies the array of local factors that the literature has analyzed in prior cases of demolitions in Chinese cities. We then detail some of that changing context, including leaders' speeches, actions on the Greater Beijing Megacity project (*Jing-Jin-Ji*), the promulgation of national *penghuqu* (棚户区) policies, and Beijing's Dispersing, Regulating, and Upgrading Action Plan. Descriptions of and reactions to the demolitions follow, including using satellite imagery to document their thoroughness. Next, we analyze how the changing context helps explain the brutality of the demolitions as well as the limitations on what context can account for. We conclude by discussing the opportunities of using satellite images as a new source of information on China's urbanization and a call for further research.

Argument

China's political structure and economic growth created expanding cities and urban villages. While ultimate political authority rests at the top, China's system is quite decentralized in terms of actual expenditures (Landry 2008). This decentralization of expenditures is paired with limitations on the ability of local governments to generate revenue, resulting in local governments being fiscally constrained, which then causes them to turn to land as a source of funds (Liu et al. 2018; Rithmire 2015; Wu and Frazier 2018, 822).

Rural and urban designations were given to Chinese land—as well as Chinese people—with regulations limiting how a given plot of land could be used. Essentially, urban land could be developed or redeveloped to a much greater extent than rural land, as the central government held on to concerns about self-sufficiency related to agricultural production.[1] Local governments held the power to convert land from rural to urban status, which dramatically increased its economic value. As workers increasingly left the agricultural sector throughout the reform era, cities grew and demand for space increased; officials interested in economic growth for corruption or promotion opportunities pursued land conversions and development, even pushing people off the land. Some villages close to the urban core retained their rural status and took advantage of this proximity by focusing on rental income from migrants wanting access to the city's labor markets (Hsing 2010, 17).

Urban villages developed as relatively underregulated spaces where cheap housing for migrant populations could proliferate and migrants could forge social bonds, making life in the city more bearable (Wang, Wang, and Wu

2009; Wu, Zhang, and Webster 2012). Such cheap housing was particularly important because the Chinese economy's turn toward real estate as a major growth sector—and site for financial speculation—led to apartment prices being above what the residential market alone could support (Woodworth and Wallace 2017). These communities housed urban laborers, and so while pressures to absorb the villages into the city proper and claim control over the land existed, they were moderated by the presence of other lands on the periphery of cities that could be converted as a substitute.

Eventually, lands on the urban periphery at a reasonable distance to the core became scarcer, leading local governments to turn their eyes to urban villages and contemplate demolitions of those communities. Of course, the demolition of migrants' homes could inflame social conflict and generate grievances among the urban poor (Hsing 2010; Smart 2002; Smart and Lam 2009).

With local officials strongly bent in favor of development, the central government balanced an overall interest in development with more concern for political and economic stability and thus acted as a constraint on local officials. On the one hand, the central government acknowledged the importance of the real estate market to GDP growth and local fiscal balance; thus, land transactions and forced demolitions were tolerated to some extent at the local level (He, Zhou, and Huang 2015). On the other hand, the central government made some efforts to protect migrant workers' rights from the overexpansion of land commercialization, including raising the barrier to entry in the real estate sector (Hsing 2010; Rithmire 2015), passing the labor contract law (Gao, Yang, and Li 2012), subsidizing migrant schools,[2] and encouraging social insurance (Gao, Yang, and Li 2012; Wu and Wang 2014). While the central government did take such pro-migrant actions, it has also long pushed to reshape China's urban system, controlling the population of its largest cities and encouraging the growth of small and medium-sized cities (Wallace 2014). Acquiring local *hukou* status and access to urban amenities was consistently easier in smaller cities than it was in those atop the urban hierarchy.

By the mid-2010s, the central government's attitude toward migrant workers became less ambiguous. It began shifting away from the dilemma of balancing stability and development toward a more strongly "pro-development" line. Under Xi's rule, the central leadership has repeatedly emphasized the necessity to accelerate housing upgrades, which implies the demolition of urban villages and the eradication of extant housing for migrant workers

(Wong, Qiao, and Zheng 2018). Local states' roles changed from the stake-holders of land grabbing to the lead actors of the national demolition plan. The Beijing city government came up with plans to disperse its non-capital functions and prioritize the development of nearby smaller cities. But push-ing growth to small cities, while having political utility for the regime, is in contrast to the desires of the migrant population, who mostly wish to move to large and medium-sized cities in order to participate in their labor markets.

Under this newly remade central-local relationship, the demolition of urban villages shows novel features. Starting from Beijing's large-scale de-molition in November 2017, we find that the eviction of migrants has become more systematic, fierce, and serving for noneconomic goals. A willingness to be more amenable or encouraging of demolition fits into the regime's general trend of being more accepting of repressive actions. This strong-handed ap-proach can be seen in crackdowns on activists, lawyers, and organizations supporting workers (Fu and Distelhorst 2018) as well as the forcible reeduca-tion facilities and mass internment of Muslims in Xinjiang (Zenz 2018; C. Zhang 2018).

Beyond this new repressive tendency, why have central priorities changed? First, China's overheated housing market has been slowing down from its rapid pace. In the metropolitan areas of big cities, ever fewer plots of land at reasonable distances to the urban core remain for real estate developers to build new commercial projects, reducing the potential volume of land rents. By pushing redevelopment of urban villages, the central government identi-fies spaces that urban governments have not controlled or profited from di-rectly. The reality of redevelopment is demolition, but its costs are borne principally by those migrants residing and working in the demolished areas, who lose their homes, their communities, and likely their access to the labor market. Those suffering the concentrated costs from demolition may protest but are unlikely to spark a broader movement, due in part to their limited incorporation into the city. Second, the central government sees the popula-tion concentration in large cities as threatening to political stability and the legitimacy of the ruling class. The soaring population growth of China's megacities has produced many urban problems (城市病), such as environ-mental pollution (Smyth et al. 2009), traffic congestion (Yang, Purevjav, and Li 2020), and harm to public health (Gong et al. 2012), and the urban middle class's discontents can turn into disapproval of the party-state's governance and strategies (Chen et al. 2015; Solinger 1999, 110–45; Sun et al. 2018).

Cleaning up urban villages is one of the most effective ways for the state to reassert control over the city's population and its level of growth. Political difficulties of governing cities increase with the population of a given city (Wallace 2014), but Chinese officials have gone beyond simply worrying about the total number of people in first-tier cities to emphasizing the "quality" of the population and arranging the population to simplify governance for the state, or making the city more legible (Scott 1998). Densely populated urban villages provide space for the emergence of poverty (Démurger et al. 2009), uncertainty, public disorder, and social resistance (Duckett and Hussain 2008; Duckett and Wang 2015; Smart and Lam 2009). China's largest cities have turned to point-based systems for giving migrants the ability to transfer their *hukou* or enroll their children in public schools. These systems are complicated, varying not just across cities but within them, as different districts often have their own policies, but overwhelmingly grant more access to those with more resources (Friedman 2017; C. Zhang 2018).

Policy and Political Context

From the mid-1990s to the mid-2010s, the central government gradually changed from a regulator to an enabler of urban village demolition in large cities. Unlike Hu and Jiang, who went back and forth between resolving social inequality and boosting the local economy, Xi's team delivers a clearer message of their attitude toward urban villages: it is crucial to control the population of migrant workers and clean up the shantytowns in Chinese metropolises. Local governments, who used to be the main actors pushing forward urban village demolition, became eager cogs in the national demolition agenda. The shifting roles of central and local governments are reflected in the promulgation of national *penghuqu* policies; leader speeches; Beijing's Dispersing, Regulating, and Upgrading Action Plan; and the Greater Beijing Megacity project (*Jing-Jin-Ji*).

The Chinese government uses the term *penghuqu* (shantytown) to refer to residential areas with high building density, poor infrastructure, and security threats (Wong, Qiao, and Zheng 2018, 601).[3] *Penghuqu* includes urban villages as well as other temporary residential buildings in mines, forest factories, and state-owned farms. According to publicly available official documents, the State Council first openly talked about the necessity of upgrading *penghuqu* in March 2008 (State Council of China 2008). However, it was in

2013 under Xi that the State Council published its first national document that solely and directly targeted *penghuqu* (State Council of China 2013). One year later, a follow-up document came out, claiming that more than 3.2 million households had been "redeveloped (改造)" in 2013, and 4.7 million were slated to be redeveloped in 2014 (State Council of China 2014).[4] Later, the central government set a target of redeveloping nine million households every year from 2015 to 2017 (Ministry of Housing and Urban-Rural Development of China, 2015). On the State Council's open document archive, twenty national documents mentioned *penghuqu* (shantytown 棚户区)/*chengzhong-cun* (urban village 城中村) from 2008 to 2010. This number increased to ninety during the period from 2016 to 2018. Moreover, the central state began to praise openly the localities in which urban village redevelopment and demolition were well implemented. In 2016, the central state applauded Anhui, Shandong, Hunan, Guizhou, and Shaanxi Provinces for their performances in urban village redevelopment (State Council of China 2017). Similar public acknowledgment of successes in *penghuqu* redevelopment was extended to almost two dozen municipal-level governments in 2018 (State Council of China 2019).

The city of Beijing responded to the national agenda of *penghuqu* redevelopment and demographic regulation with its plans of relocating non-capital functions and pushing forward *Jing-Jin-Ji* coordination. In 2017, Beijing's new party secretary, Cai Qi, who was widely believed to be nominated by Xi Jinping as his close political ally in the Beijing government, showed his loyalty to the center as soon as he took office. In Cai's first conference about Beijing's future urban plan,[5] he fixed a target maximum on the city's population—23 million—as well as hard constraints on land for urban development by the year 2020 (BASS 2019). The plan also emphasized the city's cultural development and made clear its preference for high-income denizens with references to seeing Beijing as a "world-class harmonious and habitable capital" (BASS 2019, 145, chap. 5). Another official local document that came out in early 2017, the Dispersing, Regulating, and Upgrading Action Plan (疏解整治促提升), again reiterated the city's desire to disperse low value-added economic activity and more rigorously control land use inside the city limits to upgrade the city's image and functioning (Wong, Qiao, and Zheng 2018).

These documents reflect two important themes of Beijing's migration governance plan in recent years: the relocation of non-capital functions (疏解非首都功能) and Greater Beijing Megacity project planning (*Jing-Jin-Ji* coordination). Both trends are central and state-led, followed by local-level implementation. The term "dispersing and relocating the non-capital functions" in Beijing was first proposed by Xi Jinping in the meeting of the Chinese Communist Party's economic and financial affairs team in February 2015. Five months later, the Beijing government specified the realm of non-capital functions as general manufacturing, regional logistical clusters and wholesale markets, redundant medical and educational services, and administrative services.

The relocation of non-capital functions would greatly reduce the job opportunities of migrant workers, since the majority of them work in manufacturing, logistics, and low-end services. As a substitute, the Beijing government sought to encourage the development of nearby smaller cities. This prioritization of smaller cities can be first seen in the major 2014 announcement of the National New-Type Urbanization Plan (2014–2020), which emphasized "townification" (城镇化) rather than citification (城市化) and people centered rather than land driven (Looney and Rithmire 2017).

Xi announced that more integrated planning of the *Jing-Jin-Ji* metropolitan region would be a priority in February 2014, and a June 2015 Coordinated Development Outline laid out the general plan, summarized by Kan: "Beijing will remain the center of politics, culture, and innovation; Tongzhou, beyond Chaoyang District in the city's east, will become the seat of the municipal government; Tianjin will be a hub of high-end manufacturing and technology; and Hebei is slated to be a national test site for upgrading manufacturing industries with new technologies" (2016, 6).

For Beijing proper, in addition to moving local government offices from the urban core to Tongzhou, this reconfiguration entails the removal of various industrial operations from the city, continuing a long-running process in which low-end manufacturing has been pushed out due to both market and policy pressures. However, five years on, the integration of the area remains unclear, and issues such as changes to *hukou* status have remained off the table. The scheme for the offloading of other industrial and commercial activities ("non-capital" activities) that had been taking place in Beijing to elsewhere in the region became clearer in early 2017.

On 1 April 2017, Xi inaugurated another part of the greater *Jing-Jin-Ji* plan with the announcement of the Xiong'an New Area in Hebei (Xinhua News 2017a). Xiong'an is projected by some analysts to be the most expensive investment project in Chinese history, with a Morgan Stanley analysis looking at between 1.2 and 2.4 trillion yuan, although the scale of the project remains in flux (Ren 2017). Xiong'an consists of three counties—Rongcheng County (容城县), An'xin County (安新县), and Xiong County (雄县). As in the broader *Jing-Jin-Ji* plan, certain kinds of operations are being placed in particular locations, with the government offices in Rongcheng, an ecological role for An'xin, and industrial operations centering in Xiong. While state-owned enterprises and other politically connected firms in China are dutifully complying with the central government's desire to build up the economic vitality of this area by establishing offices in Xiong'an, it is unclear if and when these investments or plans will actually occur or produce positive economic returns.[6] Apparently frustrated by the lack of progress, Xi returned to Xiong'an in January 2019 to reaffirm his commitment to the area (Shi and Jun 2019).

In summary, we see the central state as the leader in this push toward redevelopment and demolition. By ceasing to hold back cities, the politics of local development changed. Many local officials had been wary of the potential for political blowback from redevelopment and demolition of urban villages in their cities—despite having an economic interest in pursuing such actions—and so held off doing so until the central government made it clear that its priorities had changed. Local officials are implementing redevelopment and demolition as yet another piece of the hierarchy's promotion game (Landry 2003; Manion 1985).

Demolitions

With the central-local relationship changing from mutual balance to top-down coordination, the demolition of urban villages under Xi shows new features. Empirical evidence indicates that demolitions have become fiercer, more systematic, and less related to economic incentives compared to the 1990s and 2000s. In this chapter, we use the demolition in Beijing in November 2017 as a case study to examine how demolition in the new era differs from prior experiences.

The 2017 Beijing demolition wave followed a tragic fire in the Gathering Good Fortune Apartments (聚福缘公寓), which combined residences, storage, and production facilities. At 6:15 P.M. on 18 November, local firefighters responded to an alarm and were on the scene shortly thereafter (Xinhua

News 2017b). While the building was not tall, it was extensive; at twenty thousand square meters, it housed an estimated four hundred individuals (*Beijing Wan Bao* 2017). Many, perhaps dozens, were rescued from the fire's wrath, but nineteen succumbed. In its wake, the city's political leaders jumped to attention.

On 20 November, Cai Qi, the party secretary of Beijing, announced the launch of a forty-day campaign to demolish "all illegal residential structures" in the suburban areas of the city, which includes most of the outlying districts, namely Daxing, Fengtai, Chaoyang, Haidian, Tongzhou, Shunyi, and Changping (BASP 2017). In the video release of Cai's speech in an internal meeting, he said sincerely, "At the grassroots level, use 'real swords and spears (真刀真枪).' Don't be afraid of causing conflicts, our real goal is to solve the problem. . . . All district-level parties should be responsible for their territories. I want the top district leaders to be directly involved in this" (YouTube 2017).

Twenty-one bureaus of the Beijing government joined with district-level governments, identifying 25,395 places to be cleaned up within one week (Sina News 2017). The commands of the district-level party cadres to their fellows were similar to Cai's. Wang Xianyong, the party secretary of Fengtai, said in his internal meeting, "You need to be really tough! If you can demolish them today, don't leave it until tomorrow. You know what the toughest way is, arresting the troublemakers!" (Buckley 2017). As a result, media reports suggested dozens of locales were demolished and thousands of residents evicted by the end of December 2017 (Huang and Li 2017; Hornby and Zhang 2017).

The first and most important characteristic of Beijing's urban village demolition in 2017 is that it was a state-planned, systematic, and top-down process. Prior to the Daxing fire, most actions along these lines were individualized rather than citywide or systematic, and focused on residences and migrant schools (Huang and Han 2017; Friedman 2017; Wong, Qiao, and Zheng 2018). Under a market-driven logic, such demolitions took place in scattered localities where officials and commercial developers saw the potential of generating material interests. However, in 2017, the demolition became more systematic and campaign-like, incorporating all areas on Beijing's urban fringe. The decision-making process was clearly top-down—from the municipal government to the communities—with the Beijing government setting the general agenda and the district-level bureaus making detailed plans. There was minimal bottom-up negotiation, unlike what was seen in previous demolitions (Rithmire 2015).

The second characteristic of the demolition is the force and speed with which it occurred. In the past, demolitions benefited local cadres while the central government played a regulative role in setting constraints and compensating migrants and homeowners (Gao, Yang, and Li 2012; Rithmire 2015; Xiang 2004). On the contrary, the central and local government shared the same goal of evicting migrants out from large cities in 2017. With the upper-level government being supportive of population control and migrant eviction, local agents were encouraged to take more aggressive action. The central government stressed the importance of redeveloping shantytowns and created incentives for the Beijing government to push forward the demolition more fiercely. The message of being tough and aggressive was delivered through the hierarchical system of parties and executive branches. Individuals were forcibly removed from their residences, their property dumped onto sidewalks or the street. Numerous photographs document notices indicating that evictions were mandatory by 22 November, the Wednesday following the Friday night fire (Yuan, Yu, and Wu). The eviction team pushed thousands of migrants onto the streets, cutting off electrical or heating supplies and urging people to pack within forty-eight hours. In some villages, the police broke into people's homes, smashing windows and doors if the residents refused to leave (Buckley 2017).

Last but not least, the demolition targeted noneconomic goals rather than the maximization of investments and local GDP growth. The official narrative for why the fire led to the demolition wave focused on safety. Officials from the Beijing Emergency Management Bureau (北京生产安全委员会) claimed that the demolitions were undertaken to eliminate the source of the accidental fire and to protect the personal safety of migrants. They said, "Locals rent out their temporary factory buildings as residential apartments. Hundreds of people lived in a tiny factory building. The electronic wires were as dense as a spiderweb. Wide public alleys were blocked by low-quality compounds. Once an accident happens, it is hard for fire trucks and police cars to enter the village" (Sina News 2017). The government confessed that migrants involved in the eviction were not aware of the latent danger and might be upset because they had to find a new place to live immediately. From a long-term perspective, however, the officials insisted that the migrants would come to understand that the demolition was being done to protect their lives and property from the possibility of future accidents and tragedies.

In the 322-page *Analysis of the Development of Beijing (2018)*, the discussion of the fire in Daxing and subsequent demolitions is referenced only on a single page, which offers the following: "a major fire occurred in a 'three-in-one' site with storage, production, and residence functions in Daxing District." While casualties and deaths are mentioned, it lacks specifics. The rest of the discussion notes the steps that each of five governmental bodies—the Public Security Bureau, the Municipal Fire Bureau, the Capital Comprehensive Management Office, the Beijing Commission of Housing and Urban-Rural Development, and the Municipal Safety Supervision Bureau—undertook to "uncover and rectify safety hazards across the city." The analysis ends its brief description of the events and their aftermath with a more general statement: "Beijing is a mega-city. As such, for the elimination of various hazards in society it is necessary that long-term mechanisms for urban public safety be established and detailed plans be made and implemented, and that such plans are implemented in an orderly manner with strong publicity" (BASS 2019, 115).

Neither the word *development* nor the word *modernization* is placed at the center of the explanation. This rhetoric again emphasizes the idea that to ensure the safety of Beijing, some "hazards" face elimination. There is no suggestion of recognition that removing those hazards implied harming residents of the mega-city or of the deservingness of the residents to have their place in the city protected.

In sum, as the central government changed its role from mediator to initiator of urban village demolition, the demolition began to exhibit new features. Our study of the 2017 demolition wave finds that the changes in local-central incentives made the demolition more thorough and systematic and that its goal was not to enhance economic development but to remove hazards and ensure safety.

Satellite Imagery as a New Source of Information

Besides the quotes found in official statements and leaders' speeches that reveal the noneconomic purposes of the demolition, is there more evidence that shows the government's intention? Taking advantage of the newest technologies, we can use alternative tools to gather more information about Chinese cities. One of the most useful of these resources is satellite imagery. The advancement of high-resolution, high-frequency satellite images makes it possible for researchers to identify the location of urban villages and trace the changes in their spatial and temporal patterns. We see the potential of combining different evidence, conducting data analysis, and discovering new theories with the adoption of satellite imagery.

While conventional sources of information provide many valuable insights into the understanding of Chinese cities, researchers have been concerned about their limitations. Previous literature uses official documents, state-generated data, and on-site interviews and surveys to study the demolition of urban villages in China. However, the accessibility and reliability of these sources vary depending on the political circumstances. First, as China has been tightening up its policies of information security, these conventional sources of information are becoming less accessible. Many archives about contemporary China have limited the availability of documents to external researchers. In some cases, official data previously published by the government have been removed from the Internet.[7] Such restrictions appear to be expanding rather than fading at the time of this writing, making conventional data sources less fruitful for analyses going forward. Second, scholars have discovered that local cadres sometimes manipulate both qualitative and quantitative data to serve their interests in promotions (Wallace 2016) or corruption, with land transactions a prime culprit (Chen and Kung 2018). Local officials can publicize some information to show their loyalty and competence while hiding other information. It is hard to establish the credibility of state-led data—or falsify it—given the prevalence of manipulation. Third, governance of urban villages is delegated to district or township-level governments, which means that the information-collection process is fragmented. Most state-led surveys about urban villages lack a centralized agency to mandate consistency across units or concepts. The term "satisfying living conditions" has different meanings across towns and districts. Qualitative information published by local governments faces similar issues.

For these reasons, many researchers conduct on-site interviews and surveys to study urban villages in China. While fieldwork improves the reliability of empirical evidence and provides ground truth validity, it has several limitations. If the party-state continues to intensify censorship and information controls, more restrictions on field research seem likely. More-over, fieldwork cannot solve the challenges of small-N problems and limited scopes of analyses. Due to the time and budget constraints, most fieldwork covers only a few regional cases. Interviews and surveys have difficulty tracing historical circumstances that no longer exist. Comparative histori-cal studies require immense financial and time investment in long-term projects.

With the help of high-resolution satellite images and digitized street views, we are able to gather alternative information about Chinese urban villages. Free satellite imagery resources like Planet and Google Maps pro-vide their users with accurate and updated depictions of the areas under ob-servation. Google Maps updates its satellite imagery on a roughly monthly basis, while Planet, an independent satellite operator and data analysis firm, has daily imagery at a lower resolution. The street view of Baidu Maps covers most of the areas in large cities so that users can observe the details of each street and its buildings.

The combination of satellite and street-level imagery helps researchers identify the spatial locations of urban villages and observe their patterns. To examine the visual features of urban villages, we made a list of the preexist-ing urban villages reported by credible news agencies during the demolition wave in 2017. We then observed how urban villages differ from agricultural villages and middle-class residences. Figure 2.1 shows the satellite image of Xinjiancun (新建村), an urban village that appeared in many news re-ports about the demolition wave in 2017. The small brown buildings serve as residences of farmers and their families, while the large red and blue build-ings are occupied by migrant workers for residential and industrial purposes. By repetitively observing the areas known as the urban villages according to news reports and official documents,[8] we find that the urban villages in re-cent years are "three-in-one" buildings used for production, storage, and residence, with larger and brighter roofs, and are distributed irregularly. These features help us identify more urban villages not mentioned in quali-tative materials. In this way, we can use satellite imagery to incorporate a large number of observation units in the analysis.

Our research does not suggest that the urban villages in China have always been three-in-one buildings. This chapter focuses on the tempo-rary three-in-one buildings on the periphery of the metropolitan area in Beijing in recent years. However, the procedures of implementation extend across various scenarios; thus, we can locate the areas known as urban

Figure 2.1. Xinjiancun (*a*) before demolition (October 2017); (*b*) after demolition (May 2018).

villages, observe their features, and infer the places that have similar features.

Satellite imagery can provide information beyond the urban villages' location. For example, it also documents the speed of demolition. The thoroughness of the demolition can be seen in Figures 2.1a and 2.1b. In addition, the patterns of demolition in these urban villages reflect the government's intentions. Figure 2.1 shows that no commercial real estate has been built six months after the demolition.[9] Moreover, only the buildings occupied by migrant workers were demolished (large buildings with brighter roofs), while the natural villages adjacent to them survived (small buildings). The image implies that the government was targeted in its actions and did not grab all available land from village collectives and transform it for urban use. The satellite imagery also reveals that many of the demolished spots lacked a convenient traffic system and sufficient urban facilities. For instance, some demolished urban villages in Daxing District were two hours away from the city center, with no direct subway services. As a comparison, Figure 2.2 presents the demolition of Beiyuan (北苑) in 2010, in which both urban villages and natural villages were removed. Satellite images show that construction began at the earliest in June 2012, and within less than two years, new urban residential buildings rose in the same location.

This exploration shows how satellite imagery can reinforce the argument that Beijing's demolition in 2017 was not triggered by economic incentives. To improve the robustness of the findings, we recommend that researchers combine conventional sources with satellite imagery and cross-validate various types of empirical evidence. If consistent, observations from satellite imagery can provide concrete examples to compensate for the limitations of conventional sources of information. When satellite imagery goes against other forms of evidence, researchers have an opportunity to reexamine the reliability of data and explore the gap between official statements and actual implementations.

We also see the potential of building new theories based on satellite imagery. Since satellite images offer a new perspective compared with conventional sources, we expect that they can bring to light new patterns and theories to explain them. Using automated image-reading techniques, one could construct a large-scale data set of Chinese urban villages across time and place. Scholars have used remote sensing data to automatically identify the slums in South Asia and Latin America (Friesen et al. 2019; Kit, Lüdeke, and Reckien 2012; Kuffer, Pfeffer, and Sliuzas 2016). And Planet has launched an AI-based project that detects the changes in buildings and roads automatically on a global scale (Planet, n.d.). A big data set of Chinese urban villages will create more opportunities for future research.

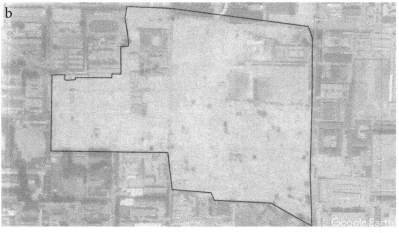

Discussion

This chapter studies the urban development of Beijing as a typical case to show how the shift in the central-local relationship impacts the demolition of urban villages in large Chinese cities. As the capital city, Beijing is more attuned to central directives and comparatively prioritizes political stability. We argue that Beijing's November 2017 demolition wave fits neatly into the political and policy context. All of the policy documents that emerged at the national and local levels suggest that China's major cities, and perhaps especially Beijing, should focus on controlling their population growth and sprawl. From the top of the government on down, support for *penghuqu* redevelopment—and attendant demolitions—has increased, with their advantages seen to outweigh their potential downsides.

Of course, these demolitions are not the first in Beijing's long history. Urban village demolition in the city and its periphery has long been a focus of study, with perhaps the most famous case being that of Zhejiangcun (浙江村) in the 1990s (Xiang 2004). The example of Beiyuan (北苑) depicted in Figure 2.2 also shows that such demolitions and redevelopments have continued to occur.

What the demolition wave shows us, then, is twofold. First, it is further evidence of the government's increased willingness to use repressive tactics, especially on populations that it desires to rectify—whether this remaking be related to religion, political attitudes, or location. Second, despite its scale and thoroughness, obviously not all urban villages or three-in-one buildings in the greater Beijing area were subject to evictions or demolition during the wave. If one can locate enough demolition sites and pair such locales with others that seem similar but were not demolished, then calculations assessing the motivations and explanations of the demolitions can be answered. For instance, are larger or smaller communities more likely to be targeted? Are different districts more aggressively pursuing demolition than others, or is proximity to urban infrastructure such as subway stations linked to demolitions?

In recent decades, China's national government has attempted to encourage the movement of migrants away from the country's largest and

Figure 2.2. Beiyuan (*a*) before demolition (June 2009); (*b*) after demolition (May 2010); (*c*) after commercial construction (September 2012).

most prestigious coastal enclaves to lower-tier cities in the interior through a variety of household registration (*hukou*) reforms. However, the vibrancy of Beijing retained its pull for migrants looking to make good wages. City officials, along with the central government, desired a population of people who have done well, with the thought that they will be the ones most inclined to do well by the regime. Following a tragedy that showed the dangers of migrants' living situations in Beijing, those officials forcibly pushed thousands of those migrants—the people who deliver goods, cook meals, and build and clean the city's towers—out of their residences into a north China winter. These actions were cold calculations that followed and flowed from the political and policy context.

Notes

1. A system of land conversion quotas was established in 2006 by the Ministry of Land Resources to ensure that farmland did not fall below a red line of 120 million hectares (Looney and Rithmire 2017).

2. "The central budget has allocated an urban-rural compulsory education fund of 117 billion yuan (17.2 billion U.S. dollars), up 6.4 percent from 2016, said the Ministry of Finance in early May" (Xinhua News 2016).

3. To clarify, the central government has been issuing "*penghuqu* reform" documents since at least 2008, but their number and significance have increased since Xi Jinping took office in late 2012.

4. The Chinese government used rhetoric strategies to describe the demolition as "reconstruction." However, most of the reconstruction was slow, insufficiently provided, and open only to homeowners (Nguyen 2017).

5. Different sources refer to the plan document as covering 2016–30 (e.g., www.gov.cn/xinwen/2017-03/29/content_5181659.htm) and 2016–35 (e.g., www.gov.cn/xinwen/2017-09/30/content_5228705.htm). Indeed, different chapters of the BASS 2019 *Analysis* use different end dates for the master plan (most use 2035, but Chapter 9 uses 2030).

6. Many have been skeptical of the planned development since its announcement, and a site visit to Rongcheng in summer 2018 did not dispel concerns that the details of the megaplan were falling into place.

7. For example, the Beijing City Lab digitalized a list of land transactions in 2013 from the official website of the Beijing Ministry of Natural Resources, www.bjgtj.gov.cn/tabid/3259/Default.aspx. (Note that the information is no longer accessible.)

8. Satellite imagery may capture the distinctiveness of urban villages in other aspects besides the shades of color. For example, it contains the emitted and reflected radiation data on the earth's surface, known as remote sensing data. Some scholars have tried to identify urban villages using remote sensing data (see Huang, Liu, and Zhang 2015; Li, Huang, and Liu 2017). Its applicability on the three-in-one buildings in Beijing will be explored in the future.

9. Later imagery indicates no construction commenced until 2020.

References

Beijing Academy of Social Sciences (BASS). 2019. *Analysis of the Development of Beijing (2018)*. Singapore: Palgrave Macmillan.

Beijing Administration of Safe Production (BASP). 2017. "21 Beijing Departments Initiate Large-Scale Investigation, Clean-up, and Renovation Campaign." [In Chinese.] 20 November. http://news.sina.com.cn/c/nd/2017-11-20/doc-ifynwxum6834517.shtml.

Buckley, Chris. 2017. "Why Parts of Beijing Look Like a Devastated War Zone." *New York Times*, 30 November. www.nytimes.com/2017/11/30/world/asia/china-beijing-migrants.html.

Chen, Juan, Deborah S. Davis, Kaming Wu, and Haijing Dai. 2015. "Life Satisfaction in Urbanizing China: The Effect of City Size and Pathways to Urban Residency." *Cities* 49 (December): 88–97.

Chen, Ting, and James Kai-sing Kung. 2018. "Busting the Princelings: The Campaign Against Corruption in China's Primary Land Market." *Quarterly Journal of Economics* 134 (1): 185–226.

Démurger, Sylvie, Marc Gurgand, Shi Li, and Ximing Yue. 2009. "Migrants as Second-Class Workers in Urban China? A Decomposition Analysis." *Journal of Comparative Economics* 37 (4): 610–28.

Duckett, Jane, and Athar Hussain. 2008. "Tackling Unemployment in China: State Capacity and Governance Issues." *Pacific Review* 21 (2): 211–29.

Duckett, Jane, and Guohui Wang. 2015. "Poverty and Inequality." In *China's Challenges*, edited by Jacques deLisle and Avery Goldstein, 25–41. Philadelphia: University of Pennsylvania Press.

Friedman, Eli. 2017. "Just-in-Time Urbanization? Managing Migration, Citizenship, and Schooling in the Chinese City." *Critical Sociology* 44 (3): 503–18.

Friesen, John, Hannes Taubenböck, Michael Wurm, and Peter F. Pelz. 2019. "Size Distributions of Slums Across the Globe Using Different Data and Classification Methods." *European Journal of Remote Sensing* 52 (sup2): 99–111.

Fu, Diana, and Greg Distelhorst. 2018. "Grassroots Participation and Repression Under Hu Jintao and Xi Jinping." *China Journal* 79:100–122.

Gao, Qin, Sui Yang, and Shi Li. 2012. "Labor Contracts and Social Insurance Participation among Migrant Workers in China." *China Economic Review* 23 (4): 1195–1205.

———. 2017. "Social Insurance for Migrant Workers in China: Impact of the 2008 Labour Contract Law." *Economic and Political Studies* 5 (3): 285–304.

Gilbert, Alan, and Peter M. Ward. 1985. *Housing, the State and the Poor: Policy and Practice in Three Latin American Cities*. New York: Cambridge University Press.

Gong, Peng, Song Liang, Elizabeth J. Carlton, Qingwu Jiang, Jianyong Wu, Lei Wang, and Justin V Remais. 2012. "Urbanisation and Health in China." *Lancet* 379 (9818): 843–52.

He, Canfei, Yi Zhou, and Zhiji Huang. 2015. "Fiscal Decentralization, Political Centralization, and Land Urbanization in China." *Urban Geography* 37 (3): 436–57.

Ho, Samuel P. S., and George C. S. Lin. 2003. "Emerging Land Markets in Rural and Urban China: Policies and Practices." *China Quarterly* 175 (175): 681–707.

Hornby, Lucy, and Archie Zhang. 2017. "Beijing's Migrant Expulsion Prompts Civic Outcry." *Financial Times*, 28 November. www.ft.com/content/892fb552-d40e-11e7-8c9a-d9c0a5c8d5c9.

Hsing, You-Tien. 2010. *The Great Urban Transformation: Politics of Land and Property in China*. Oxford: Oxford University Press.

Huang, Xin, Hui Liu, and Liangpei Zhang. 2015. "Spatiotemporal Detection and Analysis of Urban Villages in Mega City Regions of China Using High-Resolution Remotely Sensed Imagery." *IEEE Transactions on Geoscience and Remote Sensing* 53 (7): 3639–57.

Huang, Ziyi, and Wei Han. 2017. "Schools for Migrant Children Vanishing as Beijing Combats Population Growth." Caixin, 21 August. www.caixinglobal.com/2017-08-21/schools -for-migrant-children-vanishing-as-beijing-combats-population-growth-101132981 .html.

Huang, Ziyi, and Rongde Li. 2017. "Thousands Evicted in Beijing Crackdown After Fatal Fire." Caixin, 24 November. www.caixinglobal.com/2017-11-24/thousands-evicted-in-beijing -crackdown-after-fatal-fire-101175899.html.

Kan, Karoline. 2016. "Jing-Jin-Ji: Integrating a Chinese Megapolis." *World Policy Journal* 33 (2): 5–10.

Kit, Oleksandr, Matthias Lüdeke, and Diana Reckien. 2012. "Texture-Based Identification of Urban Slums in Hyderabad, India Using Remote Sensing Data." *Applied Geography* 32 (2): 660–67.

Kuffer, Monika, Karin Pfeffer, and Richard Sliuzas. 2016. "Slums from Space: 15 Years of Slum Mapping Using Remote Sensing." *Remote Sensing* 8 (6): 455.

Landry, Pierre F. 2003. "The Political Management of Mayors in Post-Deng China." *Copenhagen Journal of Asian Studies* 17 (March): 31–58.

———. 2008. *Decentralized Authoritarianism in China: The Communist Party's Control of Local Elites in the Post-Mao Era*. New York: Cambridge University Press.

Li, Yansheng, Xin Huang, and Hui Liu. 2017. "Unsupervised Deep Feature Learning for Urban Village Detection from High-Resolution Remote Sensing Images." *Photogrammetric Engineering and Remote Sensing* 83 (8): 567–79.

Liu, Yong, Peilei Fan, Wenze Yue, and Yan Song. 2018. "Impacts of Land Finance on Urban Sprawl in China: The Case of Chongqing." *Land Use Policy* 72 (March): 420–32.

Looney, Kristen, and Meg Rithmire. 2017. "China Gambles on Modernizing Through Urbanization." *Current History* 116 (791): 203–9.

Manion, Melanie. 1985. "The Cadre Management System, Post-Mao: The Appointment, Promotion, Transfer and Removal of Party and State Leaders." *China Quarterly* 102 (June): 203–33.

Ministry of Housing and Urban-Rural Development of China. 2015. "Promote Shantytown Transformation to Solve Housing Problems." www.mohurd.gov.cn/zxydt/201509/t20150902 _224630.html.

Nguyen, Victoria. 2017. "Slow Construction: Alternative Temporalities and Tactics in the New Landscape of China's Urban Development." *City* 21 (5): 650–62.

Planet. n.d. "Planet Analytic Feeds." Accessed 19 November 2021. www.planet.com/products /analytics.

Ren, Daniel. 2017. "Xi Jinping's Dream City Xiongan May Turn Out to Be China's Biggest Public Works Project, Ever." *South China Morning Post*, 13 April. www.scmp.com/business /article/2087107/xi-jinpings-dream-city-xiongan-may-turn-out-be-chinas-biggest -public-works.

Rithmire, Meg. 2015. *Land Bargains and Chinese Capitalism: The Politics of Property Rights Under Reform*. New York: Cambridge University Press.

Scott, James C. 1998. *Seeing like a State: How Certain Schemes to Improve the Human Condition Have Failed.* New Haven: Yale University Press.

Shi, Jiangtao, and Mai Jun. 2019. "Xi Jinping Visits Xiongan New Area in Show of Impatience at Lack of Progress on 'Future City' Plan." *South China Morning Post*, 27 January. www.scmp.com/news/china/article/2183804/xi-jinping-visits-xiongan-new-area-show-impatience-lack-progress-future.

Shin, Hyun Bang, and Bingqin Li. 2013. "Whose Games? The Costs of Being Olympic Citizens in Beijing." *Environment and Urbanization* 25 (2): 559–76.

Sina News. 2017. "Beijing Safety Committee Responds: There Is No Slogan to Drive Out the 'Low-End Population.'" [In Chinese.] 26 November. http://news.sina.com.cn/o/2017-11-26/doc-ifypapmz5176681.shtml.

Smart, Alan. 2002. "Agents of Eviction: The Squatter Control and Clearance Division of Hong Kongs Housing Department." *Singapore Journal of Tropical Geography* 23 (3): 333–47.

Smart, Alan, and Kit Lam. 2009. "Urban Conflicts and the Policy Learning Process in Hong Kong: Urban Conflict and Policy Change in the 1950s and after 1997." *Journal of Asian Public Policy* 2 (2): 190–208.

Smyth, Russell, Ingrid Nielsen, and Qingguo Zhai. 2009. "Personal Well-Being in Urban China." *Social Indicators Research* 95 (2): 231–51.

Solinger, Dorothy J. 1999. *Contesting Citizenship in Urban China: Peasant Migrants, the State, and the Logic of the Market.* Berkeley: University of California Press.

Song, Yan, Yves Zenou, and Chengri Ding. 2008. "Let's Not Throw the Baby Out with the Bath Water: The Role of Urban Villages in Housing Rural Migrants in China." *Urban Studies* 45 (2): 313–30.

State Council of China. 2008. "Suggestions of the State Council on Solving Difficulties of Urban Low-Income Families in Housing." [In Chinese.] 28 March. www.gov.cn/zhengce/content/2008-03/28/content_4673.htm.

———. 2013. "Suggestions of the State Council on Accelerating the Revocation of Shanty Areas." [In Chinese.] 12 July. www.gov.cn/zhengce/content/2013-07/12/content_4556.htm.

———. 2014. "The Notice of the General Office of the State Council on Further Accelerating the Revocation of Shanty Areas." [In Chinese.] 4 August. www.gov.cn/zhengce/content/2014-08/04/content_8951.htm.

———. 2017. "The Circular of the General Office of the State Council on Praising and Incentivising the Implementation of Major Policies in 2016." [In Chinese.] 27 April. www.gov.cn/zhengce/content/2017-04/27/content_5189302.htm.

———. 2019. "The Circular of the General Office of the State Council on Praising and Incentivising the Implementation of Major Policies in 2018." [In Chinese.] 10 May. www.gov.cn/zhengce/content/2019-05/10/content_5390354.htm.

Sun, Xuan, Wenting Yang, Tao Sun, and Yaping Wang. 2018. "Negative Emotion Under Haze: An Investigation Based on the Microblog and Weather Records of Tianjin, China." *International Journal of Environmental Research and Public Health* 16 (1): 86.

Wallace, Jeremy. 2014. *Cities and Stability: Urbanization, Redistribution, and Regime Survival in China.* New York: Oxford University Press.

———. 2016. "Juking the Stats? Authoritarian Information Problems in China." *British Journal of Political Science* 46 (1): 11–29.

Wang, Ya Ping, Yanglin Wang, and Jiansheng Wu. 2009. "Urbanization and Informal Development in China: Urban Villages in Shenzhen." *International Journal of Urban and Regional Research* 33 (4): 957–73.

Wong, Cecilia, Miao Qiao, and Wei Zheng. 2018. "Dispersing, Regulating and Upgrading Urban Villages in Suburban Beijing." *Town Planning Review* 89 (6): 597–621.

Woodworth, Max D., and Jeremy L. Wallace. 2017. "Seeing Ghosts: Parsing China's Ghost City Controversy." *Urban Geography* 38 (8): 1270–81.

Wu, Fulong. 2016. "State Dominance in Urban Redevelopment." *Urban Affairs Review* 52 (5): 631–58.

Wu, Fulong, Fangzhu Zhang, and Chris Webster. 2012. "Informality and the Development and Demolition of Urban Villages in the Chinese Peri-Urban Area." *Urban Studies* 50 (10): 1919–34.

Wu, Weiping, and Mark Frazier. 2018. *The SAGE Handbook of Contemporary China*. London: SAGE.

Wu, Weiping, and Guixin Wang. 2014. "Together but Unequal: Citizenship Rights for Migrants and Locals in Urban China." *Urban Affairs Review* 50 (6): 781–805.

Xiang, Biao. 2004. *Transcending Boundaries: Zhejiangcun: The Story of a Migrant Village in Beijing*. Boston: Brill.

Xinhua News. 2016. "China Focus: Education Gap Narrows for Migrant Workers' Children." 1 June. http://xinhuanet.com//english/2017-06/01/c_136331968.htm.

———. 2017a. "The Central Committee of the Communist Party of China and the State Council Announce Decision to Establish Hebei Xiong'an New District." [In Chinese.] 1 April. http://xinhuanet.com/politics/2017-04/01/c_1120741571.htm.

———. 2017b. "Fire in Xinjian Village, Daxing, Beijing Has Killed 19 People." [In Chinese.] 19 November. http://xinhuanet.com//local/2017-11/19/c_1121976989.htm.

Yang, Jun, Avralt-Od Purevjav, and Shanjun Li. 2020. "The Marginal Cost of Traffic Congestion and Road Pricing: Evidence from a Natural Experiment in Beijing." *American Economic Journal: Economic Policy* 12 (1): 418–53.

YouTube. 2017. 6 December. www.youtube.com/watch?v=_y5VnbJABbg.

Yuan, Suwen, Lu Yu, and Gang Wu. 2017. "Dislocated Migrant Workers Left in Cold and Confusion in Beijing." 26 November. www.caixinglobal.com/2017-11-26/dislocated-migrant -workers-left-cold-and-confused-in-beijing-101176307.html.

Zenz, Adrian. 2018. "'Thoroughly Reforming Them Towards a Healthy Heart Attitude': China's Political Re-Education Campaign in Xinjiang." *Central Asian Survey* 38 (1): 102–28.

Zhang, Chenchen. 2018. "Governing Neoliberal Authoritarian Citizenship: Theorizing Hukou and the Changing Mobility Regime in China." *Citizenship Studies* 22 (8): 855–81.

Zhang, Shawn. 2019. "Xinjiang Re-education Camps List by Cities." Medium, 20 May. https://medium.com/@shawnwzhang/xinjiang-re-education-camps-list-by-cities -f4ed0a6e095a.

Zhu, Jieming. 2004. "Local Developmental State and Order in China's Urban Development During Transition." *International Journal of Urban and Regional Research* 28 (2): 424–47.

CHAPTER 3

Housing Markets, Residential Sorting, and Spatial Segregation

Shin Bin Tan, Wenfei Xu, and Sarah Williams

Introduction

One of the most dramatic shifts in housing systems occurred during the 1980s and 1990s, when China transitioned from a socialist, state-led housing system toward a more market-based housing market. This transition occurred in tandem with broader economic reforms in the 1980s and 1990s that transformed China's centrally planned socialist economy to a competition-driven and market-oriented one. Prior to these reforms, almost all housing was built and owned by "work units," which were decentralized state-sector institutions. Housing units were allocated rather than sold to employees according to their status and seniority (Wang and Murie 2000; Wu et al. 2014). Given this welfare-oriented system of housing provision, Chinese cities were seen as more socially mixed and less spatially unequal than their Western counterparts (Huang 2005; Wang and Murie 2000; Yeh, Xu, and Hu 1995).

In 1998, the central government embarked on the full marketization stage in their housing reforms, abolished welfare housing distribution (Wu et al. 2014; Yang and Chen 2014) and sparked off a massive construction boom (Shi, Chen, and Wang 2016). The introduction of a private housing market allowed residents to self-sort into neighborhoods by income and associated preferences in ways previously impossible under the socialist housing framework. While the Chinese state did not withdraw completely from housing provision, the importance of public housing declined rapidly and significantly after the 1998 reforms (Shi, Chen, and Wang 2016; Wu 2015). In contrast, the private housing market grew tremendously in size and importance within China's economy and urban landscape (Wang et al. 2016; Wu 2015).

Scholars have hypothesized that this transition generated greater spatial residential segregation based on class and income (Huang 2005; Wu 2002; Wu et al. 2014; Yang, Wang, and Wang 2015). Residential segregation, which can be broadly defined as the physical separation of individuals in residential space based on their membership in socially constructed categories such as race, ethnicity, gender, class, or religion (Massey and Denton 1988; Kramer 2018), has been linked to negative effects on health, social well-being, and social equity (Massey and Denton 1993; Darden et al. 2010; Kramer and Hogue 2009). For instance, segregation can accentuate the economic advantages of high-income families and worsen the disadvantages of low-income families through neighborhood composition effects as well as the distribution of resources across space consistent with income (Reardon and Bischoff 2011). Residential segregation along socioeconomic and racial lines has also been linked to disparities in exposure to crime and violence, poorer physical and mental health status, and health-related behaviors (Kramer 2018; Williams and Collins 2001). There is also concern that rising socioeconomic segregation might lead to social unrest, decreased trust, and lower civic participation (Musterd et al. 2017; Musterd 2005).

Given the sizable negative consequences of residential segregation, there is a pressing need to understand the processes and mechanisms driving this phenomenon, as well as to track its trajectory over time. The bulk of existing urban residential segregation literature, however, has focused on the North American context, in which residential segregation is often understood through a dual race-class lens (Wilson 1987; Massey and Denton 1988; Clark 1986; Charles 2003) and as a product of racial discrimination (Yinger 1995; Galster 1988). In contrast, residential segregation in China is predominantly driven by class dynamics, with no racial component (Bian et al. 2005), which limits the applicability of insights from North American studies to China. Furthermore, there have been few empirically based multicity examinations of whether and how a transition from a state-led housing system to a market-based housing system—such as the one experienced in China—might manifest in neighborhood-level changes (Marcińczak et al. 2015). Our study seeks to address this gap in the literature by providing an empirical examination of fine-grained locational patterns of housing units constructed after China's transition toward a more market-based system of housing in terms of whether they might contribute to increased spatial segregation within neighborhoods and communities.

Furthermore, we focus on the spatial concentrations of affluence, because there has been relatively little attention paid to this important aspect of segregation. Much of the urban segregation literature has focused on the concentration of poverty (Wilson 1987), including several studies that examined the spatial segregation of poor migrant populations in Chinese cities (Shen 2017; Li, Wu, and Xiao 2015). Given that the growing inequality in China over the years has been fueled by gains at the top of the income distribution (Piketty and Qian 2009), there needs to be greater attention paid to analyzing and understanding the concentration of affluence, in addition to current studies on the concentration of poverty. Studies in this area, including this one, can help provide a fuller picture of the system of stratification and how the social lives of the rich and poor are increasingly bifurcated (Krivo et al. 2013).

By examining the relationship between housing reforms, and resultant housing construction and household residential location choices, this chapter speaks to the first theme of this volume, which focuses on how urbanization in China has been shaped by state interventions and associated social, economic, and physical interactions. Specifically, we ask: did each successive wave of construction after major urban housing reforms in 1998 contribute to more expensive residential housing units being more closely clustered together and located farther away from lower-priced housing units?

The chapter also speaks to the third theme of this volume, which considers new sources of information for conducting research on urban China. While most studies of residential segregation, including those focusing on Chinese cities, typically rely on official census data or other administrative statistics, such an approach has significant limitations due to the scale at which conclusions can be drawn. The limitations associated with using census administrative units and census unit-based segregation measures, such as the dissimilarity index, to measure residential segregation have been amply discussed in other papers (Lee et al. 2008; Reardon and O'Sullivan 2004). A challenge specific to residential segregation research in China is access to official fine-grained small-area estimates. While there have been spatial segregation studies for which researchers obtained census data aggregated at the level of resident committee areas (居委会), each of which consists of about three thousand people (Li and Wu 2008; Wu et al. 2014), such studies are rare, potentially because of data availability. Instead, most Chinese studies use census data aggregated over large administrative districts: at the level of counties (县) (Gu 2001; Huang 2005; Wu 2002), which have populations of over a million, or townships (镇 / 街道) (Liu, Dijst, and Geertman 2015; Liu and Cao 2017; Monkkonen, Comandon, and Zhu 2017), which have populations of about forty-two thousand people (Monkkonen, Comandon, and Zhu 2017). Using large administrative units makes it impossible to unpack patterns of residential segregation at the local neighborhood or community scale, which is particularly limiting for Chinese cities, where urban segregation occurs at smaller spatial scales because of high population and built density (Zhao and Wang 2018). Relying on coarsely aggregated census boundaries could thus result in underestimations of segregation.

In this chapter, we address these challenges by using a novel data set of housing listings from a popular Chinese real estate website, Fang.com. Besides real estate databases curated by government authorities or research consultancies, which may be difficult or expensive for researchers to access, the increasing proliferation and popularity of online real estate websites in China have generated a new, constantly updated, easily obtainable source of housing data that could be used for research (Li et al. 2016; Chen et al. 2016). It is important to highlight the differences between using demographic data and residential housing prices to examine socioeconomic segregation. Housing prices within a neighborhood may not fully mirror the socioeconomic status of those living within the neighborhood because an expensive neighborhood may still have residents of lower income, such as migrants co-renting an expensive apartment or households in an older, central neighborhood who obtained their homes before the neighborhood became expensive. However, while current housing prices may not wholly represent the *present* population mix of neighborhoods, they can be indicative of the *future* mix (Wu 2002), given that listed prices represent what sellers hope to get for their units and thus the types of buyers that can afford the cost. A neighborhood with many expensive housing listings is likely to be purchased by wealthy buyers over time, while a neighborhood with few expensive housing listings is unlikely to see a similar increase. Additionally, while much less common than the use of census data, using housing price data to analyze socio-spatial patterns in Chinese cities is not without precedent. Researchers have employed both asking prices and transaction prices of housing as a proxy for the socioeconomic status of residents to analyze residential patterns at a higher spatial resolution than is offered by available demographic data (Li et al. 2015; Wu 2002; Li et al. 2016; Chen et al. 2016). For these reasons, we believe residential price data can provide useful insight about socioeconomic mixing at the neighborhood scale.

By combining this novel data set with two explicitly spatial measures of segregation, instead of the conventional aspatial measures of segregation, we provide a different angle to understanding residential segregation in China. Such spatially fine-grained methods of studying socio-spatial segregation have not been much explored within the Chinese residential segregation literature. Here, using spatially fine-grained housing data and measures can help researchers identify specific locations of potentially high or low levels of spatial segregation. As an illustration, a location-specific question this study examines is whether the degree of high-end housing concentration within the historical city core differs from that in more newly built suburban areas.

Discussions in this chapter would be of specific interest to Chinese policy makers tracking neighborhood-level patterns of spatial segregation associated with rapid urban growth and housing reforms. Researchers of Chinese cities have cautioned that the increasing spatial segregation of different socioeconomic groups could negatively affect fair distribution of urban resources; exacerbate the gap in living conditions between rich and poor areas; and impair social order, harmony, and stability (Gu 2001; Huang 2005; Xu 2008; Yang, Wang, and Wang 2015). Given these potential adverse impacts, findings from our study could help policy makers identify potentially problematic city-level trends, as well as areas within cities that might benefit from targeted policies to improve housing mix.

The remainder of this chapter is organized as such: Section 2 lays out the overall analytical approach to our empirical study, explaining our choice of specific cities as case studies, discussing the unique data set of housing listings and the two spatial segregation measures used, and detailing the analytical steps taken. Section 3 presents and discusses key results that suggest a trend of growing spatial segregation. Section 4 concludes by discussing ideas for further research, limitations of the current study, and recommendations on how scholars could use nontraditional fine-grained data sources to monitor spatial segregation over time.

Analytical Approach: Context, Data, and Measures of Segregation

Selecting Case-Study Cities

An important factor linking residential segregation and the spatial heterogeneity of land and housing values is the agglomerative effect of cities, which links regional differences in urban development to differences in socioeconomic inequality and patterns of spatial segregation (Baum-Snow and Pavan 2013; Fry and Taylor 2012; Glaeser, Resseger, and Tobio 2008; Gordon and Monastiriotis 2006; Monkkonen and Zhang 2011; Morgan 1975). Due to this agglomerative effect, the size of cities can disproportionately affect wage inequality in larger cities (Baum-Snow and Pavan 2013), which in turn may affect residential segregation for affluent groups (Reardon and Bischoff 2011). A study of twenty Chinese cities, using 2000 census data, found a positive correlation, albeit a weak one, between overall segregation levels, city population size, and level of economic development, potentially because the more competitive land markets in larger, more wealthy cities led to greater neighborhood differentiation (Monkkonen, Comandon, and Zhu 2017).

To capture a spectrum of spatial segregation across Chinese cities as well as inspect the link between economic development, housing markets, and residential segregation, this study examines three Chinese cities of varying economic maturity and size: Shanghai, Chengdu, and Shenyang. Shanghai has historically been an economically successful, international port city and is now one of China's largest cities in terms of population and gross regional product (GRP). While Chengdu is generally considered a prosperous city, it nevertheless has a smaller GRP and a lower income per capita than Shanghai. Compared to Shanghai, Chengdu thus seems relatively less attractive to high-net-worth, highly educated individuals. In contrast to Chengdu and Shanghai, Shenyang has experienced uneven economic growth, which has slowed in recent years (Wang et al. 2016). Of the three cities, Shenyang has the lowest GRP, population size, and average income per capita, as well as the lowest number of top 500 companies, international schools, and multimillionaires.

A Novel Data Source for Analyzing Patterns of Segregation: Online Housing Listings

We analyzed real estate listings from Fang.com posted online between March and May 2016. While there are several online real estate portals, Fang .com is one of the most popular ones in terms of page views and visitors (Li et al. 2016). Fang.com covers many Chinese cities and thus is a good resource for comparison across multiple cities.[1] For these reasons, this study uses Fang .com as a primary data source.

The data collected from Fang.com included the locational coordinates of the housing estate (小区) each residence belonged to, asking price, size, and the year the development was built. Housing estates are planned neighborhoods, generally enclosed within a barrier of some kind, like a wall or a fence. They have their own internal circulation system, and the housing is integrated with communal facilities like kindergartens, clinics, and shops. They tend to be under the control of professional property management companies and have security guards monitoring their entrances. A housing estate can accommodate between three thousand and five thousand households, has about twenty to fifty apartment buildings, and might have an estimated area of fifteen to twenty hectares (Bray 2008; Wallenwein 2014). Given that the locational information here is of relatively small spatial resolution, especially when compared to traditional census-based administrative data, our analysis is thus comparatively less prone to the modifiable areal unit problem (MAUP) (Openshaw 1984). Furthermore, given that these housing estates are typically self-contained and gated, and residents are generally expected to interact more within the estate confines, each housing estate effectively functions as an individual residential entity and can be analyzed as such.

We restricted our analysis to resale listings, as resale prices are more stable than that of newly built commodity housing, as these prices can be arbitrarily set by developers (Wu 2002). We also included listings of presale units in our analysis, which are units in developments currently under construction but that have been sold prior to actual completion (Zheng et al.

2012). Outlier data points in terms of price and unit size were removed to avoid skewing the analysis. Appendix A provides details about the data cleaning.

To determine what is high-end housing, we adopt a definition commonly used by real estate consultancies, in which prime residential property is defined as the top 5 percent of the market by price (Chick 2019). Therefore, for our study, the most expensive units (top 5 percent) built within each year were classified as "high-end." All other units were classified as "non-high-end." Given that relatively few units were built before 1990, these units were classified as "high-end" relative to all units built before 1990, rather than in comparison to their year of being built.

We classified "high-end" and "non-high-end" within each year band in order to enable the identification of listings that may have been considered relatively high-end when first built, even if they were no longer among the top percentile of current-day prices. For instance, a high-end apartment built in 1998 may have depreciated in value by 2016 and thus may no longer fall within the top percentile of current prices. However, compared to other units built in the same year, it would still have a relative sale price premium and could be considered high-end within its cohort.

One important consideration to highlight is that a housing unit constructed in 1998 may not have been particularly expensive when it was first built, in comparison to other units built in the same year, but may have appreciated significantly in relative value if its surrounding environment improved substantially more than did other neighborhoods over the years. Similarly, a building that was relatively expensive when built in 1998 might not retain a similarly high value in 2016 vis-à-vis the rest of its cohort if the neighborhood around it has deteriorated more than have other neighborhoods over time. However, besides neighborhood characteristics, housing prices are also determined to a large extent by the structural characteristics of the unit/development, such as total unit size, number of floors, south-facing orientation of windows, architectural design features, and provision of amenities like swimming pools. Hedonic pricing studies of housing in Chinese cities suggest that these structural factors, which remain constant over time, have a larger impact on housing prices than do neighborhood or locational factors such as park access and subway proximity (Wen, Shenghua, and Xiao-yu 2005; Jim and Chen 2006; Xiao et al. 2017). Furthermore, recent studies have found evidence suggesting that buyers in higher-end housing submarkets valued characteristics such as proximity to subways, basic public services, and parks less than did buyers in lower-end housing submarkets. An explanation for this relative insensitivity to neighborhood characteristics is that rich home buyers can better afford cars and may thus be less sensitive to immediate neighborhood characteristics compared to average home buyers in China (Yang, Chau, and Wang 2019; Zhang and Yi 2017). Given these findings, one might plausibly assume that time-invariant building or unit-level structural characteristics (large unit size, villa typology) are key determinants of high-end status, and that such units maintain their high-end status even with neighborhood changes over time.

However, we acknowledge that robust verification of this assumption requires more research and data beyond the current scope of this chapter. Here, we focus on a more conservative interpretation of our findings that does not require such a strong assumption: that 2016 levels of segregation vary by each period of building construction. At the same time, we explore a more tentative interpretation: that if we hold the assumptions that the relative value of high-end housing vis-à-vis other housing stock is reasonably time-invariant (as previously discussed) and that the Fang listings capture a reasonably representative sample of housing stock in the city, then changes in the spatial segregation of high-end housing units by year built will mirror changes in levels of segregation over time. In other words, the spatial segregation of residential units listed on Fang.com in 2016 that were built before a certain year will approximate the level of spatial segregation as of that year.

Because the housing prices used for this study were obtained from one time period (March to May 2016), we did not adjust the prices further for inflation. Table 3.1 summarizes key characteristics of high-end and mass-market listings for each city.

Measuring Dimensions of Segregation: Spatial Exposure and Spatial Evenness

Over decades, researchers of residential segregation developed many measures of segregation and have categorized these into distinct conceptual dimensions (Massey and Denton 1988), which have been simplified into two: spatial exposure/isolation, and spatial evenness/clustering (Reardon and O'Sullivan 2004). Spatial exposure refers to the extent that members of one group encounter members of another group, while spatial isolation refers to the extent that members of one group encounter members of their

Table 3.1. Characteristics of high-end and mass-market listings

City	Characteristic	High-end listings	Non-high-end listings
Shanghai	Number of listings	37,124	730,692
	Mean price (RMB)	18,623,000	3,948,105
	Mean size (sq m)	217	92
	Mean year built	2000	2003
Chengdu	Number of listings	18,349	355,350
	Mean price (RMB)	3,578,000	886,298
	Mean size (sq m)	221	101
	Mean year built	2009	2009
Shenyang	Number of listings	7,370	143,633
	Mean price (RMB)	1,987,000	670,199
	Mean size (sq m)	174	91
	Mean year built	2007	2007

Note: More detailed descriptive statistics are in Appendix B.

own group (Reardon and O'Sullivan 2004). For instance, in a city where high-end housing is highly spatially isolated, areas around each high-end apartment unit would consist of mostly high-end housing units, compared to a city with low spatial isolation, where the local environment of each high-end housing unit includes more housing units of lower price points. Spatial evenness refers to the extent to which groups are similarly distributed, while its converse, spatial clustering, refers to how much groups are clustered together. A city where high-end units are closely clustered in just a few neighborhoods will have higher spatial clustering compared to a city where high-end units are dispersed evenly throughout.

We use two measures to estimate these two dimensions of segregation. The first, which estimates spatial exposure/isolation, is the spatial exposure/isolation index ($\tilde{P}^*$), a spatial extension of a much-used isolation/exposure measure (Massey and Denton 1988). Here we focus on the spatial isolation of high-end units ($_{\text{high-end}} \tilde{P}^*_{\text{high-end}}$). The higher the spatial isolation score, which ranges from 0 to 1, the more spatially separated high-end housing units are from other housing types.

The second measure, which measures spatial evenness/clustering, is the spatial information theory index ($\tilde{H}$)—an extension of the Theil's entropy measure, a commonly used measure of diversity. The spatial information theory index measures the extent that local environments of individual units differ in their group composition, and can be interpreted as a measure of the variation in diversity of local environments of each unit (Iceland 2004). If there is deviation between the group composition of individual listings' local environment and overall city group composition, it would suggest clustering of different unit types in different parts of the city. $\tilde{H}$ would thus be non-zero, with a maximum value of 1, where the local environments of all individual listings consist of only one type of housing. If $\tilde{H}$ is negative, this suggests hyperintegration, where there is greater diversity in the local environments than in the population as a whole (Reardon et al. 2009; Reardon and O'Sullivan 2004).

Additional details of these two measures and how they are applied to our analysis are included in Appendix C.

Examining Intracity Patterns

As a demonstration of how fine-grained spatial housing data and spatial segregation measures can be used to analyze intracity spatial patterns, we identified a five-kilometer-radius area for each city that approximated the urban historic core. This core was then used as a basis to answer the location-specific question of whether the distribution of high-end housing within the more historic city core differs from that in more suburban areas.

Analyzing Segregation over Separate and Cumulative Time Periods

To analyze how units built after the major 1998 housing reforms contributed to each city's overall levels of segregation, we grouped the listings into five-year periods based on their built year, then calculated the degree of high-end housing segregation that occurred within each five-year block. The last block, 2014–20 stretches seven years to include presale listings that were sold before actual completion and thus can be interpreted as a rough estimate of the future spatial distribution of housing stock. For ease of reference, we refer to these time periods loosely as "five-year blocks."

We then considered the cumulative patterns of spatial segregation by calculating segregation measures for all units built within a window that widened by five-year increments: 1900 to 1998, 1900 to 2003, 1900 to 2008, 1900 to 2013, and finally a larger seven-year increment covering the years 1900 to 2019. Doing so allows us to understand how each successive period of development contributed to overall levels of segregation in 2016.

An Empirical Analysis of Residential Spatial Segregation Patterns

Spatial Patterns of Units Built, Summarized by Five-Year Blocks

Figure 3.1 summarizes the two segregation measures calculated for units built within each five-year block.

For units built after 1998, both measures of spatial segregation showed an upward trend in all three cities. This finding suggests that each successive five-year period of building produced a batch of high-end housing that was more isolated and clustered than the previous batch. The highest levels of isolation and clustering is projected to be contributed by developments built between 2014 and 2020, taking into consideration presales for buildings still under construction. Spatial segregation was consistently highest in Shanghai, as was its rate of increase over each five-year period, indicated by a steeper slope in Figure 3.1. The rate of increase in spatial segregation in Chengdu and Shenyang was comparatively less steep and moved within a fairly similar range. Interestingly, though, for Shanghai and Chengdu, units

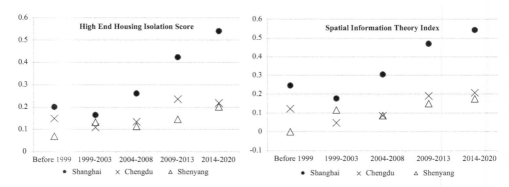

Figure 3.1. Spatial information theory index and high-end housing isolation score for units completed within five-year blocks.

built prior to 1999 seemed more spatially segregated on both $\tilde{P}^*$ and $\tilde{H}$ measures, compared to units built immediately after, from 1999 to 2003.

Analysis of City Core, by Five-Year Blocks

We analyzed whether there were perceptible differences in the spatial segregation of high-end housing within each city's urban core versus housing located outside the core. To do so, we calculated the average localized $\tilde{P}^*$ high-end housing isolation score for each housing estate, defined here as the distance-weighted proportion of high-end units within the local environment of each housing estate that has at least one high-end housing unit listed, which we will refer to as high-end housing estates henceforth for brevity. Localized $\tilde{P}^*$ high-end housing isolation scores of high-end housing estates within the city core were then compared against those of high-end housing estates outside the core. Figure 3.2 maps out the high-end housing isolation scores for the three cities for units built before 1999 and those built between 2014 and 2020.

Shanghai's high-end housing estates within the city center were much more spatially isolated from non-high-end housing compared to high-end estates outside the city center throughout all five-year blocks of development. The average localized high-end $\tilde{P}^*$ score of high-end housing estates within the defined city center increased from 0.26 for units built before 1999 to 0.47 for units built between 2014 and 2020. High-end housing estates outside the city center had average localized high-end $\tilde{P}^*$ scores, which increased from 0.04 to 0.12 between 1999 and 2020.

For Chengdu and Shenyang, higher levels of spatial isolation of high-end housing estates within the city core were observable for some but not all five-year periods. Compared to Shanghai, however, the differences between city core and non-city core levels of segregation in Chengdu and Shenyang were relatively small, ranging from 0.02 to 0.03 for Chengdu and 0.03 to 0.14 for Shenyang.

Cumulative Spatial Pattern of Units, by Five-Year Increments

We then examined how the accumulation of building stock over each period of building contributed to overall spatial housing segregation (see Figure 3.3).

SHANGHAI Localized Luxury Isolation Score

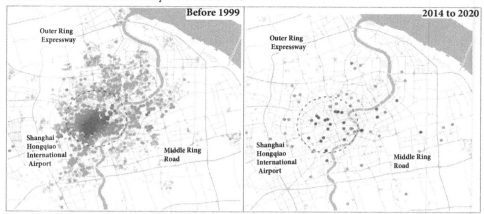

CHENGDU Localized Luxury Isolation Score

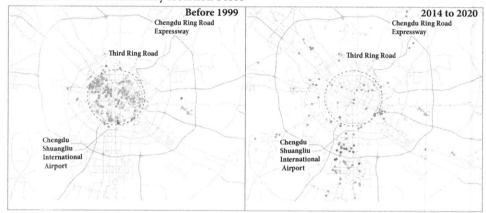

SHENYANG Localized Luxury Isolation Score

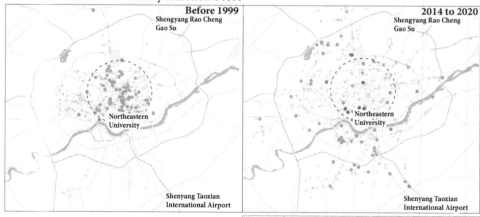

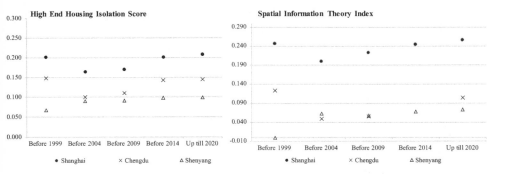

Figure 3.3. Spatial information theory index and high-end housing isolation score for developments built before a specified year.

Our analysis of the change in spatial segregation that occurred with the accumulation of building stock was consistent with the earlier analysis of each individual five-year period of development. Units in Shanghai and Chengdu prior to 1999 were more spatially segregated than those in the periods after, which suggests that the new developments built after 1999 reduced overall spatial segregation. However, new units built at each successive five-year junction from 1999 onward increased citywide spatial segregation. Units built in Shenyang from 1999 onward contributed to an increase in overall spatial segregation from pre-1999 levels, and absolute spatial segregation seemed consistently highest in Shanghai.

Analysis of City Core, by Five-Year Increments

Figure 3.4 maps out the accumulated high-end housing isolation scores for the three cities. Consistent with our earlier analysis of each discrete five-year time block, the average localized $\tilde{P}^*$ scores within Shanghai's city core, which ranged from 0.21 to 0.26, were substantially higher than the average $\tilde{P}^*$ score of high-end housing outside the city center, which ranged from

Figure 3.2. Localized $\tilde{P}^*$ scores for Shanghai, Chengdu, and Shenyang, by year blocks.

0.04 to 0.07. In contrast, for Chengdu, the average localized $\tilde{P}^*$ score of high-end estates within the city center were not much different from the average localized $\tilde{P}^*$ score of high-end estates outside the city center, across all time periods. Instead of the city core, Figure 3.4 suggests that south of the city core, outside the Third Ring Road and close to the Tianfu International Finance Center (天府国际金融中心) seemed to be the neighborhood where high-end housing was becoming most segregated over time.

For Shenyang, while there were some differences between the average localized $\tilde{P}^*$ scores of units within the city center and those outside the city center, these differences were again very small, ranging from 0.01 to 0.02. As indicated in Figure 3.4, the area south of the Hunhe River and Shenyang's Northeastern University (东北大学) was where spatial segregation of high-end housing seemed more concentrated, rather than in the city center.

Collectively, our analysis suggests that areas farther from the urban cores of Chengdu and Shenyang may be growing more segregated than the urban cores themselves.

Discussion and Conclusions: Possible Implications for Chinese Cities

The introduction and consolidation of a housing market in China post-1998 has been hypothesized to have facilitated residential sorting along socio-economic lines. Thus, one would expect to see greater spatial segregation of high-end housing units built after 1998. In our analysis, we indeed found that high-end housing units built from 2004 onward appeared more clustered and isolated from lower-priced housing, which suggests that each period of new construction beginning in 2004 contributed to increasing levels of segregation. However, we also found some interesting city-specific patterns emerging from our analysis. First, we found that units built within the first five years of housing policy reform did not contribute to increased segregation in Chengdu and Shanghai, but they did in Shenyang. Second, we found that high-end private housing was most highly segregated in Shanghai and least so in Shenyang. Third, we found that high-end private housing was more clustered along the urban fringes of the two Tier 2 cities than within their city centers, in contrast to Tier 1 Shanghai. Finally, our analysis demonstrates that a widely available online data source such as Fang.com can facilitate analyses and comparisons of socio-spatial segregation across

SHANGHAI Localized Luxury Isolation Score

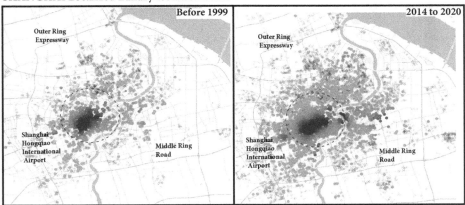

CHENGDU Localized Luxury Isolation Score

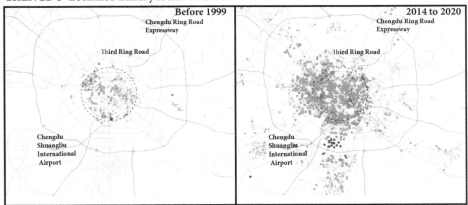

SHENYANG Localized Luxury Isolation Score

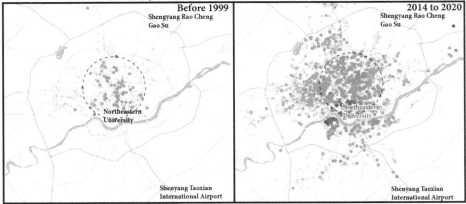

Figure 3.4. Localized P̌* scores for Shanghai, Chengdu, and Shenyang, cumulative.

multiple Chinese cities. The following paragraphs explore each of these findings in greater detail.

An unexpected finding was that there was an initial drop in the spatial segregation of high-end units from pre-1999 levels in Chengdu and Shanghai compared to new developments built between 1999 and 2004. The first batch of new developments built within five years of the 1998 reforms actually lowered both the $\tilde{P}^*$ and $\tilde{H}$ measures of segregation. In contrast, for Shenyang, we do not observe a similar decline of measured segregation when comparing the building units constructed pre-1999 to those constructed 1999 and onward. These findings suggest that the introduction of a housing market may not automatically or immediately generate new housing stock that increases overall spatial clustering in cities, particularly in cities where high-end housing stock built prior already exhibits strong spatial clustering and isolation. For instance, housing types built before 1999 were much more spatially mixed in Shenyang compared to Shanghai and Chengdu, possibly because Shenyang had comparatively slower and patchier growth and urbanization during China's initial phase of market liberalization in the 1980s and 1990s (Liu et al. 2014). The initial influx of new housing encouraged by market reforms may thus have ultimately improved the spatial mix in cities like Chengdu and Shanghai that had pre-reform housing stock that was spatially more segregated, but not in cities with a more mixed pre-reform housing stock. Differences in regional or city-level urban and housing policies could also have potentially affected the specific spatial patterning of new housing sold on the market. Future research could focus on this period of transition to examine the policy and market mechanisms at play in these different cities.

If one adopts the previously discussed assumption that the value of high-end housing units is relatively impervious to neighborhood change over time, one may therefore further extrapolate from the findings that actual levels of segregation (not just relative contributions of each period of construction) have increased over time across all three cities. This is an observation broadly in line with existing literature on residential segregation in Chinese cities, where researchers observed socio-spatial restructuring and increasing urban social segregation post-reform (Gu 2001; Huang 2005; Wu 2002; Wu et al. 2014; Yang, Wang, and Wang 2015). This chapter thus provides some evidence that Chinese cities across the spectrum of economic development are experiencing an increase in spatial segregation of the market housing over time.

To date, there has been little empirical work that specifically analyzes the patterns and impact of spatial segregation of affluence, and none, to our knowledge, specific to Chinese cities. While research from elsewhere, primarily Western jurisdictions, suggests a link between spatial segregation and poorer health, economic development, and social outcomes (Massey and Denton 1988; Darden et al. 2010; Kramer and Hogue 2009; Reardon and Bischoff 2011; Musterd et al. 2017), more research is needed to definitively ascertain the actual impact of increasing spatial segregation in Chinese cities. As a result, we can only offer speculative hypotheses about the potential social impact of the spatial patterns we observe in our analysis, drawing from available literature on spatial inequality and residential segregation in China and elsewhere. China scholars have noted that spatial segregation in Chinese cities worsened low-income residents' access to urban resources like green spaces (Shen, Sun, and Che 2017) and jobs (Zhou, Wu, and Cheng 2013), and have also expressed concern that increasing residential segregation would widen the gap in living conditions between rich and poor areas and thus impair social order, harmony, and stability (Gu 2001; Huang 2005; Xu 2008; Yang, Wang, and Wang 2015). Increases in spatial segregation may exacerbate and reinforce societal fissures created by the broader trend of growing income and wealth inequality in China since its 1978 economic reforms (Piketty, Yang, and Zucman 2019; Xie and Zhou 2014; Zhou and Song 2016). This growing rich–poor gap is seen by the public as a major problem (Xie and Zhou 2014), and policy makers—concerned about its implications on social harmony—have sought to mitigate this gap through various income distribution policies (Zhou and Song 2016).

Given spatial segregation's potential adverse impacts on social well-being and associated stability, we recommend that scholars and policy makers pay close attention to this worrying trend of increasing levels of spatial segregation. Just as local governments, including Shanghai's and Chengdu's, have over the years demonstrated a willingness to intervene in the housing market through various policies in order to stabilize housing prices and maintain housing affordability (Shi, Chen, and Wang 2016; Sun et al. 2017), they should consider how these policies could also address the increasing segregation of affluence.

Our analysis also found high-end private housing to be the most highly segregated in Shanghai across the board, and least so in Shenyang, which supports our initial hypothesis that more economically developed cities with larger population sizes and a more affluent, educated population would see more intensive residential sorting and high-end housing segregation. Our findings here also align with findings from a previous study that larger, richer Chinese cities tended to be more segregated (Monkkonen, Comandon, and Zhu 2017). The social implications here are that the more affluent Chinese cities may experience the effects of social segregation more acutely. Accordingly, policy makers concerned with preventing spatial polarization should place higher priority on monitoring and managing housing mix in such larger, richer cities.

In terms of location-specific characteristics of segregation, our analysis shows clear differences between our case-study cities. Shanghai's city core showed intense spatial segregation of high-end housing, where high-end estates located within the city center had localized $\tilde{P}^*$ scores at least twice that of the high-end estates located outside the city center across individual five-year periods and cumulatively. This finding is consistent with results from other empirical studies that highlight how local-government-led redevelopment within older inner-city cores in Shanghai resulted in low-rise, working-class neighborhoods being displaced by modern, expensive high-rise condominiums (Ren 2008; Yang, Wang, and Wang 2015) and further suggests that city-center gentrification is a major driver of the spatial concentration of affluence in Shanghai.

Interestingly, though, such a large difference in measured segregation between the city core and the rest of the city was not observed for either Chengdu or Shenyang. Rather, the differences between the average localized $\tilde{P}^*$ scores of high-end estates within the city center and those of high-end estates outside the city center were fairly marginal for both cities. Our results suggest that housing development patterns in these two cities are substantially different from Shanghai's, and that high-end private housing is more clustered along the urban fringes than it is within the center. Our estimates of localized segregation highlighted pockets of developments outside the city core, such as the areas close to the Tianfu International Finance Center in Chengdu and south of the Hunhe River in Shenyang, which show increasingly intense spatial isolation of high-end housing. One possible reason is that Shanghai's city center, compared to that of Shenyang or Chengdu, may have more attractive locational features, such as historical buildings and riverfront access, that further concentrate the development of high-end housing there. More research would be valuable to better understand the localized influences behind finer-grained patterning of spatial segregation.

In terms of social implications, our exploratory findings echo the findings of other scholars, who have documented and critiqued the way inner-city redevelopment efforts in Chinese cities displaced residents, particularly the socioeconomically vulnerable, in favor of luxury residential and commercial projects (Zhang and Fang 2004; He 2010; Zhang 2006). Our study's findings support these calls to examine and mitigate displacement of low-income groups and entrenchment of concentrated affluence within urban centers, but potentially only for specific cities, as not all cities follow the same localized spatial patterns of segregation.

Our analysis provides a demonstration of the potential utility of applying localized spatial measures of segregation to real estate listings, as this enables the identification of more localized, neighborhood-level patterns of segregation in ways that aggregated census data cannot. Planners and researchers can use such methods to identify more precisely which areas are undergoing spatial polarization and formulate policies as necessary, such as encouraging more affordable housing units there. Additionally, as real estate listings provide a constantly updated snapshot of urban developments, they provide a more timely way to monitor socio-spatial changes compared to relying on census data only.

At the same time, our analysis demonstrates the limitations of using a data set of real estate listings to analyze spatial patterns in Chinese cities. Our data set may not be completely representative of the entire salable housing stock because it is a selection of apartments that were listed online. Thus, it may have excluded housing stock that real estate agencies responsible for generating such listings find less profitable to market, such as those in more suburban, less expensive areas (Li et al. 2019). There is also a likelihood that the most luxury properties might not be listed online but rather transacted via private brokers to maintain privacy of the buyers and sellers. This study's findings should thus be understood in terms of capturing the majority of the housing stock but potentially underrepresenting the tail ends of housing price distribution. Nevertheless, given that Fang .com was one of the most popular sites in China at the point of data collection, our data set is likely to be as comprehensive as can be expected when using such online housing listings. A recent study comparing secondhand residential listing prices in Guangzhou from various real estate websites, including Fang.com, found good correlation with official city data (Li et al. 2019).

In short, this study demonstrates how a widely available online data source such as Fang.com can facilitate analyses and comparisons of sociospatial segregation across multiple Chinese cities, which is currently rare (Monkkonen, Comandon, and Zhu 2017). The increasing proliferation of real estate listing websites not just in China but across the globe further presents opportunities for multicity studies, which can in turn broaden analyses of urban patterns beyond major cities like Beijing and Shanghai, where research attention has been concentrated to date. Our analysis here is an exploratory first step in examining how different cities exhibit different locational patterns of housing segregation. Additional research comparing a larger data set of cities could help uncover factors driving these differences.

Appendix A: Filtering Criteria

The following table summarizes the year built, range of reasonable unit prices, and apartment sizes used for our analysis.

Price and Size Ranges of Fang Listings Included in Analysis

	Shanghai	*Chengdu*	*Shenyang*
Year built	1900 to 2020	1900 to 2020	1900 to 2020
Price (RMB)	<350,000,000	<100,000,000	<70,000,000
Size (sq. m)	20 to 1000	20 to 900	20 to 900
Price per square meter (PSM)	<200,000	<60,000	<40,000

In order to establish reasonable upper ends of listed prices, we reviewed reports, studies, and broker listings on high-end developments that quoted actual sale or listed prices. These were used as a realism check on our proposed filtering figures.

Shanghai

- A 2012 study of upmarket residential enclaves in Shanghai provides the following upper-end benchmark:
  - Units in a development in Luwan cost RMB 90,000 per square meter, with unit sizes ranging up to 312 square meters, and a total price of RMB 28.08 million
  - Villas in Changning cost RMB 75,000 per square meter, with a maximum size of 876 square meters, and a total price of RMB 65.7 million

- A 2015 report provides the following information:[2]
  - A Shanghai apartment in Tomson Riviera was sold on 19 June 2015 for RMB 240 million
  - A high-end apartment in Lujiazui, Shanghai, sold for RMB 150,328 per square meter

According to a Savills Q2 2016 property report on Chengdu, the average transaction price for the main urban area reached RMB 10,528 per square meter (Macdonald, Law, and Wo 2016). A similar Q2 2016 report showed that Shanghai's average transaction price was RMB 35,500 per square meter (Macdonald et al. 2016). Similarly, a 2016 study reported that average residential prices in Shanghai were about RMB 35,000 per square meter, while those for a second-tier city like Wuhan were about RMB 10,000 per square meter (Glaeser et al. 2016). We thus made a broad assumption that Shanghai's prices were about 3.5 times higher than Chengdu's.

For Shenyang, a Jones Lang Lasalle report estimated that, as of late 2015, Shenyang's average residential prices was approximately RMB 6,500 per square meter (Wang et al. 2016). We thus assumed that Shanghai's prices were about five times more than Shenyang's.

Appendix B: Descriptive Statistics for Fang.com Listings

	Shanghai	Chengdu	Shenyang
No. of filtered listings	767,816	373,699	151,003
No. of unique developments	10,665	6,070	2,715
Year built	Mean: 2003	Mean: 2009	Mean: 2007
	Min: 1900	Min: 1900	Min: 1900
	25%: 1998	25%: 2006	25%: 2005
	50%: 2004	50%: 2010	50%: 2008
	75%: 2008	75%: 2013	75%: 2011
Price (RMB)	Mean: 4,657,635	Mean: 1,018,468	Mean: 734,453
	Min: 120,000	Min: 68,000	Min: 30,000
	25%: 2,050,000	25%: 600,000	25%: 462,683
	50%: 3,300,000	50%: 800,000	50%: 660,000
	75%: 5,600,000	75%: 1,150,000	75%: 870,000
Characteristics of high-end listings (top 5 percentile)	$n = 37,124$	$n = 18,349$	$n = 7,370$
	Mean size: 217	Mean size: 221	Mean size: 174
	Mean price: 18,622,943	Mean price: 3,578,099	Mean price: 1,986,708
	Mean year: 2000	Mean year: 2009	Mean year: 2007

Appendix C: Calculating Spatial Exposure/Isolation and Spatial Entropy

The two measures—spatial exposure/isolation ($\tilde{P}^*$) and spatial information theory index ($\tilde{H}$)—were chosen for our analysis because they do not rely on data aggregated to the polygon, like census data, but can work with distinct address locations, thus making the analysis more spatially precise. The two measures also have population density invariance, which means that if the population density of each group at each location is multiplied by a constant factor, the estimated segregation score remains unchanged (Reardon and O'Sullivan 2004). As our case study cities have different overall housing densities, this characteristic facilitates cross-city comparisons of segregation estimates.

While there are many other measures of clustering—such as global and local indicators of spatial autocorrelation Moran's I and Getis-Ord's G*—that are prevalent in geographical analysis and have been used in some residential segregation studies (Johnston, Poulsen, and Forrest 2011; Li et al. 2015), we decided to adopt measures that are more empirically and theoretically grounded in the sociological residential segregation literature, which our current study draws from. Doing so facilitates cross-referencing against existing socio-spatial segregation studies (Lee et al. 2008; Monkkonen, Comandon, and Zhu 2017; Reardon et al. 2009).

The influence of units within each localized environment is spatially weighted based on the Euclidean distance from the individual unit of interest—in other words, a distance-decay effect. We used a negative exponential function to represent a distance-decay effect, in which shorter distances between housing units increases the probability of their residents interacting. The weight given to these listings was defined as $w(d) = e^{-\beta d}$, where d is the Euclidean distance in kilometers between the listings' locations, and β is the distance-decay factor. We chose an exponential function because empirical research on intra-urban mobility patterns in cities suggested that an exponential law better reflected the distance-decay effect on individuals' daily activity range (Kang et al. 2012) and trip length distributions (Liang et al. 2013) than did a power law.

As walking is a mode of travel that provides more opportunities for chance encounters and social interactions (Middleton 2018) and has been associated with a greater sense of community within neighborhoods (Wood, Frank, and Giles-Corti 2010), we examined available empirical studies that modeled the distribution of walking trips using negative exponential functions. These studies generally pegged the distance-decay factor for walking trips between 0.6 and 2.1 per kilometer. As we could not find studies on distance-decay effect specific to the walking behavior of Chinese urban residents, we assumed a rate of decay of $\beta = 1.0$, which falls within the range of other studies (Iacono, Krizek, and El-Geneidy 2008; Yang and Diez-Roux 2012).

As a sensitivity analysis, we also tested distance-decay factors of 0.5 and 2. This sensitivity analysis using different distance-decay factors yielded consistent findings for citywide measures of segregation, as well as the difference between city-core and non-core areas. Using a larger, more aggressive distance decay factor gave rise to higher absolute scores of clustering and isolation, compared to smaller β's, which suggests that if we assume that residents of high-end units tend to travel and interact within a highly constrained radius of activity around their homes, the resultant socioeconomic segregation of interaction may be higher than if we assume they travel outside their home area more.

Effectively, we calculated a "surface" of information, which provided for each listing's location the weighted proportion of the housing units within the local neighborhood that are either high-end housing units or non-high-end units. This surface of weighted population proportion for each listing's localized environment was used to calculate $\tilde{P}^*$ and $\tilde{H}$. Both measures were calculated using R software package "seg." Additional details about the calculation of both measures, including formulas, are published in Reardon and O'Sullivan (2004) and Hong and Sullivan (2019).

Notes

This work was supported by funding from the Sam Tak Lee Lab at the Massachusetts Institute of Technology.

1. As of July 2018, listings from 658 cities were available from the website (www.fang.com /SoufunFamily.htm).

2. "Look: Shanghai's Most Expensive Apartment, Sold for 240 Million RMB," 2 July 2015, http://shanghaiist.com/2015/07/02/shanghais-most-expensive-apt.php.

References

Baum-Snow, Nathaniel, and Ronni Pavan. 2013. "Inequality and City Size." *Review of Economics and Statistics* 95 (4): 1535–48.

Bian, Yanjie, Ronald Breiger, Joseph Galaskiewicz, and Deborah Davis. 2005. "Occupation, Class, and Social Networks in Urban China." *Social Forces* 83 (4): 1443–68.

Bray, David. 2008. "Designing to Govern: Space and Power in Two Wuhan Communities." *Built Environment* 34 (4): 392–407.

Charles, Camille Z. 2003. "The Dynamics of Racial Residential Segregation." *Annual Review of Sociology* 29 (1): 167–207.

Chen, Yimin, Xiaoping Liu, Xia Li, Yilun Liu, and Xiaocong Xu. 2016. "Mapping the Fine-Scale Spatial Pattern of Housing Rent in the Metropolitan Area by Using Online Rental Listings and Ensemble Learning." *Applied Geography* 75 (October): 200–212.

Chick, Sophie. 2019. "The Changing Face of Global Prime Residential." *Impacts* 2 (April): 38–41. www.savills.com/impacts/market-trends/the-changing-face-of-global-prime-residential .html.

Clark, W. A. V. 1986. "Residential Segregation in American Cities: A Review and Interpretation." *Population Research and Policy Review* 5 (2): 95–127.

Darden, Joe, Mohammad Rahbar, Louise Jezierski, Min Li, and Ellen Velie. 2010. "The Measurement of Neighborhood Socioeconomic Characteristics and Black and White Residential Segregation in Metropolitan Detroit: Implications for the Study of Social Disparities in Health." *Annals of the Association of American Geographers* 100 (1): 137–58.

Fry, Richard, and Paul Taylor. 2012. *The Rise of Residential Segregation by Income*. Washington, DC: Pew Research Center's Social and Demographic Trends Project.

Galster, George. 1988. "Residential Segregation in American Cities: A Contrary Review." *Population Research and Policy Review* 7 (2): 93–112.

Glaeser, Edward, Wei Huang, Yueran Ma, and Andrei Shleifer. 2016. "A Real Estate Boom with Chinese Characteristics." NBER Working Paper No. 22789, National Bureau of Economic Research, November. https://doi.org/10.3386/w22789.

Glaeser, Edward L., Matthew G. Resseger, and Kristina Tobio. 2008. "Urban Inequality." Working Paper No. 14419. National Bureau of Economic Research, October. https://doi.org/10.3386/w14419.

Gordon, Ian, and Vassilis Monastiriotis. 2006. "Urban Size, Spatial Segregation and Inequality in Educational Outcomes." *Urban Studies* 43 (1): 213–36.

Gu, Chao-lin. 2001. "Social Polarization and Segregation in Beijing." *Chinese Geographical Science* 11 (1): 17–26.

He, Shenjing. 2010. "New-Build Gentrification in Central Shanghai: Demographic Changes and Socioeconomic Implications." *Population, Space and Place* 16 (5): 345–61.

Hong, Seong-Yun, and David O'Sullivan. 2019. "Seg: Measuring Spatial Segregation." 18 December. https://cran.r-project.org/web/packages/seg/index.html.

Huang, Youqi. 2005. "From Work-Unit Compounds to Gated Communities." In *Restructuring the Chinese City: Changing Society, Economy and Space*, edited by Laurence J. C. Ma and Fulong Wu, 172–98. London: Routledge.

Iacono, Michael, Kevin Krizek, and Ahmed El-Geneidy. 2008. *Access to Destinations: How Close Is Close Enough? Estimating Accurate Distance Decay Functions for Multiple Modes and Different Purposes.* St. Paul: Minnesota Department of Transportation.

Iceland, John. 2004. "Beyond Black and White: Metropolitan Residential Segregation in Multi-Ethnic America." *Social Science Research* 33 (7): 248–71.

Jim, C. Y., and Wendy Y. Chen. 2006. "Impacts of Urban Environmental Elements on Residential Housing Prices in Guangzhou (China)." *Landscape and Urban Planning* 78 (4): 422–34.

Johnston, Ron, Michael Poulsen, and James Forrest. 2011. "Evaluating Changing Residential Segregation in Auckland, New Zealand, Using Spatial Statistics: Evaluating Changing Residential Segregation." *Tijdschrift voor Eeconomische en SocialeGgeografie* 102 (1): 1–23.

Kang, Chaogui, Xiujun Ma, Daoqin Tong, and Yu Liu. 2012. "Intra-Urban Human Mobility Patterns: An Urban Morphology Perspective." *Physica A: Statistical Mechanics and Its Applications* 391 (4): 1702–17.

Kramer, Michael R. 2018. "Residential Segregation and Health." In *Neighborhoods and Health*, edited by Dustin T. Duncan, Ichirō Kawachi, and Ana V. Diez Roux. New York: Oxford University Press.

Kramer, Michael R., and Carol R. Hogue. 2009. "Is Segregation Bad for Your Health?" *Epidemiologic Reviews* 31 (1): 178–94.

Krivo, Lauren J., Heather M. Washington, Ruth D. Peterson, Christopher R. Browning, Catherine A. Calder, and Mei-Po Kwan. 2013. "Social Isolation of Disadvantage and Advantage: The Reproduction of Inequality in Urban Space." *Social Forces* 9 (21): 141–64.

Lee, Barrett A., Sean F. Reardon, Glenn Firebaugh, Chad R. Farrell, Stephen A. Matthews, and David O'Sullivan. 2008. "Beyond the Census Tract: Patterns and Determinants of Racial Segregation at Multiple Geographic Scales." *American Sociological Review* 73 (5): 766–91.

Li, Huiping, Qingfang Wang, Wei Shi, Zhongwei Deng, and Hongwei Wang. 2015. "Residential Clustering and Spatial Access to Public Services in Shanghai." *Habitat International* 46 (April): 119–29.

Li, Ming, Guojun Zhang, Yunliang Chen, and Chunshan Zhou. 2019. "Evaluation of Residential Housing Prices on the Internet: Data Pitfalls." *Complexity* 2019 (February): 1–15.

Li, Shengwei, Xinyue Ye, Jay Lee, Junfang Gong, and Chenglin Qin. 2016. "Spatiotemporal Analysis of Housing Prices in China: A Big Data Perspective." *Applied Spatial Analysis and Policy* 10 (3): 421–33.

Li, Zhigang, and Fulong Wu. 2008. "Tenure-Based Residential Segregation in Post-Reform Chinese Cities: A Case Study of Shanghai." *Transactions of the Institute of British Geographers* 33 (3): 404–19.

Li, Zhigang, Fulong Wu, and Yang Xiao. 2015. "Residential Segregation of New Migrants in Guangzhou, China: A Study of the 6th Census." *Geographical Research* 33 (11): 2056–68.

Liang, Xiao, Jichang Zhao, Li Dong, and Ke Xu. 2013. "Unraveling the Origin of Exponential Law in Intra-Urban Human Mobility." *Scientific Reports* 3 (1): 2983–90.

Liu, Miao, Yanyan Xu, Yuanman Hu, Chunlin Li, Fengyun Sun, and Tan Chen. 2014. "A Century of the Evolution of the Urban Area in Shenyang, China." *PLoS ONE* 9 (6): e98847.

Liu, Yafei, Martin Dijst, and Stan Geertman. 2015. "Residential Segregation and Well-Being Inequality over Time: A Study on the Local and Migrant Elderly People in Shanghai." *Cities* 49 (December): 1–13.

Liu, Ziwei, and Huhua Cao. 2017. "Spatio-Temporal Urban Social Landscape Transformation in Pre-New-Urbanization Era of Tianjin, China." *Environment and Planning B: Urban Analytics and City Science* 44 (3): 398–424.

Macdonald, James, Siu Wing Chu, Shirley Tang, and Kitty Tan. 2016. *Briefing: Residential Sales*. Savills World Research, Shanghai, August. https://pdf.savills.asia/asia-pacific-research/china-research/shanghai-research/shanghai-residential/16q2-sh-resi-sales-en.pdf.

Macdonald, James, Dave Law, and Eric Wo. 2016. *Briefing: Residential Sector*. Savills World Research, Chengdu, July. https://pdf.savills.asia/asia-pacific-research/china-research/chengdu-research/chengdu-residential/16q2-cd-residential-en.pdf.

Marcińczak, Szymon, Tiit Tammaru, Jakub Navák, Michael Gentle, Zoltán Kovács, Jana Temelová, Vytautas Valatka, Anneli Kährik, and Balázs Szabó. 2015. "Patterns of Socioeconomic Segregation in the Capital Cities of Fast-Track Reforming Postsocialist Countries." *Annals of the Association of American Geographers* 105 (1): 183–202.

Massey, Douglas S., and Nancy A. Denton. 1988. "The Dimensions of Residential Segregation." *Social Forces* 67 (2): 281–315.

———. 1993. *American Apartheid: Segregation and the Making of the Underclass*. Cambridge, MA: Harvard University Press.

Middleton, Jennie. 2018. "The Socialities of Everyday Urban Walking and the 'Right to the City.'" *Urban Studies* 55 (2): 296–315.

Monkkonen, Paavo, Andre Comandon, and Jiren Zhu. 2017. "Economic Segregation in Transition China: Evidence from the 20 Largest Cities." *Urban Geography* 38 (7): 1039–61.

Monkkonen, Paavo, and Xiaohu Zhang. 2011. "Socioeconomic Segregation in Hong Kong: Spatial and Ordinal Measures in a High-Density and Highly Unequal City." Working Paper 2011-03, Berkeley Institute of Urban and Regional Development, June.

Morgan, Barrie S. 1975. "The Segregation of Socio-economic Groups in Urban Areas: A Comparative Analysis." *Urban Studies* 12 (1): 47–60.

Musterd, Sako. 2005. "Social and Ethnic Segregation in Europe: Levels, Causes, and Effects." *Journal of Urban Affairs* 27 (3): 331–48.

Musterd, Sako, Szymon Marcińczak, Maarten van Ham, and Tiit Tammaru. 2017. "Socioeconomic Segregation in European Capital Cities: Increasing Separation Between Poor and Rich." *Urban Geography* 38 (7): 1062–83.

Openshaw, Stan. 1984. "The Modifiable Areal Unit Problem (Concepts and Techniques in Modern Geography)." Norwich, UK: Geo Books.

Piketty, Thomas, and Nancy Qian. 2009. "Income Inequality and Progressive Income Taxation in China and India, 1986–2015." *American Economic Journal: Applied Economics* 1 (2): 53–63.

Piketty, Thomas, Li Yang, and Gabriel Zucman. 2019. "Capital Accumulation, Private Property, and Rising Inequality in China, 1978–2015." *American Economic Review* 109 (7): 2469–96.

Reardon, Sean F., and Kendra Bischoff. 2011. "Income Inequality and Income Segregation." *American Journal of Sociology* 116 (4): 1092–1153.

Reardon, Sean F., Chad R. Farrell, Stephen A. Matthews, David O'Sullivan, Kendra Bischoff, and Glenn Firebaugh. 2009. "Race and Space in the 1990s: Changes in the Geographic Scale of Racial Residential Segregation, 1990–2000." *Social Science Research* 38 (1): 55–70.

Reardon, Sean F., and David O'Sullivan. 2004. "Measures of Spatial Segregation." *Sociological Methodology* 34 (1): 121–62.

Ren, Xuefei. 2008. "Forward to the Past: Historical Preservation in Globalizing Shanghai." *City and Community* 7 (1): 23–43.

Shen, Jie. 2017. "Stuck in the Suburbs? Socio-spatial Exclusion of Migrants in Shanghai." *Cities* 60 (February): 428–35.

Shen, Y., F. Sun, and Y. Che. 2017. "Public Green Spaces and Human Wellbeing: Mapping the Spatial Inequity and Mismatching Status of Public Green Space in the Central City of Shanghai." *Urban Forestry & Urban Greening* 27:59–68.

Shi, Wei, Jie Chen, and Hongwei Wang. 2016. "Affordable Housing Policy in China: New Developments and New Challenges." In "Housing the Planet: Evolution of Global Housing Policies," edited by Xing Quan Zhang and Michael Ball, special issue, *Habitat International*, 54, pt. 3 (May): 224–33.

Sun, Weizeng, Siqi Zheng, David M. Geltner, and Rui Wang. 2017. "The Housing Market Effects of Local Home Purchase Restrictions: Evidence from Beijing." *Journal of Real Estate Finance and Economics* 55 (3): 288–312.

Wallenwein, Fabienne. 2014. "The Housing Model *Xiaoqu*: The Expression of an Increasing Polarization of the Urban Population in Chinese Cities?" Master's thesis, Institut für Sinologie, Universität Heidelberg, February.

Wang, Michael, Steven McCord, Alex Wang, and Carol Lin. 2016. "Shenyang City Profile." JLL research report. http://www.joneslanglasalle.com.cn/china/en-gb/Research/city-profile-sy2016-en.pdf.

Wang, Y. P., and A. Murie. 2000. "Social and Spatial Implications of Housing Reform in China." *International Journal of Urban and Regional Research* 24 (2): 397–417.

Wen, Hai-zhen, Jia Sheng-hua, and Guo Xiao-yu. 2005. "Hedonic Price Analysis of Urban Housing: An Empirical Research on Hangzhou, China." *Journal of Zhejiang University—Science A* 6 (8): 907–14.

Williams, David R., and Chiquita Collins. 2001. "Racial Residential Segregation: A Fundamental Cause of Racial Disparities in Health." *Public Health Reports* 116 (5): 404–16.

Wilson, William J. 1987. *The Truly Disadvantaged: The Inner City, the Underclass, and Public Policy*. Chicago: University of Chicago Press.

Wood, Lisa, Lawrence D. Frank, and Billie Giles-Corti. 2010. "Sense of Community and Its Relationship with Walking and Neighborhood Design." *Social Science and Medicine* 70 (9): 1381–90.

Wu, Fulong. 2002. "Sociospatial Differentiation in Urban China: Evidence from Shanghai's Real Estate Markets." *Environment and Planning A* 34 (9): 1591–1615.

———. 2015. "Commodification and Housing Market Cycles in Chinese Cities." *International Journal of Housing Policy* 15 (1): 6–26.

Wu, Qiyan, Jianquan Cheng, Guo Chen, Daniel J. Hammel, and Xiaohui Wu. 2014. "Sociospatial Differentiation and Residential Segregation in the Chinese City Based on the 2000 Community-Level Census Data: A Case Study of the Inner City of Nanjing." *Cities* 39 (August): 109–19.

Xiao, Yixiong, Xiang Chen, Qiang Li, Xi Yu, Jin Chen, and Jing Guo. 2017. "Exploring Determinants of Housing Prices in Beijing: An Enhanced Hedonic Regression with Open Access POI Data." *ISPRS International Journal of Geo-Information* 6 (11): 358–70.

Xie, Yu, and Xiang Zhou. 2014. "Income Inequality in Today's China." *Proceedings of the National Academy of Sciences—PNAS* 111 (19): 6928–33.

Xu, Feng. 2008. "Gated Communities and Migrant Enclaves: The Conundrum for Building 'Harmonious Community/Shequ.'" *Journal of Contemporary China* 17 (57): 633–51.

Yang, Linchuan, K. W. Chau, and Xu Wang. 2019. "Are Low-End Housing Purchasers More Willing to Pay for Access to Basic Public Services? Evidence from China." *Research in Transportation Economics* 76 (September): 100734.

Yang, Shangguang, Mark Y. L. Wang, and Chunlan Wang. 2015. "Socio-spatial Restructuring in Shanghai: Sorting Out Where You Live by Affordability and Social Status." In "Current Research on Cities," edited by Andrew Kirby, special issue, *Cities* 47 (February): 23–34.

Yang, Yong, and Ana V. Diez-Roux. 2012. "Walking Distance by Trip Purpose and Population Subgroups." *American Journal of Preventive Medicine* 43 (1): 11–19.

Yang, Z., and J. Chen. 2014. "Housing Reform and the Housing Market in Urban China." In *Housing Affordability and Housing Policy in Urban China*, 15–43. Berlin: Springer.

Yeh, Anthony Gar-On, Xueqiang Xu, and Huaying Hu. 1995. "The Social Space of Guangzhou City, China." *Urban Geography* 16 (7): 595–621.

Yinger, John. 1995. *Closed Doors, Opportunities Lost: The Continuing Costs of Housing Discrimination*. New York: Russell Sage Foundation.

Zhang, Lei, and Yimin Yi. 2017. "Quantile House Price Indices in Beijing." *Regional Science and Urban Economics* 63 (March): 85–96.

Zhang, Li. 2006. "Contesting Spatial Modernity in Late-Socialist China." *Current Anthropology* 47 (3): 461–84.

Zhang, Yan, and Ke Fang. 2004. "Is History Repeating Itself? From Urban Renewal in the United States to Inner-City Redevelopment in China." *Journal of Planning Education and Research* 23 (3): 286–98.

Zhao, Miaoxi, and Yiming Wang. 2018. "Measuring Segregation Between Rural Migrants and Local Residents in Urban China: An Integrated Spatio-social Network Analysis of Kecun in Guangzhou." *Environment and Planning B: Urban Analytics and City Science* 45 (3): 417–33.

Zheng, Siqi, Jing Wu, Matthew E. Kahn, and Yongheng Deng. 2012. "The Nascent Market for 'Green' Real Estate in Beijing." *European Economic Review* 56 (5): 974–84.

Zhou, Suhong, Zhidong Wu, and Luping Cheng. 2013. "The Impact of Spatial Mismatch on Residents in Low-income Housing Neighbourhoods: A Study of the Guangzhou Metropolis, China." *Urban Studies* 50 (9): 1817–35.

Zhou, Yixiao, and Ligang Song. 2016. "Income Inequality in China: Causes and Policy Responses." *China Economic Journal* 9 (2): 186–208.

CHAPTER 4

Has the Economic Situation of Rural Migrant Workers in Urban China Been Improving? An Updated Assessment

Shi Li and Binbin Wu

Introduction

In the 1980s, due to the government's control over the food distribution system and strict enforcement of the *hukou* (household registration) system, rural laborers were monitored closely when they entered cities. By the early and mid-1990s, the loosening control over the household registration system allowed for more labor mobility. This, coupled with the reform of the urban employment system and the growing wage gap between agricultural and nonagricultural employment, has drawn an unprecedented number of rural migrants to cities for work. In the late 1990s, as the urban labor market became increasingly saturated and locals found themselves competing with migrants for employment, municipal governments adopted policies to restrict employment opportunities for rural migrant workers.

Since 2005, the central government has implemented a successive series of policies to improve the employment status and market position of migrant workers. In 2014, the State Council issued *Opinions on Further Promoting the Reform of the Household Registration System*. This opinion marked a transition from the first wave of household registration reforms to a stage of comprehensive implementation. This shift has been made possible in part by rapid economic growth, which has relieved the pressure of competition over urban employment and increased the demand for labor. The latest data show that at the end of 2018, there were nearly 173 million rural migrant workers in urban China,[1] accounting for 39.77 percent of total urban employees (National Bureau of Statistics of China 2019). However, China's unique *hukou* system still restricts the individual rights of rural migrant workers, including their right to equal employment opportunities, equal pay for equal work, and equal access to social security and public services (S. Li 2014).

Previous studies have shown that before 2010, rural migrant workers in China's urban labor market were relegated to what has been called "second-class citizen" status (Démurger et al. 2009). First, rural migrant workers did not enjoy the same employment opportunities as did urban workers. They were more likely to be excluded from the highest-paying jobs in the labor market, and often held the market's lowest-paid positions (Meng and Zhang 2001; Zhao 2004; Yan 2006; Tian 2010; Li and Gu 2011; Zhang, Li, et al. 2016). Second, in terms of working conditions, rural migrant workers had fewer labor protections in place, often working long hours in physically demanding positions (Zheng and Huang 2007; Ye and Yang 2015; Wang and Ye 2016). Third, especially from the end of the twentieth and into the first decade of the twenty-first century, rural migrant workers' income was substantially lower than that of their urban worker counterparts (Wang 2003; Wang 2005; Deng 2007; Zhang and Cai 2017). Lu (2012) found that in the first thirty years of the economic transition, the wage ratio between rural migrant workers and formal urban workers first increased and then decreased. Part of the resulting income disparity between rural migrant workers and urban workers was due to growing wage discrimination—that is, unequal pay for equal work. Fourth, there has been little to no improvement in migrant workers' limited access to social security programs, and many have been excluded from urban social security systems (Lin and Zhu 2009; Qin and Chen 2014).

In the past decade, rural migrant workers' economic standing has improved. The central government has implemented policies to improve employment opportunities and the overall market status of rural migrant workers. The increasing demand for rural migrant workers in the urban labor market has also helped improve their economic status. For example, the portion of the wage gap that has been attributed to wage discrimination has decreased significantly, suggesting that rural migrant workers are being more equitably compensated for their work (Deng and Li 2012; Zhu 2016;

Sun 2017). In recent years, the average rise in rural migrant workers' income has exceeded that of urban workers, narrowing the wage gap between the two groups.

This chapter uses the two latest data sets derived from national household surveys conducted by China Household Income Project and China Family Panel Studies to analyze the changes in the economic status of rural migrant workers compared to urban workers. Specifically, this chapter will use analytical methods (such as decomposition and counterfactual analysis) to discuss the employment structure of rural migrant workers, the gap between their wages and those of urban workers, and their accessibility to urban social security programs. The results indicate that the differences in employment opportunities and income level between the two groups have reduced significantly in the period under study, but rural migrant workers still face barriers to accessing social security and public services in urban areas. Finally, the chapter puts forth some policy suggestions to further improve the economic status of rural migrant workers.

Data and Variables

Data sets from two national household surveys—China Household Income Project (CHIP) and China Family Panel Studies (CFPS)—are used in this chapter. To date, CHIP has conducted five waves of household surveys: in 1988, 1995, 2002, 2007, and 2013. The first three surveys were organized by the Institute of Economics at the Chinese Academy of Social Sciences and foreign researchers, and the latter two surveys by the China Institute for Income Distribution at Beijing Normal University, with the support of international team members. The sampled households of the CHIP surveys were drawn from the large sample of the National Bureau of Statistics of China (NBS), and the surveys were implemented with the assistance of NBS. The surveys covered both urban and rural households, yet no migrant households were included until the latter three surveys, in which samples of rural migrant households were added. This chapter uses the data of the CHIP surveys in 2002, 2007, and 2013 by selecting rural migrant workers and urban local workers aged sixteen to sixty-five who reported being actively employed at the time of the survey. The sample size from each year's survey was 3,230, 6,513, and 1,189 rural migrant workers and 9,777, 6,621, and 8,699 urban workers, respectively.

The CFPS survey was carried out by the Institute of Social Science Survey of Peking University in 2010, 2012, 2014, and 2016. The CFPS sample covers twenty-five provinces, municipalities, or autonomous regions in China, and the respondents include all household members in the sample. This chapter uses data from the surveys in 2010, 2014, and 2016 (CFPS data from the 2012 survey do not distinguish between employees and self-employed workers). We've included in our analysis both rural migrant workers and urban workers aged sixteen to sixty-five who reported being actively employed at the time of the survey. The sample size from the three surveys was 504, 742, and 590 rural migrant workers and 3,178, 2,789, and 2,346 urban workers, respectively.

Classifying employment sector variables in the same way that Démurger et al. (2009) and Zhang, Wu, et al. (2016) did, the chapter refers to family and self-run businesses as self-employed; government agencies, public institutions, and state-owned enterprises as the public sector; and enterprises of other owners, such as private, foreign-invested firms, as the private sector. Service industries are categorized as high end, low end, and other, as illustrated in Chen and Chen (2018). The high-end service industry includes finance, technology and research, education, and media. The low-end service industry includes transportation, retail, catering and accommodation, and leasing services. In addition to the employment sector, the chapter distinguishes between white-collar and blue-collar professions, with managers, professionals, and clerks constituting white-collar workers, and manual laborers making up the blue-collar workers (Li 2012).

Differences in Employment Status Between Rural Migrant Workers and Urban Workers

Chinese rural migrant workers have long been excluded from the relatively high-end job market because they cannot enjoy the same employment opportunities as their urban counterparts. In general, the public sector provides better compensation and social security, as well as more stable work. Due to these benefits, the public sector is often flooded with people seeking employment, which in turn leads to a higher entry threshold. These conditions raise the question of how hard it is for rural migrant workers to enter the public sector. Past studies show that the proportion of urban workers employed in the public sector is much higher than that of rural migrant workers. In this chapter, we use the latest data to understand how rural migrant workers' employment opportunities have changed in recent years.

Statistical Description

Table 4.1 shows the employment ratio of rural migrant workers to urban workers in the public sector, private sector, as well as those self-employed. The table also uses the more intuitive Duncan coefficient (Duncan and Duncan 1955) to reveal the distributional differences between rural migrant workers and urban workers.[2]

As shown in Table 4.1, according to the results calculated from CHIP data, 55.90 percent of urban workers and 9.66 percent of rural migrant workers were employed in the public sector in 2007, a difference of about 46 percentage points. In 2013, this difference shrank to about 32 percentage points. Moreover, from 2007 to 2013, the Duncan coefficient decreased from 46.24 percent to 32.37 percent. The results calculated from CFPS data show the same trend, with a difference between urban workers and rural migrant workers in the public sector decreasing, from nearly 38 percent in 2010 to nearly 28 percent in 2016. The Duncan coefficient is also decreasing in the CFPS data, from 37.69 percent in 2010 to 27.90 percent in 2016.

These results indicate that the gap in the share of rural migrant workers and urban workers employed in the public sector is narrowing. This may be partly related to the rapid increase in the human capital of rural migrant workers. As shown in Table 4.1, the difference in educational attainment between urban workers and rural migrant workers has also been significantly reduced over time. This can be largely attributed to the fact that rural migrant workers' average educational attainment has grown more than that of urban workers in recent years.

There are observable differences between urban workers and rural migrant workers across employment sectors and occupations. First, the proportion of urban workers working in the high-end service industry or white-collar occupations exceeds that of rural migrant workers. White-collar occupations have higher wages, often carry a more prestigious professional reputation, are more stable over time, and are tied to better welfare programs.

According to CHIP data in Table 4.2a, the Duncan coefficient of the gaps in industry distribution between the two groups decreased by more than two percentage points from 2007 to 2013, while it decreased by more than

Table 4.1. Human capital and employment sector of rural migrant workers and urban workers

	2007		2013		2010		2014		2016	
	Urban workers	Migrant workers	Urban workers	Migrant workers	Urban workers	Migrant workers	Urban workers	Migrant workers	Urban workers	Migrant workers
Human capital										
Year of education	12.16	9.13	11.65	9.54	11.98	8.96	11.51	9.41	11.67	9.78
Work experience (year)	22.00	15.85	23.70	21.93	21.61	19.20	23.62	19.45	23.81	20.09
Employment sector										
Self-employed (%)	7.37	23.35	10.99	27.77	12.37	33.93	16.96	27.22	16.50	28.31
Public sector (%)	55.90	9.66	41.43	9.06	45.63	7.94	38.01	8.09	38.75	10.85
Private sector (%)	36.73	66.99	47.58	63.17	42.01	58.13	45.03	64.69	44.76	60.85
Duncan coefficient (%)		46.24		32.37		37.69		29.92		27.90
Observations	6,621	6,513	8,699	1,189	3,178	504	2,789	742	2,346	590

Sources: CHIP 2007, CHIP 2013; CFPS 2010, CFPS 2014, CFPS 2016, authors' calculations.

Table 4.2a. Counterfactual industries and occupations of employed urban workers and rural migrant workers (2002, 2007, and 2013)

	2002		2007		2007 (Counterfactual)		2013		2013 (Counterfactual)	
	Urban workers	Migrant workers	Urban workers	Migrant workers	Urban workers	Migrant workers	Urban workers	Migrant workers	Urban workers	Migrant workers
Industry										
Secondary industry (%)	34.68	21.45	27.60	37.66	28.43	36.73	27.50	35.62	28.55	36.84
Low-end service industry (%)	17.43	30.91	25.37	38.94	26.63	40.65	22.83	35.97	24.17	41.94
High-end service industry (%)	5.98	2.66	18.28	8.43	16.45	7.51	16.09	7.33	14.30	3.34
Other industry (%)	41.90	44.97	28.75	14.96	28.48	15.12	33.58	21.07	32.98	17.88
Duncan coefficient (%)		16.55		23.63		22.32		21.27		26.06
Occupation										
White-collar worker (%)	55.29	14.66	57.18	8.59	52.39	6.76	45.03	23.17	42.12	16.03
Blue-collar worker (%)	30.03	14.59	22.96	34.86	25.96	37.50	21.51	30.62	22.96	33.37
Services and other (%)	14.68	70.75	19.86	56.55	21.65	55.73	33.46	46.22	34.92	50.60
Duncan coefficient (%)		56.08		48.59		45.63		21.86		26.09

Sources: CHIP 2002, CHIP 2007, CHIP 2013, authors' calculations.

Table 4.2b. Counterfactual industries and occupations of employed urban workers and rural migrant workers (2010, 2014, and 2016)

	2010		2014		2014 (Counterfactual)		2016		2016 (Counterfactual)	
	Urban workers	Migrant workers	Urban workers	Migrant workers	Urban workers	Migrant workers	Urban workers	Migrant workers	Urban workers	Migrant workers
Industry										
Secondary industry (%)	33.59	53.85	34.76	50.33	34.71	50.61	33.33	42.42	34.06	41.36
Low-end service industry (%)	21.57	28.21	24.83	27.77	24.58	28.59	24.65	27.76	24.96	29.79
High-end service industry (%)	14.68	2.24	15.36	7.81	15.91	6.65	18.45	11.31	18.88	9.55
Other industry (%)	30.16	15.71	25.04	14.10	24.81	14.15	23.57	18.51	22.10	19.31
Duncan coefficient (%)		26.90		18.49		19.91		12.20		12.12
Occupation										
White-collar worker (%)	48.88	20.51	43.82	23.86	45.35	21.02	45.85	31.11	47.15	24.13
Blue-collar worker (%)	27.81	42.63	28.87	44.90	28.42	45.33	26.27	35.48	26.29	38.07
Services and other (%)	23.32	36.86	27.32	31.24	26.23	33.64	27.89	33.42	26.56	37.80
Duncan coefficient (%)		28.37		19.96		24.33		14.74		23.02

Sources: CFPS 2010, CFPS 2014, CFPS 2016, authors' calculations.

14 percentage points from 2010 to 2016, according to CFPS data in Table 4.2b. Data also suggest that the spread between the two groups across occupations is narrowing. The Duncan coefficient of the occupational distribution gap between the two groups decreased by nearly 27 percent from 2007 to 2013 (CHIP data in Table 4.2a) and by more than 13 percent from 2010 to 2016 (CFPS data in Table 4.2b), respectively.

These results suggest that rural migrant workers' employment options have expanded in recent years, which also implies that employment discrimination against rural migrant workers in the urban labor market has somewhat subsided, and the division between the two groups across the labor market has become less pronounced.

Hukou Discrimination in Employment

The analysis above provides only a statistical description. As the human capital and personal characteristics of both the rural migrant workers and the urban workers changed during the period under study, the supply and demand in the labor market also changed. To further understand the differences in employment choices between the two groups and their influencing factors, especially trying to investigate the role of *hukou* in their employment choices, we need to control for these changes in our next analysis.

Here we use the employment choice model, designed to analyze trends in job selection across different industries or occupations. As an example, to understand industry choice, we use a multinomial logit model to estimate the distributional probability of employees in each of the industries (Bazen 2011). The distribution of rural migrant and urban workers are explained in two parts: first, differences in individual characteristics, such as years of education, age, or gender; and second, differences in estimated coefficients of explanatory variables in two industry selection models. Here we refer to the difference in the estimated coefficients as *hukou* restriction.

To control for the impact of the changes on individual characteristics, we further conducted a counterfactual estimation under the assumption that the characteristics of urban workers and rural migrant workers would remain unchanged over time to isolate the changing role of the *hukou* in employment choices.[3]

Tables 4.2a and 4.2b show the counterfactual analysis results. The data suggest that rural migrant workers have been facing less *hukou* restriction across industries and occupations in recent years. Although the industry restrictions in the urban labor market appeared to increase slightly from 2002 to 2013 as the counterfactual Duncan coefficient increased slightly from 16.55 percent in 2002 to 26.06 percent in 2013, a downward trend began in 2010 as the counterfactual Duncan coefficient decreased from 26.90 percent in 2010 to 12.12 percent in 2016.

We also examined the opportunities available to rural migrant workers to enter the high-end service sector. CHIP data shows that the counterfactual proportion of rural migrant workers entering the high-end service sector increased from 2.66 percent in 2002 to 7.51 percent in 2007, a nearly three-fold increase. Although the proportion of rural migrant workers entering the counterfactual high-end service industry in 2013 (3.34 percent) was lower than in 2007, it was still higher than in 2002. The results from CFPS data indicate that the counterfactual proportion of rural migrant workers entering the high-end service industry has also increased year by year, from 2.24 percent in 2010 to 6.65 percent in 2014 to 9.55 percent in 2016.

Differences in Wages Between Rural Migrant Workers and Urban Workers

How has the gap in wages between rural migrant workers and urban workers changed over the past decade? Has it narrowed or widened? Chinese academics and policy makers alike have been working to answer this question. In theory, a growing acceptance of rural migrant workers in cities should show a decline in discrimination and a narrowing of the wage gap. We used our micro-data analysis to test this hypothesis.

Statistical Description

The results from several data sets show that although the average wage of rural migrant workers is below that of urban workers in the labor market, the gap between the two groups has been closing year by year.

As shown by the CHIP data in Table 4.3a, the annual and hourly wages of urban workers in 2002 were 38.60 percent and 96.39 percent higher, respectively, than those of rural migrant workers. By 2013, the differences had dropped to 15.42 percent and 33.88 percent. Similarly, the results from CFPS data in Table 4.3b indicate that from 2010 to 2014, the ratio of urban workers' annual wage to that of rural migrant workers decreased from 1.19 to 1.01, and the hourly wage ratio decreased from 1.35 to 1.14.[4]

The annual wage gap between rural migrant workers and urban workers is smaller than the gap between their respective hourly wages. This suggests that rural migrant workers have longer working hours than do urban workers. Studies show that long working hours can take a toll on mental health, which in turn makes it more difficult for rural migrant workers to integrate into urban society.[5]

In recent years, the two groups' working hours have also begun to level. As shown in Tables 4.3a and 4.3b, the average number of hours urban workers worked per week in 2002 was 30.73 percent less than that of rural migrant workers. In 2010, this difference fell to 13.43 percent. The difference continued to narrow from 2010 to 2014.

Hukou-Related Wage Discrimination

It is also important to understand the degree to which the *hukou* system plays a role in the wage gap between rural migrant workers and urban workers. To answer this question requires further analysis. The analysis method used here is the commonly used decomposition method developed by Blinder-Oaxaca (1973). With the results from the decomposition analysis, we conducted a counterfactual analysis to examine the change in the *hukou* system's effect.

We used the following Mincer (1974) wage equation to estimate the wage level of rural migrant workers and local workers. The wage equation (1) is written as follows:

$$lnw_i = X_i\beta + u_i \qquad (1)$$

The logarithm of individual wage (annual wage or hourly wage) lnw_i in equation (1) is a function of the demographic characteristic variables (X_i) that affect wage (including years of education, years of work experience, years of work experience squared, gender, industry, occupation, and region), β is the corresponding coefficient estimates, and u_i is the error term.

Table 4.3a. Wage and working hours of employed urban workers and rural migrant workers (2002, 2007, and 2013)

	2002			2007			2013		
	(1) Urban workers	(2) Migrant workers	Ratio of (1)/(2)	(1) Urban workers	(2) Migrant workers	Ratio of (1)/(2)	(1) Urban workers	(2) Migrant workers	Ratio of (1)/(2)
Annual wage (yuan)	11,247	8,115	1.39	21,840	14,551	1.50	28,659	24,830	1.15
Hourly wage (yuan)	5.35	2.72	1.96	11.27	5.56	2.03	12.84	9.59	1.34
Average week working time (hour)	43.32	62.53	0.69	43.22	58.33	0.74	45.96	51.81	0.89
Observations	9,327	1,501	—	6,133	4,992	—	7,737	859	—

Sources: CHIP 2002, CHIP 2007, CHIP 2013, authors' calculations.
Note: Wages are calculated in 2002 prices.

Table 4.3b. Wage and working hours of employed urban workers and rural migrant workers (2010 and 2014)

	2010			2014		
	(1) Urban workers	(2) Migrant workers	Ratio of (1)/(2)	(1) Urban workers	(2) Migrant workers	Ratio of (1)/(2)
Annual wage (yuan)	26,208	22,113	1.19	30,662	30,464	1.01
Hourly wage (yuan)	13.43	9.93	1.35	15.21	13.30	1.14
Average week working time (hour)	50.35	58.15	0.87	45.52	52.31	0.87
Observations	2,629	312	—	1,933	461	—

Sources: CFPS 2010, CFPS 2014, authors' calculations.
Note: Wages are calculated in 2010 prices.

Next, with the estimated results of the wage equation, we applied the Blinder-Oaxaca decomposition method to break down the wage gap into two parts. Equation (2) is written as follows:

$$ln\bar{w}_u - ln\bar{w}_m = \bar{X}_u\beta^u - \bar{X}_m\beta^m = \left(\bar{X}_u - \bar{X}_m\right)\beta^*$$
$$+ \left\{\bar{X}_u(\beta^u - \beta^*) + \bar{X}_m(\beta^* - \beta^m)\right\}$$

(2)

In equation (2), u and m represent urban workers and rural migrant workers, respectively; β^* refers to the coefficients of nondiscriminatory labor market wage;[6] $\left\{\bar{X}_u(\beta^u - \beta^*) + \bar{X}_m(\beta^* - \beta^m)\right\}$ represents the differences in demographics (the difference in individual characteristics between two groups); and $\left(\bar{X}_u - \bar{X}_m\right)\beta^*$ represents the difference between the coefficients (the difference of estimated coefficients for the wage equation between two groups). Here, the wage gap caused by the coefficient differences is considered the *hukou* effect.

Finally, we made a counterfactual estimation. Considering that the demographics of urban workers and rural migrant workers differ from year to year, to control for demographic changes we assumed that the individual characteristics of urban workers and rural migrant workers remain unchanged.[7]

As shown in Tables 4.4a and 4.4b, urban workers' annual and hourly wages were 38.60 percent and 96.39 percent higher than those of rural migrant

Table 4.4a. *Hukou*-related wage discrimination against rural migrant workers, 2002–2013

		2002	2007	2007 (counterfactual)	2013	2013 (counterfactual)
Annual wage (yuan)	(1) Urban workers	11,247	21,840	20,015	28,659	28,236
	(2) Migrant workers	8,115	14,551	13.583	24,830	22,395
	((1)–(2)) / (2) (%)	38.60	50.09	47.36	15.42	26.08
Hourly wage (yuan)	(1) Urban workers	5.35	11.27	10.26	12.84	12.67
	(2) Migrant workers	2.72	5.56	5.03	9.59	8.50
	((1)–(2)) / (2) (%)	96.39	102.69	103.90	33.88	49.17

Sources: CHIP 2002, CHIP 2007, CHIP 2013, authors' calculations.
Note: Counterfactual results of 2007 and 2013 are estimated by using demographic characteristics of 2002 samples.

Table 4.4b. *Hukou*-related wage discrimination against rural migrant workers, 2010–2014

		2010	2014	2014 (counterfactual)
Annual wage (yuan)	(1) Urban workers	26,208	30,662	31,871
	(2) Migrant workers	22,113	30,464	29,896
	((1)–(2)) / (2) (%)	18.52	0.65	6.61
Hourly wage (yuan)	(1) Urban workers	13.43	15.21	15.67
	(2) Migrant workers	9.93	13.30	12.93
	((1)–(2)) / (2) (%)	35.28	14.35	21.20

Sources: CFPS 2010, CFPS 2014, authors' calculations.
Note: Counterfactual results of 2014 are estimated by using demographic characteristics of 2010 samples.

workers in 2002. In the urban labor market in 2013, the wage gap between the two groups narrowed, suggesting that the *hukou* effect weakened. As CFPS data also indicate, the wage discrimination against rural migrant workers diminished from 2010 to 2014.

These results are based on the hypothesis that the workers' choices of industry and occupation are exogenous. However, the choices are also influenced by workers' characteristics. Treating "industry" and "occupation" as exogenous control variables in the wage equation results in certain endogenous problems (Guo, Jiang, and Lu 2011). To address these issues, we used the Appleton decomposition method (Appleton, Hoddinott, and Krishnan 1999; Guo, Jiang, and Lu 2011) to estimate the impact that the *hukou* had on the wage gap. As shown in Table 4.5, during the periods 2002–13 and 2010–14, which are covered by the two data sets, the overall *hukou* effect on wage differentials has generally weakened; for example, the contribution of the *hukou* effect to the annual wage gap was 22.13 percent in 2002, which declined to −93.24 percent in 2013. In addition, the impact of *hukou* discrimination in wage determination has reduced. The wage difference between the two groups mainly comes from the difference in demographic characteristics, especially the difference in human capital level, such as year of education.

This decomposition analysis yields results worthy of further discussion. What does it mean for the measured effect of the *hukou* on the wage gap to be negative? Are urban workers discriminated against in the urban labor market? Or are rural migrant workers overpaid? From a labor market policy standpoint, there is no evidence to suggest that there is discrimination against urban workers. How, then, should these results be interpreted?

There are two explanations for the results. The first is that rural migrant workers' wages are set to compensate for their lack of access to social security, as stipulations of the *hukou* system prevent them from enjoying the same welfare benefits and social security programs that urban workers do. Social benefits must then be internalized in the market price of labor. That is to say, the market price of labor consists of two parts: wage and welfare. In this context, welfare can be understood as social security benefits provided by employers, in-kind income, and access to public services. This welfare can be valued in the labor market, which, together with monetary wages, constitutes

Table 4.5. The effect of *hukou* on the urban and rural migrant worker wage gap (%)

	2002	2007	2013	2010	2014
Industry (annual wage)	22.13	24.68	−93.24	−65.31	−189.66
Industry (hourly wage)	42.54	35.99	−10.03	−29.47	15.81
Occupation (annual wage)	22.65	17.87	−93.08	−112.33	−272.53
Occupation (hourly wage)	44.13	35.59	−9.01	−67.75	−6.94

Sources: CHIP 2002, CHIP 2007, CHIP 2013, CFPS 2010, CFPS 2014, authors' calculations.

the total market price of labor. Therefore, rural migrant workers who cannot access these baseline welfare benefits will be compensated instead with a wage increase. As a result, rural migrant workers with the same personal characteristics as urban workers will receive a higher wage.

The second explanation for the negative coefficients observed in Table 4.5 is the variation in qualifying characteristics across groups that are otherwise unobserved in the equation. For example, the average intelligence, physical strength, or other personal characteristics among rural migrant workers may contribute to their overall labor productivity, making them more likely to be eligible for bonuses or financial rewards.

Differences in Social Security Accessibility Between Rural Migrant Workers and Urban Workers

Rural migrant workers' inability to access social security has been an ongoing point of contention in China. Their social security coverage and benefit levels have improved slightly, but not significantly in recent years. There is still a large gap between rural migrants and urban workers. One of the main reasons is that the city governments still consider rural migrant workers to be outsiders and therefore feel no responsibility or urgency to integrate them into existing systems of urban welfare. In addition to this, rural migrant workers are high mobility groups, which presents its own set of difficulties in providing services. To have a more detailed understanding of the improvement of social security benefits for rural migrant workers, we made relevant analyses using the latest data.

Statistical Description

Table 4.6 shows the difference in rural migrant workers' and urban workers' social security participation rates. On the one hand, the rate of migrant worker participation in urban social security programs is growing; however, urban workers' participation rate is also increasing. The question is, How have these two groups' participation rates changed in relation to each other?

In terms of accessing pension, urban workers' participation rate has not increased significantly, and the gap with rural migrant workers' participation has narrowed. Specifically, the CHIP data shows that in 2002, the participation rate of rural migrant workers in the pension was 11.43 percent that of urban workers' participation. By 2013, it had risen to 39.53 percent. A similar trend can be observed in the share of workers who accessed medical insurance. In 2002, the participation rate of rural migrant workers was 10.41 percent that of urban workers. In 2013, this number rose to 33.88 percent. CFPS data shows a similar trend.

Hukou Discrimination in Social Security

It is also important to analyze further the extent to which *hukou* has a bearing on access to social welfare programs. Cai, Du, and Wang (2005) found that rural migrant workers experience more discrimination in their access to social welfare programs than in wages. Indeed, rural migrant workers who participate in urban social security programs often have higher contribution rates, experience barriers to transferring benefits between cities, and have no guarantee of benefits in the future. At the same time, employers looking to reduce labor costs are reluctant to pay contribution fees for rural migrant workers. Taken together, these factors disincentivize participation in the programs and explain, at least in part, the gaps between groups.

To find relevant evidence from the micro-data, we use the logit model as follows:

$$P(y_i = 1|Z_i) = F(Z_i \delta) \tag{3}$$

Taking three insurances as an example, whether an individual$_i$ participates in three insurances is a binary dummy variable: yes ($y_i = 1$) and no ($y_i = 0$). Z_i represents the personal characteristics that affect participation in three insurances (including age, age squared, gender, marital status, education level, industry, occupation, labor contract, and region), and δ is the coefficient estimate of the variables. Because insurance participation is a discrete variable, the decomposition of the social security gap between the two groups can be based only on the nonlinear Blinder-Oaxaca model (Sinning, Hahn, and Bauer 2008). In a nonlinear case, the Blinder-Oaxaca decomposition is rephrased in the form of conditional expectations expressed as follows:

$$\begin{aligned}\bar{y}_u - \bar{y}_m = &\{E_{\delta^u}(y_u|Z_u) - E_{\delta^u}(y_m|Z_m)\} \\ &+ \{E_{\delta^u}(y_m|Z_m) - E_{\delta^m}(y_m|Z_m)\}\end{aligned} \tag{4}$$

Table 4.6. Participation of employed urban workers and rural migrant workers in social security programs (%)

	2002		2007		2013		2010		2014	
	Urban workers	Migrant workers	Urban workers	Migrant workers	Urban workers	Migrant workers	Urban workers	Migrant workers	Urban workers	Migrant workers
Sub-item										
Medical insurance	46.08	4.80	78.82	11.30	87.28	29.57	70.25	21.47	82.10	37.96
Pension insurance	60.63	6.93	73.34	21.41	79.23	31.32	52.53	15.06	63.42	37.09
Injury insurance	—	—	52.41	21.63	41.68	24.80	28.30	21.15	43.40	33.84
Unemployment insurance	38.79	3.06	59.48	14.46	44.72	19.56	43.55	13.14	47.34	25.38
Housing fund	56.41	—	53.77	8.61	44.04	11.18	44.69	6.09	42.73	15.62
Maternity insurance	—	—	—	—	31.47	15.13	13.81	7.37	31.04	21.04
Complex										
Three insurances	26.15	2.13	54.70	6.25	42.91	16.88	30.35	7.37	46.15	24.73
Five insurances	—	—	—	—	25.90	11.29	8.41	4.49	28.45	19.96
Five insurances and one fund	—	—	—	—	20.05	6.40	5.82	1.60	20.85	9.76
Observations	9,327	1,501	6,133	4,992	7,737	859	2,629	312	1,933	461

Sources: CHIP 2002, CHIP 2007, CHIP 2013, CFPS 2010, CFPS 2014, authors' calculations.
Note: "Three insurances" refers to medical insurance, pension insurance, and unemployment insurance. "Five insurances" refers to medical insurance, pension insurance, injury insurance, unemployment insurance, and maternity insurance.

In equation (4), u represents urban workers and m represents rural migrant workers. $E_{\delta^m}(y_m | Z_m)$ is the conditional expectation of y_m, which indicates rural migrant workers' observable choice of three insurances. $E_{\delta^u}(y_m | Z_m)$ is the counterfactual participation rate of rural migrant workers using the estimated coefficient of urban workers. $\bar{y}_u - \bar{y}_m$ is the gap in the participation rate between the two groups. $E_{\delta^u}(y_m | Z_m) - E_{\delta^m}(y_m | Z_m)$ represents the gap in social security choices due to the difference in the estimated coefficients, which we refer to as the unexplained part or *hukou* discrimination.

Table 4.7 shows the counterfactual participation and *hukou* discrimination against rural migrant workers in social security programs. The counterfactual participation rate of rural migrant workers in urban social programs is higher than the observed participation rate shown in Table 4.6. For example, the counterfactual participation rate of rural migrant workers in three insurances was 15.28 percent in 2002, while their actual participation rate was only 2.13 percent. The difference in coefficients of social security equations between the two groups to some extent reflects the *hukou* discrimination against rural migrant workers in access to social security.

The data spanning from 2002 to 2013 and 2010 to 2014 suggest that *hukou*-based discrimination against rural migrant workers' ability to access social security declined. For example, the difference in participation attributed to *hukou* discrimination accounted for 54.74 percent of the total difference in 2002 and dropped to 45.37 percent in 2013. To summarize, data indicates that rural migrant workers' participation rate in social security is rising, and the gap with urban workers' participation is narrowing. In other words, *hukou*-based discrimination is decreasing. That said, the gap still exists, and barriers for rural migrant workers to access social security programs in China do still exist.

Conclusion and Discussion

Based on the latest data of three household surveys, this chapter describes and analyzes current employment, wage, and social security access trends among rural migrant workers in urban China. The main conclusions are as follows: First, with several public policies introduced in favor of rural migrant workers in the last decade, the gradual strengthening of the overall labor market, and shifts in labor supply and demand, rural migrant workers have more choices in urban employment—that is, more opportunities to

Table 4.7. Counterfactual participation in urban social programs and *hukou* discrimination against rural migrant workers (%)

	2002		2007		2013		2010		2014	
	Counter-factual	Hukou discrimi-nation	Counter-factual	Hukou discrimi-nation	Counter-factual	Hukou discrimi-nation	Counter-factual	Hukou discrimi-nation	Counter-factual	Hukou discrimi-nation
Three insurances	15.28	54.74	34.18	57.63	28.69	45.37	26.88	84.87	34.99	47.92
Five insurances	—	—	—	—	17.72	44.01	9.02	115.58	19.86	−1.13
Five insurances and one fund	—	—	—	—	11.40	36.60	4.58	70.64	13.42	33.00

Sources: CHIP 2002, CHIP 2007, CHIP 2013, CFPS 2010, CFPS 2014, authors' calculations.
Note: "Three insurances" refers to medical insurance, pension insurance, and unemployment insurance. "Five insurances" refers to medical insurance, pension insurance, injury insurance, unemployment insurance, and maternity insurance.

enter high-end service industries and choose white-collar occupations. Moreover, discrimination against rural migrant workers in the workplace has been shown to be declining.

In most small and mid-sized cities, *hukou* is no longer a restricting factor for rural migrant workers to enter their choice of employment sector. However, there still exist marked differences between rural migrant workers and urban workers in the industries and occupations in which they are employed. This difference can be attributed not only to differences in human or social capital but also to local employment policies for rural migrant workers in cities where the *hukou* system is still an institutional barrier to labor mobility.

Second, rural migrant workers' wages have increased rapidly in recent years to slowly close the wage gap between rural migrant workers and local workers. Data even suggest that there is a reverse discrimination effect at work that can be understood as additional compensation paid to rural migrant workers who are unable to access social security.[8]

Third, rural migrant workers' participation rate in urban social security programs has increased to a certain extent, but due to the system's design, a large number of rural migrant workers are still excluded from the urban social security system. Furthermore, even if rural migrant workers were to participate in social security programs, the existing system prevents them from receiving the same benefits as urban employees.

Overall, rural migrant workers' economic status has improved in recent years, both relative to their past conditions and when compared to marginal improvements for urban workers. But the improvement is still uneven across cities and groups. In areas where market forces play an adequate role, such as in wage determination, the relative position of rural migrant workers has improved more significantly, while in areas where governments have more restrictions on employment and social security, their relative position has slowly progressed.

There are several policy implications and suggestions from our findings. First, rural migrant workers should still be understood as a marginalized group in urban China. As such, we must continue to promote household registration reforms, especially in large cities. Second, cities must facilitate the process of urban-rural integration and promote in situ transformation through the development and upgrading of small towns and local industrial structures. In doing so, cities would be investing in the stability and long-term employment of migrant workers. Third, there must be a push to equalize access to public services, focusing on improving equal opportunities for rural migrant workers in the fields of education, medical care, housing, and other public services.

Notes

1. Rural migrant workers here refer to those whose *hukou* (household registration) is still in rural areas and who have been working outside their original township for six months or more.

2. The Duncan coefficient formula is $D = 0.5\sum_{i}^{k}|u_i - m_i|$, where u_i and m_i represent the employment ratio of urban workers and rural migrant workers in the i-th position. The bigger the Duncan coefficient is, the bigger the difference of jobs between the two groups.

3. The specific steps were as follows: First, the multinomial logit model was used to estimate the coefficients of the urban workers' industry selection equation in 2007 and 2013. Then, the population distribution of urban workers in 2002 and the coefficients of the industry selection equations of urban workers in 2007 and 2013 were used to estimate the industry distribution of urban workers in the counterfactual situation in 2007 and 2013. In addition, the counterfactual distribution of the urban workers' industry in 2014 and 2016 was estimated using the demographic variables of local urban workers in 2010 and the coefficients of the urban workers' industry selection equation in 2014 and 2016. Similarly, we calculated the counterfactual distribution of rural migrant workers in 2007, 2013, 2014, and 2016. Counterfactual estimates of occupational distribution are similar.

4. In the CFPS 2016 survey, CFPS neglected to collect information on those who did not change their job between CFPS 2014 and CFPS 2016, resulting in a lack of reported wages for this group of major jobs (Wu et al. 2018). Although researchers used the model to generate the imputed value of the main work income in 2016, the working hours and social security status of this part of the population were missing. Therefore, CFPS 2016 data is not used for analysis of working hours and social security status.

5. Pan and Lin (2015) used the data of the 2012 "Three Inclusions" survey of rural migrant workers in Hunan Province to find that rural migrant workers generally have longer working hours, which has a significant negative impact on social interaction and social integration of rural migrant workers.

6. For the choice of nondiscriminatory labor market wage structure coefficient in this chapter, refer to the detailed discussion on index benchmark issues in Zhang et al. (2014).

7. The counterfactual estimate of annual and hourly wages is similar to that of industry and occupational distribution.

8. In reality, there may be a problem of self-selection—that is, migrants remaining in cities have higher income on average, and low-income migrants have returned to the countryside (Li, Sato, and Sicular 2013). This is a theoretical hypothesis about self-selection, and we need to find empirical evidence to test it. Based on the data of CHIP 2007, Wei, Yang, and Zhu (2019) used the sample selection model of Heckman (1979) to overcome the sample self-selection problem and found that migrants with stronger abilities and higher income choose to return to rural areas. However, in the data of CHIP 2002, CHIP 2013, CFPS 2010, CFPS 2014, and CFPS 2016 used in this chapter, the information of return migrants cannot be obtained. We will further evaluate the self-selection of migrants and its impact on their income growth in the future.

·

References

Appleton, Simon, John Hoddinott, and Pramila Krishnan. 1999. "The Gender Wage Gap in Three African Countries." *Economic Development and Cultural Change* 47 (2): 289–312.

Bazen, Stephen, ed. 2011. *Econometric Methods for Labour Economics*. Oxford: Oxford University Press.

Blinder, Alan S. 1973. "Wage Discrimination: Reduced Form and Structural Estimates." *Journal of Human Resources* 8 (4): 436–55.

Cai, Fang, Yang Du, and Meiyan Wang, eds. 2005. *Transformation and Development of China's Labor Market*. Beijing: Commercial Press.

Chen, Binkai, and Siyu Chen. 2018. "Flowing Social Capital: Can Traditional Clan Culture Affect Migrants' Employment in Modern Society?" *Economic Research Journal* 53 (3): 35–49.

Démurger, Sylvie, Marc Gurgand, Shi Li, and Ximing Yue. 2009. "Migrants as Second-Class Workers in Urban China? A Decomposition Analysis." *Journal of Comparative Economics* 37 (4): 610–28.

Deng, Quheng. 2007. "Earnings Differential Between Urban Residents and Rural Migrants: Evidence from Oaxaca-Blinder and Quantile Regression Decompositions." *Chinese Journal of Population Science* (2): 8–16.

Deng, Quheng, and Shi Li. 2012. "Low-Paid Workers in Urban China." *International Labour Review* 151 (3): 157–71.

Duncan, Otis Dudley, and Beverly Duncan. 1955. "A Methodological Analysis of Segregation Indexes." *American Sociological Review* 20 (2): 210–17.

Guo, Jiqiang, Li Jiang, and Lili Lu. 2011. "Decomposition Methods for Wage Differentials: A Survey." *China Economic Quarterly* 10 (2): 363–414.

Heckman, James J. 1979. "Sample Selection Bias as A Specification Error." *Econometrica* 47 (1): 153–62.

Li, Jun, and Yanfeng Gu. 2011. "Hukou-Based Stratification in China's Urban Labor Market." *Sociological Studies* 25 (2): 48–77.

Li, Qiang. 2012. *Rural Migrant Workers and Chinese Social Stratification*. 2nd ed. Beijing: Social Sciences Academic Press.

Li, Shi. 2014. "Economic Situation of Rural Migrant Workers in the Chinese Labour Market." *Human Resources Development of China* 11:6–9.

Li, Shi, Hiroshi Sato, and Terry Sicular. 2013. *Analysis on the Change of Income Gap in China—Research on Income Distribution of Chinese Residents IV*. Beijing: People's Publishing House.

Lin, Liyue, and Yu Zhu. 2009. "An Analysis on Influencing Factors for Floating Population's Participation in Social Security: A Survey in Six Cities in Fujian Province." *Population and Economics* (3): 89–95.

Lu, Feng. 2012. "Wage Trends Among Chinese Rural Migrant Workers: 1979–2010." *Social Sciences in China* (7): 47–67.

Meng, Xin, and Junsen Zhang. 2001. "The Two-Tier Labor Market in Urban China: Occupational Segregation and Wage Differentials Between Urban Residents and Rural Migrants in Shanghai." *Journal of Comparative Economics* 29 (3): 485–504.

Mincer, Jacob, ed. 1974. *Schooling, Experience, and Earnings*. New York: National Bureau of Economic Research. Distributed by Columbia University Press.

National Bureau of Statistics of China. 2019. "2018 Migrant Worker Monitoring Survey Report." [In Chinese.] www.stats.gov.cn/tjsj/zxfb/201904/t20190429_1662268.html.

Oaxaca, Ronald. 1973. "Male-Female Wage Differentials in Urban Labor Markets." *International Economic Review* 14 (3): 693–709.

Pan, Zequan, and Tingting Lin. 2015. "Working Time, Social Interactions and Rural Migrant Workers' Social Inclusion: Based on 'Three Inclusions' of Rural Migrant Workers Survey in the Hunan Province." *Chinese Journal of Population Science* (3): 108–15.

Qin, Lijian, and Bo Chen. 2014. "Impact of Medical Insurance on Rural Migrant Workers' Urban Integration." *Management World* (10): 91–99.

Sinning, Mathias, Markus Hahn, and Thomas K. Bauer. 2008. "The Blinder-Oaxaca Decomposition for Nonlinear Regression Models." *Stata Journal* 8 (4): 480–92.

State Council of the People's Republic of China. 2014. *Opinions on Further Promoting the Reform of the Household Registration System*. Beijing: State Council.

Sun, Jingfang. 2017. "Changes to Hukou Discrimination in China's Labor Market: Employment and Wages of Rural Migrant Workers." *Economic Research Journal* 52 (8): 171–86.

Tian, Feng. 2010. "A Study of the Income Gap Between Urban Workers and Rural Migrant Workers." *Sociological Studies* 25 (2): 87–105.

Wang, Meiyan. 2003. "Wage Differential During the Transition: The Quantitative Analysis of Discrimination." *Quantitative and Technical Economics* (5): 94–98.

———. 2005. "Employment Opportunities and Wage Gaps in the Urban Labor Market: A Study of the Employment and Wages of Migrant Laborers." *Social Sciences in China* (5): 36–46.

Wang, Qiong, and Jingyi Ye. 2016. "Health Status, Income and Overtime Work of Rural Migrant Workers." *Chinese Rural Economy* (2): 2–12.

Wei, Lv, Mo Yang, and Dongming Zhu. 2019. "Could Rural Immigrants Be Assimilated into the Urban Labor Market?" *Journal of Finance and Economics* 45 (2): 86–99.

Wu, Qiong, Lihong Dai, Qi Zhen, Jingshen Zhang, Liping Gu, Cong Zhang, and Fangyuan Zhao. 2018. "Introduction to the 2016 Database and Data Cleanup Report of China Family Panel Studies." [In Chinese.] www.isss.pku.edu.cn/cfps/docs/20181229160348287861.pdf.

Yan, Shanping. 2006. "The Flow of Personnel in China's Urban Labor Market and the System That Decides Thereon." *Management World* (8): 8–17.

Ye, Jingyi, and Yang. 2015. "Minimum Wage Standard and Its Implementation Difference: Violation Rate and Violation Depth." *Economic Perspectives* (8): 51–63.

Zhang, Li, and Wenxin Cai. 2017. "The Income Discrimination by Hukou in China's Labor Market—an Analysis Based on Unconditional Quantile Decomposition." *Journal of Fudan University (Natural Science)* 56 (1): 12–18.

Zhang, Li, Shi Li, William A. Darity Jr., and Rhonda Vonshay Sharpe. 2014. "Hukou Discrimination on Wage Income in China's Labor Market." *Management World* (11): 35–46.

———. 2016. "The Discrimination in Job Obtainment by Hukou in Labor Market in China and Its Change Trend." *Journal of Finance and Economics* 42 (1): 4–16.

Zhang, Li, Binbin Wu, Shi Li, and Sylvie Démurger. 2016. "The Sectoral Effect on Income Discrimination by Hukou: A Decomposition Analysis based on Microsimulation." *Chinese Rural Economy* (2): 36–51.

Zhao, Zhong. 2004. "Rural-Urban Migration in China—What Do We Know and What Do We Need to Know?" *China Economic Quarterly* (2): 517–36.

Zheng, Gongcheng, and Liruolian Huang, eds. 2007. *Rural Migrant Workers and Social Protection in China*. Beijing: People's Publishing House.

Zhu, Rong. 2016. "Wage Differentials Between Urban Residents and Rural Migrants in Urban China During 2002–2007: A Distributional Analysis." *China Economic Review* 37 (February): 2–14.

CHAPTER 5

Urban Poverty in China: Has *Dibao* Been an Effective Policy Response?

Qin Gao

Introduction

China has made dramatic progress in poverty reduction in the past forty years, contributing significantly to anti-poverty efforts globally. Within China, the government's focus has long been on rural poverty. In 2013, the central government launched its latest anti-poverty campaign to eradicate extreme rural poverty by 2020, involving heavy financial and human resource investments and mass sociopolitical mobilization. Urban poverty, meanwhile, has been receiving less attention and is all but forgotten in policy debates and public discourse.

In this chapter, I place urban poverty against the backdrop of rapid urbanization in China to gain a deeper understanding of its driving forces and policy responses. In particular, I focus on the primary social safety net that addresses urban poverty, the Minimum Livelihood Guarantee (or *dibao*), and investigate whether it has served as an effective policy response within the broader social policy and urban studies contexts. Rather than presenting findings based on new analysis, I provide a review of the existing evidence on four aspects of *dibao*'s anti-poverty effectiveness: income poverty, family consumption, employment and welfare dependency, and subjective well-being.

I begin by presenting trends in urban poverty alongside trends in China's urbanization. I then summarize the predictors of urban poverty at the individual, household, and community levels. Next, I provide a comprehensive review of the empirical evidence on the effectiveness of *dibao* as a policy response to urban poverty. Finally, I conclude by drawing lessons from the existing evidence and suggest policy implications and possible immediate next steps.

Urban Poverty: Definitions, Trends, and Predictors

Poverty Definitions

It is essential to first define the urban population in order to estimate urban poverty. The literature has primarily defined the urban population in China as those who hold an urban household registration status, or *hukou* (Wang and Zhang 2013). Official statistics show that the urban population increased from 731 million in 2013 to 848 million in 2019. These figures include the estimated 245 million and 236 million rural-to-urban migrants, in 2013 and 2019 respectively, who lived and worked in cities while holding a rural *hukou* (National Bureau of Statistics of China 2020). Still, most empirical studies are unable to include migrants in their estimates due to lack of data available on these groups (Guo, Tan, and Qu 2018; Wang and Zhang 2013).

Within the urban population, the estimation of urban poverty mainly uses two measures: absolute poverty and relative poverty (Zhang, Jia, and Shen 2019). Absolute poverty refers to when the income or consumption level of an individual or family falls below an established poverty threshold (or poverty line). Like most low- and middle-income countries, China still mainly uses absolute poverty measures. Worldwide, the measure most often used is the World Bank poverty line set at $1.90 per person per day at 2015 purchasing power parity (PPP). Another widely used absolute poverty measure is defined based on the cost of basic needs method. This method divides people's basic needs into food demand and non-food demand and accounts for the cost differences of obtaining basic needs in different periods and regions (Ravallion 1998).

However, the absolute poverty measure is unable to reflect people's living conditions relative to changes in the societal context. To address this limitation, Townsend (1979) proposed the use of relative poverty measures, so that poverty is estimated and understood relative to the average standard of living in the society. Most member countries of the Organisation for Economic Co-operation and Development have adopted the relative poverty measure, with the poverty line set at 50 percent or 60 percent of the median income in a society. As the median income level increases, the relative poverty

line automatically increases. As urban China has rapidly achieved an economic development level closer to that in high-income countries, scholars
have urged the use of relative rather than absolute poverty measures (Lin 2020;
Wang, Yang, and Gao 2019).

It is important to note that there exists a third type of poverty measure
that is still not widely considered in China: subjective poverty. A subjective
poverty measure determines the poverty line based on people's perceptions
of their own well-being. This requires a clear description of the well-being
function of the residents and, to some extent, a shared understanding of such
well-being (Kapteyn et al. 1977). Policy makers and scholars may need to
consider this poverty measure in the future.

Urban Poverty Trends

Empirical evidence based on China Household Income Project (CHIP) data
shows that the urban poverty rate based on absolute poverty measures has
been largely declining from 1988 to 2013, while the rate based on relative
poverty measures has been mostly increasing during the same period. This
reflects both improvement in absolute living standards and the rising income inequality in urban areas over the past thirty years. CHIP has been a
repeated cross-sectional national survey of household income and consumption since 1988. The survey is carried out every five to seven years and
was conducted in 1988, 1995, 2002, 2007, 2013, and 2018. Because of its extensive questions on income sources and amount, it remains one of the best
data sets to study poverty and income distribution in China (Gustafsson, Li,
and Sato 2014; Sicular et al. 2020).

Table 5.1 presents select results from the literature on absolute poverty
rates based on the CHIP data. These are reported alongside the population
urbanization rate, estimated as the share of the total national population who
hold urban *hukou* by the National Bureau of Statistics of China (2020). Column 1 shows that population urbanization in China increased rapidly from
1988 to 2013. The share of urban residents (those living in urban areas for six
months or more in a year) in the national population was just over a quarter in
1988, but it increased to nearly 54 percent by 2013, having risen steadily over
that period.

Columns 2–4 in Table 5.1 present three sets of estimates of absolute poverty rates in urban China. Regardless of the absolute poverty line used, the

Table 5.1. Trends in urbanization rate and absolute urban poverty rates (%)

Definition	Urbanization rate	Urban poverty rate (all estimations are based on CHIP data)		
	(1) Share of people with urban hukou in total population	(2) Poverty line = $2/ person/day	(3) Poverty line = necessary food and non-food cost	(4) Poverty line = Yunnan dibao line in 2013
1988	25.81	8.04	4.18	8.03
1995	29.04	7.40	5.90	7.97
2002	39.09	6.32	2.91	3.00
2007	45.89	3.62	2.34	0.25
2013	53.73	2.04	1.69	1.16

Sources: NBS, Zhang et al. (2019), Gustafsson and Ding (2019).

urban poverty rate dropped significantly from 1988 to 2013. Based on the poverty line of $2.00 that is close to the World Bank poverty line of $1.90 per person per day, Zhang, Jia, and Shen (2019) estimated the absolute poverty rate to decline from 8.04 percent in 1988 to 2.04 percent in 2013. Following Ravallion (1998), the authors also adopted a poverty line estimate based on the necessary food and non-food costs for sustenance, which is lower than the $2.00 per person per day poverty line. Accordingly, the absolute poverty rate estimated (column 3) was much lower than that based on the $2.00 per person per day poverty line (column 2). Taking into account changes in food and non-food costs over time also led to some fluctuations in the estimated absolute poverty rate during this period, with a higher poverty rate (5.90 percent) in 1995 than in 1988 (4.18 percent).

Gustafsson and Ding (2019) adopted the 2013 dibao line in Yunnan—one of the poorest provinces in China—as an absolute poverty line to estimate national urban poverty. Dibao, or the Minimum Livelihood Guarantee, is China's primary safety net program to support the poor. Dibao line is the income threshold used to determine eligibility for receiving the cash assistance. Each locality sets up its own dibao line according to local cost of living and fiscal capacity, and families whose income falls below the line can receive dibao benefits that supplement their income so that it reaches the dibao line. Similar to the trends revealed by Zhang, Jia, and Shen (2019), the estimated poverty rate based on the Yunnan dibao line also declined significantly from 1988 to 2013, with a substantial dip in 2007 to reach 0.25 percent, and then a slight bounce back to 1.16 percent by 2013.

The urban poverty trends based on relative poverty measures tell a different story. As shown in Table 5.2, the relative poverty rate increased from 1988 to 2013 regardless of the relative poverty line used. The poverty rate was relatively low in 1988—at 4.45 percent when the poverty line was set at 50 percent of median per capita income and 2.67 percent when the poverty line was set at 50 percent of median equivalence scale income (household income calculated by dividing by the equivalence scale, which takes the value of 1 for the first person and 0.5 for each additional person). By 2007, these estimates rose to 11.82 percent and 14.79 percent respectively, with the former rising to 12.81 percent and the latter falling slightly to 14.02 percent by 2013. When the relative poverty line was set higher—at 60 percent or 70 percent of median equivalence scale income—the estimated relative poverty rate was also higher, but the overall trend remained unchanged. In other words, the relative poverty rate increased from 1988 to 2013, while the absolute poverty rate decreased during this period, reflecting the rising average standard of living as well as growing income inequality in urban China during this period.

Predictors of Urban Poverty

Existing studies have examined the predictors of urban poverty at the individual, household, and community levels (Gustafsson and Ding 2019; Yang,

Table 5.2. Trends in relative urban poverty rates (%, all estimations are based on CHIP data)

	(1) Poverty line = 50% of median per capita income	(2) Poverty line = 50% of median equivalence scale income	(3) Poverty line = 60% of median equivalence scale income	(4) Poverty line = 70% of median equivalence scale income
1988	4.45	2.67	6.42	13.16
1995	5.52	7.97	14.00	22.64
2002	10.65	10.70	18.07	26.47
2007	11.82	14.79	21.37	28.50
2013	12.81	14.02	20.44	27.69

Sources: Zhang et al. (2019), Gustafsson and Ding (2019).

Chen, and Jin 2019; Zhang, Jia, and Shen 2019). At the individual level, the head of household's educational attainment was identified as the strongest and most consistent predictor, with higher educational attainment associated with a lower chance of living in poverty. At the household level, a larger household size and more children were associated with both income and asset poverty. At the community level, the higher the average income level in the region, the lower the poverty rate; and the more pronounced the income inequality in the region, the higher the poverty rate.

Dibao's Effectiveness in Addressing Urban Poverty

A growing body of literature has examined the effectiveness of various social policies in addressing urban poverty in China. Westmore (2018) found that overall, government transfers to low-income households were effective in significantly reducing poverty rates. Huang (2017) found the Urban Resident Basic Medical Insurance program effective in supporting low-income families with medical care costs, a burden that can otherwise trap families in cycles of poverty. Zhu (2017) studied the effect of pensions on poverty rate, finding limited reduction in poverty rates in urban areas. Wei and Wang (2013) examined housing support policies, which proved to support low- and middle-income urban households in maintaining stable housing.

Having served as the primary safety net since 1999, *dibao* is urban China's main poverty alleviation program. How effective has it been? Drawing from a review of the existing empirical literature in both English and Chinese, I examine in this section four aspects of *dibao*'s anti-poverty effectiveness: income poverty, family consumption, employment and welfare dependency, and subjective well-being. Overall, the existing literature suggests that *dibao* has had a modest effect on reducing income poverty and has enabled recipient families to spend more on education and health care. At the same time, *dibao* has been found to create some work disincentives and may lead to reduced subjective well-being for recipients.

Income Poverty

A substantial set of literature has focused on *dibao*'s role in addressing income poverty. Most of these studies use large-scale household survey data and quantitative analysis. This body of evidence shows that *dibao* has had a modest impact on poverty reduction, leading to a rise in family income at both the national and local levels.

At the national level, Yang and Gao (2019) used CHIP 2013 data to examine the effect of urban *dibao* on income poverty. To address the issue of selectivity bias, they used a propensity score matching (PSM) method to match *dibao* recipients with their nonrecipient peers based on a wide range of family characteristics. They used the *dibao* line and $3.10 per person per day PPP as the poverty lines to measure absolute poverty. Yang and Gao found that the lower the poverty line adopted, the greater urban *dibao*'s poverty reduction effect. They also found that urban *dibao* was most effective in reducing poverty in the western region of China and less so in the central region. This difference may be attributable to a failure in the central provinces to target those who needed the support most.

Luo and Wang (2018) estimated urban *dibao*'s effectiveness by using 2014 data of the China Family Panel Studies (CFPS) and selecting a sample of urban households in eight provinces in the eastern, central, and western regions. They used two absolute poverty lines, including the World Bank poverty line of $1.90 per person per day and the national average urban *dibao* line, and one relative poverty line, measured at 50 percent of median pre-*dibao* per capita income. They found that the poverty reduction effect of urban *dibao* was significant for the recipient sample but limited for the eligible sample, as some who were eligible did not receive the *dibao* benefits. As a result, urban *dibao*'s poverty reduction in the general urban population was also very limited. Luo and Wang proposed to enhance urban *dibao*'s targeting performance and benefit level in order to improve its anti-poverty effectiveness.

At the local level, Gao (2013) used household survey data collected from five hundred low-income families from 2009 to 2010 in Shanghai to estimate the poverty reduction effect of urban *dibao*. By using different poverty lines, Gao found that *dibao*'s poverty reduction effect was most prominent when a low poverty line was used. As the poverty line rose, the poverty reduction effect of *dibao* became smaller. When the most widely used relative poverty line (set at 50 percent of median per capita income in Shanghai in 2009) was used, poverty rate, gap, and severity were all drastically higher than when the much lower absolute poverty lines were used. Therefore, Gao concluded that urban *dibao* was far from sufficient in lifting the relative positions of the recipient families in the context of the overall income distribution in Shanghai.

Qualitative studies overall support these quantitative findings. Using in-depth interviews with *dibao* recipients in Chengdu, Zhang (2015) examined the anti-poverty effectiveness of urban *dibao*. The interviews were conducted from April to August 2013, usually in *dibao* recipients' homes. Zhang found that urban *dibao* provided insufficient cash support, and other special assistance programs were more tokenistic and did not offer much help to these families in need.

Guan (2019) evaluated the *dibao* standards through two approaches: an assessment of its overall anti-poverty effectiveness and an international comparative analysis. Drawing from both administrative and survey data as well as fieldwork evidence, Guan concluded that *dibao*'s role in narrowing the income gap between rich and poor was limited. *Dibao* recipients also faced other difficulties in daily life, such as demanding family care responsibilities, and were at higher risk of suffering from psychological distress. An international comparison revealed that the *dibao* standard lagged far behind programs in developed countries, which typically adopted relative poverty lines as their social assistance standards.

Family Consumption

Does urban *dibao* change family consumption and affect the structure of household expenditures? A series of studies found that urban *dibao* boosts family expenditures on education and health. Most empirical studies also found that for the most part, recipient families did not use their *dibao* supplements on basic needs such as food, clothing, housing, and transportation (Gao, Zhai, and Garfinkel 2010; Gao et al. 2014).

Wang, Yang, and Gao (2019) used CHIP 2002, 2007, and 2013 data to track the changes in the effects of urban *dibao* on family consumption over time. They found a positive correlation between receiving urban *dibao* and total household consumption, a trend that was statistically significant in 2002 and 2007 but became nonsignificant in 2013. Delving into the structure of consumption, they found that in all three years, urban *dibao* recipients prioritized spending on education and health compared to their nonrecipient counterparts. In addition, in 2013, urban *dibao* recipients tended to spend less on food, clothing, and socializing.

Using CHIP 2013 data, Yang and Gao (2019) further investigated the regional differences in the effects of urban *dibao* on family consumption. They found regional differences in urban *dibao*'s impact on total family consumption: *dibao* recipients in the eastern region reduced their total family spending, those in the central region increased their spending, and those in the western region had no significant change in total family consumption. Compared to nonrecipients, recipients in the eastern and central regions (but not the western region) were more likely to use *dibao* funds for education, while those in the western and central regions (but not the eastern region) were more likely to use the funds for health care.

Employment and Welfare Dependency

Welfare dependency is the state in which individuals or households rely on government welfare benefits as their sole or main income source for a prolonged period of time, and without which they would not be able to afford the expenses of daily living. As in other societies, *dibao* could encourage welfare dependency and discourage recipients from seeking work. Existing evidence suggests that urban *dibao* might deter recipients from seeking employment and have the unintended consequence of encouraging welfare dependency.

For example, Ci and Lan (2015) examined *dibao* recipients' employment behaviors by using 2014 survey data from Hubei and Liaoning Provinces and binary logistic regressions. They found that *dibao* participation was associated with increased probability of job loss and reduced willingness to reemploy, indicating that the phenomenon of welfare dependency might be real in urban China, at least to some extent. The authors further found that low personal income and substantial family care responsibilities were associated with reduced possibility of *dibao* recipients returning to work.

Using household survey data and focus groups with *dibao* beneficiaries, administrators, and policy makers in three cities (Jinan, Changsha, and Baotou) in summer 2012, Xu and Carraro (2017) investigated the extent to which *dibao* recipients looked for work. They found that individual and household circumstances were important factors in determining the recipients' long-term unemployment. At the individual level, nearly half of the study sample were approaching retirement age and chronically ill. At the household level, family caregiving responsibilities were a major constraining factor for many *dibao* recipients—particularly women—seeking a job or a higher income. Xu and Carraro also identified several policy-level barriers, such as the lack of coordination between *dibao* cash assistance and employment services and the absence of universally accessible basic social services that could benefit not only *dibao* recipients but other population groups.

One unique feature of *dibao* is its link to a series of other benefits, including medical, education, and housing assistance. Gao (2017) referred to this as "tied eligibility," which is efficient for program administration purposes but deters *dibao* beneficiaries from leaving the welfare roll, often out of fear of losing the various associated supplementary benefits and ultimately falling back into poverty.

To address this issue at least partially, the Chinese government established an employment assistance program in 2014 to mobilize welfare recipients to seek employment. Using qualitative interviews and related document reviews in Chengdu from March to May 2017, Zhang (2019) evaluated the effectiveness of these employment assistance programs. The participants expressed dissatisfaction and confusion about the program's participation requirements, citing a lack of clarity on what "no work potential" meant as a condition of exemption. Zhang found that for those who participated in the programs, employment assistance was unable to help them move off welfare and become self-sufficient.

Subjective Well-Being

How does *dibao* affect the subjective well-being of recipients? Most existing studies found *dibao* participation to have some unintended negative behavioral and subjective consequences. For example, *dibao* recipients were found to be less likely to engage in leisure, enrichment, or social activities. Most of this body of research focused on adult recipients. Only one recent study (Huo et al. 2020) investigated the effects of *dibao* participation on adolescent mental health. The study found that compared to nonrecipients, adolescent boys who were new urban *dibao* recipients showed declines in mental health. This effect did not exist for adolescent girls.

Gao and Zhai (2017) examined the effect of urban *dibao* on recipients' subjective well-being using CHIP 2002 data. They found that *dibao* recipients tended to be less optimistic about their economic prospects and less happy than their nonrecipient peers of similar demographics. The authors attributed these negative effects to the application and receipt process, which they found highly degrading and demoralizing. Using CFPS 2010 data, Gao, Wu, and Zhai

(2015) examined how *dibao* participation affected time allotted to different activities. They found that urban *dibao* reduced the amount of time recipients spent on education, leisure, and social activities and increased the amount of time they spent on unspecified activities or being idle.

Such negative effects on recipients' subjective well-being may be due to the stigma associated with *dibao* application and receipt. For example, using survey data collected in twenty-nine provinces in 2015, Huo and Lin (2016) found that 37 percent of *dibao* recipients reported feeling inferior when interacting with people, and 55 percent reported feeling depressed and anxious often or sometimes. Using the same data, Huo and Lin (2019) found that the stigma attached to the *dibao* application process and receipt also plays an important role in negatively impacting recipients' subjective well-being.

Not all findings about the subjective well-being effects of urban *dibao* are negative. Using CFPS 2010 data, Huang and Gao (2019) offered one of the first empirical tests on the political impact of *dibao* receipt. They found *dibao* neither improved nor worsened urban recipients' assessment of local government performance. In rural areas, *dibao* was found to have improved perceptions of government performance. Using CFPS 2012 and 2014 panel data and a combined method of propensity score matching and difference-in-differences (PSM-DID), Han and Gao (2018) found that overall, urban *dibao* helped improve recipients' subjective well-being. Still, urban *dibao* recipients viewed themselves as lower class and had less confidence about the future than did nonrecipients.

A set of qualitative studies also focused on urban *dibao*'s subjective well-being effects, mostly offering in-depth evidence on its negative effects. Drawing from fieldwork on the periphery of Harbin, Cho (2010) found that *dibao* eligibility screening was conducted not merely based on income, but through complex relationships among the poor and different levels of government officials.

Chen and colleagues (2013) conducted a longitudinal qualitative study of forty families receiving urban *dibao* in a district of Shanghai and interviewed the families five times over a twenty-four-month period. They found that the recipients' feelings toward *dibao* varied. Many recipients, especially those who were older, appreciated the *dibao* benefits. Other recipients, particularly laid-off workers, resented the economic and behavioral constraints of the *dibao* program.

Conducting in-depth interviews with fifteen people from households receiving urban *dibao* in the Wuhou and Qingyang districts of Chengdu,

Zhang (2015) found that many *dibao* recipients held pessimistic outlooks on life and had little access to mental health services. Zhang also found most *dibao* recipients felt shame and a sense of failure in life. This was attributed to not only the recipients' personal experiences in poverty but also the stigma attached to receiving *dibao*, made clear in the contempt of some neighborhood cadres who administered the *dibao* disbursements.

Conclusion and Policy Implications

In this chapter, I provide an overview of China's urban poverty trends and review the existing evidence on the anti-poverty effectiveness of urban *dibao*, the primary social safety net program. The urban poverty rate in China has been declining based on absolute poverty measures but increasing based on relative poverty measures. This reflects the parallel trends of increasing living standards and rising income inequality in urban China during the past thirty years. Urban *dibao* has helped reduce income poverty modestly, though unevenly across different regions in China. It has enabled recipient families to spend more money on education and health care but has shown unintended negative effects on recipients' employment and subjective well-being.

Drawing from existing evidence and building on the review in this chapter, future reforms of urban *dibao* should focus on five key areas, with some possible immediate steps that can be taken. First, urban *dibao*'s targeting performance needs to be improved, which will lead to more effective poverty reduction. *Dibao* assistance lines need to be adjusted in accordance with changes in local living standards and supported financially so that all in need can benefit from this last-resort safety net program (Luo and Wang 2018). One immediate step that can take place is to use multidimensional measures to identify families with specific needs in health, education, housing, or utilities more precisely and provide *dibao* and other assistance quickly and appropriately (Gao, Zhai, and Wang 2021).

Second, greater emphasis should be placed on work support programs that would enable *dibao* recipients to obtain sustainable employment and income. Equally important, those shouldering family care responsibilities should either be fully compensated for their work or have access to social services and other support that can help relieve some of their burden (Xu and Carraro 2017). Positive work incentives should also be provided to encourage employment and deter welfare dependency. This is especially important given the ongoing challenges in the labor market associated with the COVID-19 pandemic. Work support programs are arguably more important than ever to offer both immediate and sustainable employment and income to urban families in poverty.

Third, a comprehensive social assistance system centering on but not limited to *dibao* should be fully established and implemented. Currently, *dibao* is the largest social assistance program, supplemented by other programs such as medical, education, housing, employment, and other temporary support. Still, only a small subgroup of *dibao* recipients gain access to these additional benefits, and even then, the support is usually limited. These other assistance programs—in the form of cash or goods and services—should be expanded to meet the multidimensional needs of low-income families (Gao and Zhai 2019). As a particularly vulnerable group, children in low-income families should be a specific focus in both policy interventions and the evaluation of outcomes (Ci and Lan 2015; Gao and Wang 2021).

Fourth, urban *dibao*'s coverage should be broadened to include rural migrants who work and live in the cities (see Chapter 4 in this book for related evidence and arguments). Many migrants can be classified as the urban poor, yet currently most of them are unable to access urban benefits, including *dibao* (Luo and Wang 2018). The *hukou* system should be reformed or at least decoupled from social benefit eligibility so that rural migrants can obtain the necessary social protection against poverty and other hardships (Wang and Zhang 2013). Some cities are already experimenting with reforms in this regard. For example, following a plan issued by the central government, during 2020–25 Shenzhen will remove the differential treatment of migrant workers and include them in its social insurance and social assistance system, at the same level as those with local *hukou*.

Lastly, the central and local governments should work toward the full unification and integration of urban and rural *dibao* programs. The central authority should develop an efficient and consistent nationwide *dibao* targeting system for identifying poor households and determining appropriate subsidy amounts. The central authority should also provide local administration officials and communities training and monitoring to implement the *dibao* targeting system (Zhai and Gao 2019). Such a unification would greatly facilitate the equalizing of access to and benefit from not only *dibao* but its associated supplementary programs to better support the livelihood of those struggling with poverty (Xu and Yu 2019).

References

Chen, Honglin, Yu-cheung Wong, Qun Zeng, and Juha Hämäläinen. 2013. "Trapped in Poverty? A Study of the Dibao Programme in Shanghai." *China Journal of Social Work* 6 (3): 327–43.

Cho, Mun Young. 2010. "On the Edge Between 'the People' and 'the Population': Ethnographic Research on the Minimum Livelihood Guarantee." *China Quarterly* 201 (2–3): 20–37.

Ci, Qinying, and Jian Lan. 2015. "'Welfare' and 'Anti-welfare Dependence'—Analysis of Unemployment and Reemployment Based on Urban Dibao Groups." [In Chinese.] *Wuhan University Journal (Philosophy and Social Sciences)* 68 (4): 111–19.

Gao, Qin. 2013. "Public Assistance and Poverty Reduction: The Case of Shanghai." *Global Social Policy* 13 (2): 193–215.

Gao, Qin. 2017. *Welfare, Work and Poverty: Social Assistance in China*. New York: Oxford University Press.

Gao, Qin, and Yi Wang. 2021. *Child Multidimensional Poverty in China: From 2013 to 2018.* Beijing: UNICEF China. https://www.unicef.cn/en/reports/child-multidimensional-poverty -china.

Gao, Qin, Shiyou Wu, and Fuhua Zhai. 2015. "Welfare Participation and Time Use in China." *Social Indicators Research* 124 (3): 863–87.

Gao, Qin, and Fuhua Zhai. 2017. "Public Assistance, Economic Prospect, and Happiness in Urban China." *Social Indicators Research* 132 (1): 451–73.

———. 2019. "Improving Dibao Monitoring and Evaluation: Methodologies and Roadmap." *China: An International Journal* 17 (1): 130–48.

Gao, Qin, Fuhua Zhai, and Irwin Garfinkel. 2010. "How Does Public Assistance Affect Family Expenditures? The Case of Urban China." *World Development* 38 (7): 989–1000.

Gao, Qin, Fuhua Zhai, and Yi Wang. 2021. "Welfare Participation Reduced Severe Child Multidimensional Poverty in Rural China: Better Targeting Can Lead to Greater Poverty Reduction." *Child Indicators Research* (forthcoming). https://doi.org/10.1007/s12187-021 -09885-2.

Gao, Qin, Fuhua Zhai, Sui Yang, and Shi Li. 2014. "Does Welfare Enable Family Expenditures on Human Capital? Evidence from China." *World Development* 64 (December): 219–31.

Gao, Qin, Yanxia Zhang, and Fuhua Zhai. 2019. "Social Assistance in China: Impact Evaluation and Policy Implications." *China: An International Journal* 17 (1): 3–9.

Guan, Xingping. 2019. "Goals, Principles and Adequacy: An Analysis of China's Dibao Standards." *China: An International Journal* 17 (1): 10–28.

Guo, Junping, Qingxiang Tan, and Wei Qu. 2018. "Measurement and Analysis of Family Poverty of Migrant Workers in Cities—Based on the Perspective of 'Revenue-Consumption-Multidimensional.'" [In Chinese.] *China Rural Economy* 9:94–109.

Gustafsson, Björn, and Sai Ding. 2019. "Growing into Relative Income Poverty: Urban China, 1988–2013." *Social Indicators Research* 147 (1): 73–94.

Gustafsson, Björn, Shi Li, and Hiroshi Sato. 2014. "Data for Studying Earnings, the Distribution of Household Income and Poverty in China." *China Economic Review* 30 (September): 419–31.

Han, Huawei, and Qin Gao. 2018. "Subjective Welfare Effect of Low-Aid Insurance in Chinese Cities: A Study based on the Data of Chinese Family Tracking Survey." [In Chinese.] *Social Security Review* 2 (3): 82–97.

Huang, Wei. 2017. "Study on the Effect of Medical Insurance Policy on Poverty Alleviation—Based on the URBMI Pilot Evaluation of Household Survey Data." [In Chinese.] *Economic Research* 52 (9): 117–32.

Huang, Xian, and Qin Gao. 2019. "Alleviating Poverty or Discontent: The Impact of Social Assistance on Chinese Citizens' Views of Government." *China: An International Journal* 17 (1): 76–95.

Huo, Xuan, Qin Gao, Fuhua Zhai, and Mingang Lin. 2020. "Effects of Welfare Entry and Exit on Adolescent Mental Health: Evidence from Panel Data in China." *Social Science and Medicine* (1982) 253:112969.

Huo, Xuan, and Mingang Lin. 2016. "Influencing Factors and Effects of the Implementation of the Minimum Living Security Policy in Urban and Rural Areas." [In Chinese.] *Journal of Suzhou University (Philosophy and Social Science)* 37 (6): 28–35.

———. 2019. "Understanding Welfare Stigma in China: An Empirical Study of the Implementation of Urban Dibao." *China: An International Journal* 17 (1): 29–47.

Kapteyn, Arie, Theo Goedhart, Victor Halberstadt, and Bernard van Praag. 1977. "The Poverty Line: Concept and Measurement." *Journal of Human Resources* 12 (4): 503–20.

Lin, Mingang. 2020. "Theoretical and Policy Focus of Relative Poverty: Establishing a Governance System for Relative Poverty in China." [In Chinese.] *Chinese Social Security Review* 4 (1): 85–91.

Luo, Wenjian, and Wen Wang. 2018. "An Analysis of the Poverty Reduction Effect of the Urban Dibao System: An Empirical Study Based on the Chinese Family Tracking Survey (CFPS)." [In Chinese.] *Journal of Jiangxi University of Finance and Economics* 5:62–70.

National Bureau of Statistics of China. 2020. *Statistical Communiqué of the People's Republic of China on the 2019 National Economic and Social Development.* Beijing: China Statistics Press.

Ravallion, Martin. 1998. "Poverty Lines in Theory and Practice." Working Paper No.133, Living Standards Measurement Studies, World Bank, Washington, DC.

Sicular, Terry, Shi Li, Ximing Yue, and Hiroshi Sato. 2020. *Changing Trends in China's Inequality: Evidence, Analysis, and Prospects.* Oxford: Oxford University Press.

Townsend, Peter. 1979. *Poverty in the United Kingdom: A Survey of Household Resources and Standards of Living.* Ewing, NJ: University of California Press.

Wang, Xiaolin, and Deliang Zhang. 2013. "Urban Poverty Analysis in China (1989–2009)." [In Chinese.] *Journal of Guangxi University (Philosophy and Social Sciences)* 35 (2): 76–81.

Wang, Yi, Sui Yang, and Qin Gao. 2019. "Social Assistance and Household Consumption in Urban China: From 2002 to 2013." *Journal of the Asia Pacific Economy* 24 (2): 182–207.

Wei, Houkai, and Ning Wang. 2013. "Participatory Anti-poverty: The Direction of Urban Poverty Governance." [In Chinese.] *Jianghuai Forum* 5:9–17.

Westmore, Ben. 2018. "Do Government Transfers Reduce Poverty in China? Micro Evidence from Five Regions." *China Economic Review* 51 (October): 59–69.

Xu, Yuebin, and Ludovico Carraro. 2017. "Minimum Income Programme and Welfare Dependency in China." *International Journal of Social Welfare* 26 (2): 141–50.

Xu, Yuebin, and Lu Yu. 2019. "The Unification of Rural and Urban Dibao in China: A Case Study." *China: An International Journal* 17 (1): 109–29.

Yang, Sui, and Qin Gao. 2019. "The Impact of Minimum Living Security on Income Poverty and Consumption Expenditure." [In Chinese.] *Social Security Research* 5:63–78.

Yang, Yuanyuan, Jun-Hong Chen, and Minchao Jin. 2019. "Who Are the Asset-Poor in China: A Comprehensive Description and Policy Implications." *Journal of Social Policy* 48 (4): 765–87.

Zhai, Fuhua, and Qin Gao. 2019. "Strengthening Coordination Between Rural and Urban Dibao: Evidence and Implications." *China: An International Journal* 17 (1): 96–108.

Zhang, Bingzi, Jing Jia, and Guangjun Shen. 2019. "Characteristic Evolution of Urban Poverty." [In Chinese.] *Statistical Research* 36 (2): 11–22.

Zhang, Haomiao. 2015. "The Social Assistance Policy in Urban China: A Critical Review." *International Journal of Sociology and Social Policy* 35 (5/6): 403–18.

———. 2019. "The Limits of the Chinese Welfare State: Evidence from the Dibao Program in Chengdu." *Asian Studies Review* 43 (3): 512–26.

Zhu, Huoyun. 2017. "Evaluation of the Poverty Reduction Effect of Urban and Rural Residents' Endowment Insurance—Based on the Perspective of Multidimensional Poverty." [In Chinese.] *Beijing Social Sciences* 9:112–19.

CHAPTER 6

Implementing the National New-Type Urbanization Plan: Regional Variations

Juan Chen, Pierre F. Landry, and Deborah Davis

Introduction

Across the globe, millions of people leave their village homes to find work and live in towns and cities. Since 1980, the trend has accelerated, and in the Chinese case the acceleration has been particularly pronounced. In 1978, only 17.9 percent of the population were classified as urban; by 2019, the number had soared to over 60 percent (National Bureau of Statistics of China 2020). Two distinct and independent phenomena drive this transformation (Chen et al. 2015). The first is the sustained migration of more than two hundred million rural residents (Chan 2013). The second is the lesser-studied process of in situ urbanization, whereby villagers become urban residents when their land is reclassified as urban (Friedmann 2005; Lin 2007; Liu et al. 2010). In the second situation, villagers do not move to the city; instead, the city comes to them.

China is not the only country to hasten industrialization and spur economic growth by repurposing agricultural land or creating new administrative boundaries, but the Chinese reliance on administrative reclassification of both settlements and people has been unusually sustained and extensive. Between 1981 and 2018, urban land in China increased eightfold, bringing over two hundred million rural residents into new urban folds without them having to leave their homes (Ministry of Housing and Urban-Rural Development of China 2019; Yeh, Xu, and Liu 2011). A comparison between the growth rate of urban land and the growth rate of the urban population further documents the centrality of administrative reclassification for understanding the process and consequences of rapid urbanization in China (see Figure 6.1).

Even in the second decade of economic reform, the gap persisted; for example, between 1990 and 2014, urban space grew 5.5 percent per year, whereas the urban populations grew only 2.9 percent annually (Hu and Zhang 2018, 457; Shen 2018, 31).[1] Moreover, until recently the Chinese government continued to promote increased urbanization via administrative reclassification. In a project undertaken by the National Development and Reform Commission, 145 of the 156 prefectural cities and 67 of the 161 county-level cities were approved to have sites for new towns. And among these prefectural cities, the average planned area for development of 63.6 square kilometers equaled or exceeded half the area of all current municipalities, which suggests that to populate these new towns it may be necessary to relocate all nearby rural residents to the prefectural municipalities (Li and Fan 2013).

Scholars who have examined China's rapid urbanization of the physical land ahead of its actual settlement by urban residents have raised multiple concerns. First, they argue that because reclassification of rural land is primarily a tool for local governments to augment short-term revenues and

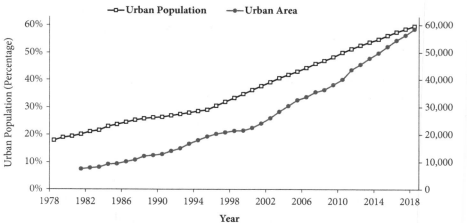

Figure 6.1. Growth in urban population and urban built-up areas, 1978–2018. *Data source:* China Urban Construction Statistical Yearbook 2018; China Statistical Yearbook 2019.

local cadres' promotions (Landry 2008; Landry, Lü, and Duan 2018; Wang et al. 2015), higher levels of urbanization did not optimize land use, population densities did not rise, and urban sprawl and underagglomeration characterized Chinese urbanization (Han et al. 2014).

Second, scholars argue that rapid urbanization has not improved quality of life, particularly among those residents newly incorporated into urban districts (Ong 2014). For many years, scholars have criticized the Chinese household registration system—first implemented in the 1950s to ensure economic stability and social control by restricting outmigration from villages— for denying access to local education, employment, housing, health care, and social services to rural-to-urban migrants who lacked an urban *hukou* even as they became long-term city residents (Chan and Zhang 1999; Solinger 1999; Wang 2005). In 2012, for instance, 52.6 percent of the Chinese population considered the city their home, but only 35.3 percent held urban *hukou*. The 17 percent gap reflects the approximately 250 million new urban residents who were unable to obtain an urban *hukou* despite their resettlement in a city and therefore did not qualify for urban welfare benefits (Chen, Davis, and Landry 2017).

In response to these issues—particularly to the inability of new urban residents to access urban education, health, housing, and welfare services— the central government rolled out the National New-Type Urbanization Plan in 2014. Specifically, the plan aimed to raise the proportion of the urban population to 60 percent by 2020, an increase that would have relocated or reclassified one hundred million villagers as permanent urban residents. The plan further stressed that going forward, China's urbanization would be people oriented and designed to improve quality of life through infrastructure investment and *hukou* and housing reforms (Guan et al. 2018). Local governments were also requested to expand access to social welfare and benefits (Wang et al. 2015).

Even in advance of 2020, 60 percent of the nation resided in towns and cities, and the total number of urban *hukou* holders had increased by one hundred million. However, because only 45 percent of that 60 percent held urban *hukou*, with full access to urban welfare and benefits (National Bureau of Statistics of China 2020), scholars are insisting not only that all those living in towns and cities should have permanent urban *hukou* but that the restrictive and divisive *hukou* system should be either dropped or, more realistically, downgraded to a means of tracking residency (Chen, Davis, and Landry 2017).

Reforming the *hukou* system, however, will not resolve all the inequalities arising from the Chinese urbanization process. In particular, because China's urbanization is unevenly spatially distributed, there needs to be more attention paid to the degree and drivers of regional disparities. To date, cities with higher administrative rank—such as Beijing and Shanghai—enjoy more favorable consideration and thus have expanded much faster, even after controlling for other economic and demographic drivers of urban expansion (Li et al. 2015). There is also poor coordination between the levels of government, and as a result, the consequences of urbanization often vary and are unpredictable (Chen, Davis, and Landry 2017; Shih and Cartier 2011). Moreover, given China's regional and administrative heterogeneity, it is unlikely that one policy will work across the entire nation (Wang et al. 2015). In anticipation of this issue, the National Development and Reform Commission (NDRC) launched a series of pilot programs to allow a small number of localities to experiment with how best to meet the broad goals of a more people-centered and equitable urban society (NDRC 2014).

Pilot Programs

Decentralized experimentation (*shidian* [试点]) is a well-established policy process that Chinese leaders have repeatedly adopted to generate institutional and policy innovations for various economic and social reforms, particularly when confronting intensely disputed policy issues (Zhou 2013). For example, pilots were conducted before introducing health-care reforms in the 1990s and when revising the one-child policy in the 2000s. During the policy process, the central government permits local governments chosen as *shidian* to design and implement new approaches to solve officially targeted problems. If successful, these local experiences serve as a model for national policy formulation (Heilmann 2008).

With regard to the National New-Type Urbanization Plan, the central government asked the NDRC (2014) to choose the pilot sites of different administrative levels. In the first year, the agency selected sixty-two cities and towns and two provinces: Jiangsu and Anhui (see Figure 6.2). In line with historical practice, the program did not specify a mandatory policy agenda (Heilmann 2008; Zhou 2013); instead, the participating cities were encouraged to initiate various *hukou*, land, finance, and administrative reforms,

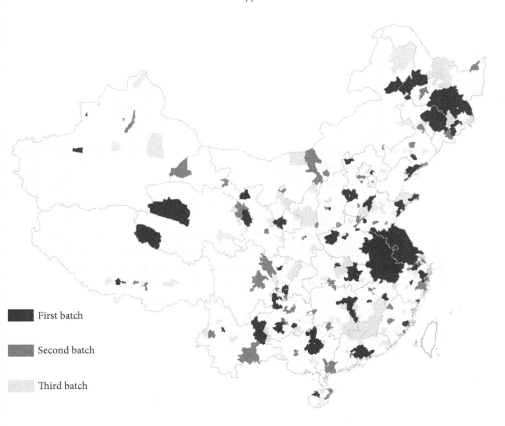

Figure 6.2. Pilot areas in the National New Urbanization Comprehensive Pilot Program.

and be innovative in promoting people-oriented urbanization that suits local circumstances and conditions. Each pilot locality submitted a working plan outlining overall goals, main tasks, and follow-ups that the local government would employ in order to achieve its plan. All selected localities were expected to initiate their pilot programs before the end of 2014 and make their initial results available for review by 2017. Ideally, the successful pilot experiments would be replicated nationally between 2018 and 2020.

Following the first batch of selected pilot areas, the NDRC selected a second batch of 73 cities and towns (NDRC 2015) and a third batch of 111 cities and towns (NDRC 2016) (see Figure 6.2). The localities in these second and third batches were expected to initiate their pilot programs before the end of 2015 and 2016 in order to achieve initial results in 2017 and 2018 and become the basis of national initiatives—together with the first batch—by 2020.

As is usually the case with local Chinese experiments, the choice of pilot locations was not random and did not follow randomized control trial (RCT) best practices. Instead, the pilot sites were likely chosen based on their capacity to act as exemplary models (Yang 2013). There is also a risk that participating local governments manipulated the pilot program as an opportunity to extract more funding and additional land quotas for urban construction and prioritize raw urban growth over the improvement of human welfare (Chen, Davis, and Landry 2017; Guan et al. 2018; Wang et al. 2015). Any assessment of the pilot program must therefore consider characteristics of selected localities. In the following section, we use county-level demographic and socioeconomic data to identify the types of localities most likely to have been selected as pilots, patterns of variation in their policies, and whether local experimentation influences in situ urbanization. We then further discuss the potential consequences of nonrandom selection for rapid but uneven urbanization in China.

Who Joined the Pilot Program? Batch Characteristics and Regional Variations

To discover whether pilot areas differed from non-pilot areas and whether pilot areas varied across the three batches, we coded all 2,869 de facto county-level administrative units in China into four categories. We identified 521 county-level administrative units (from two provinces; two sub-provincial cities; seven provincial capitals; twenty-five prefecture-level cities; twenty-five county-level cities, counties, and urban districts; and two townships) affected by the first batch of localities chosen for the 2014 National New Urbanization Comprehensive Pilot Program. Similarly, 153 county-level administrative units (associated with 73 cities and towns) joined the second batch, while 245 county-level units (associated with 111 cities and towns) joined the third one. The remaining 1,950 county-level administrative units were coded into the category of non-pilot areas. With the exception of population density, county-level variables are computed as shares of individual demographic and socioeconomic attributes. In addition to census data, we compiled the GDP of each county for the year 2010 based on data from online sources, statistical yearbooks, and government reports.

The descriptive statistics reported in Table 6.1 show that the first batch of counties chosen for the pilot program had a significantly larger share of cross-county migrants, a higher population density, and higher GDPs than counties belonging to either the third batch or the non-pilot areas. In the first batch, counties were more concentrated in eastern China than those in the second batch and the non-pilot areas, mainly because Jiangsu and Anhui—the two provincial-level pilots—were included in the first batch of the program. The second batch of counties has more in common with the first (in terms of share of cross-county migrants and level of economic development) than with the third batch or the non-pilot areas, except that the second batch of counties was more concentrated in southwestern China.

We next estimated a multinomial logistic regression model to determine what characteristics of county-level administrative units were associated with inclusion in the pilot program and whether these characteristics differed by batch. The dependent variables were coded as follows: 1 = in the first batch, 2 = in the second batch, 3 = in the third batch, and 0 = not in the pilot program. County-level characteristics reported in Table 6.1 are included as independent variables in the multinomial logistic regression model. Robust standard errors are estimated that account for heteroskedasticity across clusters at the provincial level. The statistical results are presented in Table 6.2.

Our estimates suggest that counties with a larger working-age population and a higher GDP were more likely to be selected into the first batch of the pilot program. Higher GDP was also a significant predictor for selection into the second batch. In terms of regional distribution, using north China as reference, counties in the east and south central regions had higher probabilities of being included in the first batch of the pilot program. When demographic and economic factors are controlled for, counties located in the southwest and northwest were more likely to be included in the second batch.

In contrast to the first and second batches, county GDP was not a significant predictor for selection into the third batch of the pilot program. The clear regional division observed between the first and second batches also

Table 6.1. Descriptive statistics of county-level administrative units ($N = 2{,}869$)

County characteristics	First batch pilot areas (n = 521)	Second batch pilot areas (n = 153)	Third batch pilot areas (n = 245)	Non-pilot areas (n = 1,950)
Ages 15–64 (%)	75.853	74.915	74.018	73.504
Age 65+ (%)	9.428	9.085	8.965	8.553
Gender (female, %)	49.089	48.654	48.781	48.571
Ethnicity (ethnic minority, %)	5.498	12.750	8.155	20.388
Marital status (married, %)	72.302	72.324	72.667	70.927
Education (years, mean)	9.172	8.820	8.917	8.558
Occupation (professional/ managerial, %)	6.596	5.624	5.262	5.174
Homeowners (%)	85.419	84.611	88.863	88.264
Urban population (%)	56.475	49.116	49.013	43.924
Urban *hukou* (%)	35.478	29.227	32.034	27.646
Cross-county migrants (%)	9.043	9.078	4.329	4.372
Population density (per square kilometer, mean)	2,043.026	1,336.779	516.766	1,135.712
Population density (natural logarithm, mean)	6.506	5.990	5.392	5.293
GDP (100 million yuan, mean)	261.390	227.009	147.097	121.026
GDP (natural logarithm, mean)	5.089	4.833	4.416	4.109
Regions (%)				
North China	5.566	13.072	6.122	18.564
Northeast China	14.587	4.575	11.429	9.282
East China	51.631	13.072	34.286	13.795
South Central China	18.234	16.340	23.265	23.641
Southwest China	6.718	37.909	11.429	20.000
Northwest China	3.263	15.033	13.469	14.718

Table 6.2. Multinomial logistic regression predicting associations of county-level administrative units with three batches of pilot program (N = 2,869)

County characteristics	First batch pilot areas		Second batch pilot areas		Third batch pilot areas	
Ages 15–64	11.137**	(3.606)	11.004	(8.568)	-2.665	(4.036)
Age 65+	4.676	(7.654)	8.615	(7.308)	-7.127	(8.103)
Gender (female)	18.836*	(8.180)	6.673	(10.071)	16.337	(10.518)
Ethnicity (ethnic minority)	-0.308	(1.106)	0.536	(0.676)	-1.747*	(0.798)
Marital status (married)	0.681	(2.106)	8.661**	(3.355)	4.393	(2.253)
Education (years)	-0.413	(0.298)	-0.250	(0.286)	0.582**	(0.217)
Occupation (professional/ managerial)	1.322	(5.233)	-5.917	(8.742)	-18.681*	(7.667)
Homeowners	3.263	(2.971)	0.025	(1.661)	1.547	(2.333)
Urban population	-1.364	(1.369)	-0.952	(1.673)	0.218	(1.153)
Urban hukou	1.830	(1.594)	0.106	(1.692)	1.502	(1.047)
Cross-county migrants	3.324	(1.861)	2.406	(1.284)	1.530	(2.367)
Population density (natural logarithm)	0.144	(0.110)	0.150	(0.180)	-0.432***	(0.083)
GDP (natural logarithm)	0.447**	(0.171)	0.718***	(0.165)	0.150	(0.199)
Regions						
North China (reference)	—		—		—	
Northeast China	0.938	(0.826)	-0.697	(0.717)	0.716	(0.388)
East China	2.192**	(0.823)	-0.311	(0.638)	2.520***	(0.441)
South Central China	1.085*	(0.522)	0.198	(0.579)	1.452***	(0.398)
Southwest China	0.610	(0.676)	1.670*	(0.728)	1.763***	(0.372)
Northwest China	0.304	(0.816)	1.371*	(0.669)	1.309*	(0.567)
Constant	-23.157**	(7.489)	-22.980*	(11.720)	-16.296*	(6.843)

Note: Coefficients are reported; robust standard errors are in parentheses; * $p < 0.05$, ** $p < 0.01$, *** $p < 0.001$.

diminishes, with counties in the east, southwest, northwest, and south central regions all more likely to have been included in the pilot program than those in the north and northeast. These differences indicate that while county GDP was a strong predictor of inclusion in the first batch, over the next two batches, the Chinese central government tried to reduce regional disparities and granted opportunities to more remote areas in the western provinces regardless of their level of economic development.

Localities Selected for the Pilot Program: Striving for Growth

As all the locales in the three batches of the pilot program were expected to achieve initial results in either 2017 or 2018 and become the basis of national initiatives by 2020, we next considered the three batches together to further explore the association between level of economic development and selection into the pilot program, while teasing out whether there were any regional differences in the association. We estimated logistic regression models for selection in the pilot program without differentiating the three batches as the dependent variable. Table 6.3 reports the coefficients and the robust standard errors that account for heteroskedasticity across clusters at the provincial level. Model 1 and Model 2 are estimated with all counties included ($N = 2,869$). In Model 1, the independent variables are the county-level characteristics as described in Table 6.1. In Model 2, we added an interaction term between county GDP and region. To better illustrate the relationship of the pilot program to county economic development and regional variation, we graphed the interaction results shown in Figure 6.3.

As shown in Figure 6.3, of the counties with lower GDPs, those located in northeast China have a slightly higher chance of being selected into the pilot program, while counties in east China have a much higher chance of being in the pilot program than units located in the other four regions. However, for counties with higher GDPs, the regional differences become less pronounced. Counties with higher GDPs are significantly more likely to be included in the pilot program except in the northeast and east. The graph clearly demonstrates the regional differences and the preferences of the central government when selecting pilot sites. It is also clear that county-level economic development is an indication of the potential for further urbanization.

Table 6.3. Logistic regressions predicting associations of pilot program with county GDP and regions

County Characteristics	All counties (N = 2,869)				Excluding counties in pilot prefectures and provinces (N = 2,114)			
	Model 1		Model 2		Model 3		Model 4	
Ages 15–64	6.215**	(2.192)	7.043**	(2.453)	2.289	(2.989)	1.754	(2.894)
Age 65+	2.205	(5.602)	2.541	(5.482)	-2.309	(4.993)	-2.835	(5.267)
Gender (female)	14.103*	(6.278)	15.258*	(6.360)	5.282	(8.765)	4.823	(9.124)
Ethnicity (ethnic minority)	-0.643	(0.600)	-0.200	(0.574)	0.541	(0.458)	0.514	(0.478)
Marital status (married)	3.036	(1.577)	2.554	(1.633)	3.229	(2.741)	3.012	(2.535)
Education (years)	-0.062	(0.208)	-0.122	(0.223)	0.021	(0.166)	0.036	(0.171)
Occupation (professional/ managerial)	-4.591	(3.871)	-1.973	(3.878)	-7.406	(5.561)	-6.769	(5.820)
Homeowners	1.941	(1.933)	2.202	(1.818)	-0.914	(1.238)	-0.733	(1.281)
Urban population	-0.852	(0.864)	-1.099	(0.831)	0.357	(0.924)	0.376	(0.968)
Urban hukou	1.601	(1.050)	1.509	(1.093)	-0.726	(1.125)	-0.857	(1.144)
Cross-county migrants	2.750*	(1.374)	2.815*	(1.357)	-0.680	(1.340)	-0.689	(1.371)
Population density (natural logarithm)	-0.067	(0.087)	-0.048	(0.090)	-0.292***	(0.074)	-0.299***	(0.072)
GDP (natural logarithm)	0.400**	(0.140)	0.639***	(0.154)	0.870***	(0.110)	0.836***	(0.134)
Regions								
North China (reference)	—		—		—		—	
Northeast China	0.669	(0.492)	3.292*	(1.513)	0.391	(0.280)	1.645	(1.619)
East China	1.958***	(0.496)	4.411**	(1.611)	0.152	(0.257)	-1.299	(1.191)
South Central China	0.977***	(0.227)	1.051	(1.014)	0.307	(0.262)	0.498	(1.406)
Southwest China	1.264***	(0.245)	0.848	(1.027)	0.640	(0.414)	0.706	(1.046)
Northwest China	0.909*	(0.445)	1.167	(1.072)	0.706*	(0.326)	-0.374	(1.190)

(Continued)

Table 6.3. (Continued)

County Characteristics	All counties (N = 2,869)				Excluding counties in pilot prefectures and provinces (N = 2,114)			
	Model 1		Model 2		Model 3		Model 4	
Interactions								
GDP (natural logarithm) × North China (reference)			—	—			—	—
GDP (natural logarithm) × Northeast China			−0.569*	(0.286)			−0.253	(0.343)
GDP (natural logarithm) × East China			−0.503	(0.282)			0.274	(0.203)
GDP (natural logarithm) × South Central China Cina China			−0.024	(0.199)			−0.042	(0.278)
GDP (natural logarithm) × Southwest China			0.105	(0.202)			−0.025	(0.214)
GDP (natural logarithm) × Northwest China			−0.038	(0.179)			0.262	(0.236)
Constant	−18.208***	(4.123)	−20.019***	(3.908)	−10.522*	(5.296)	−9.795	(5.522)

Note: Coefficients are reported; robust standard errors are in parentheses; * $p < 0.05$, ** $p < 0.01$, *** $p < 0.001$.

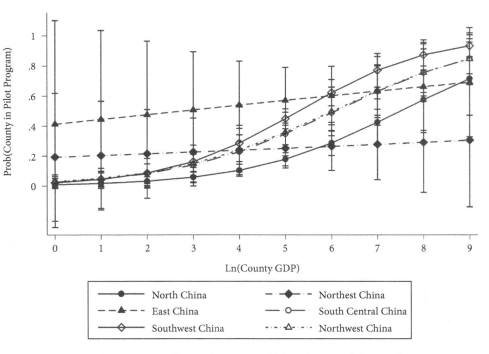

Figure 6.3. Pilot program selection by county GDP and region ($N = 2,869$).

We collected and analyzed data at the county level. Still, it is important to note that most county-level units were included in the pilot program as one part of a larger prefecture or province. To further explore the relationship between the pilot program and county-level economic development and potential regional differences, we replicated the first two logistic regression models in Table 6.3 and excluded those counties belonging to the pilot prefectures or provinces ($N = 2,114$). The regression results are reported as Model 3 and Model 4 in Table 6.3. The interactive effects are further illustrated in Figure 6.4.

When counties in the pilot prefectures or provinces are excluded from the analysis, the regional differences are no longer significant. County GDP is the most prominent determinant of membership in the pilot program. Counties in different regions of China more or less follow the same pattern: those with low GDPs are unlikely to be included in the pilot program, whereas those with high GDPs are likely to be included. The results indicate that

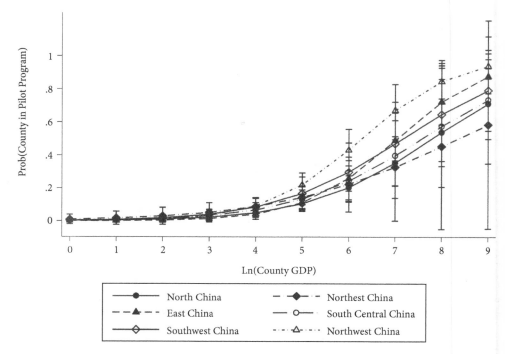

Figure 6.4. Pilot program selection by county GDP and region, excluding counties in pilot prefectures and provinces ($N = 2{,}114$).

when selecting prefecture and provincial-level pilots, the central government may exhibit certain regional preferences, but for county-level pilots, the particular county's economic development appears to be the decisive factor both in the local government's initiative to apply for the pilot scheme and in the central government's process of selection.

Discussion

In this chapter, we focused on the National New Urbanization Comprehensive Pilot Program, which extended from 2014 through 2020. We made novel use of county-level population and GDP data for assessing site selection and potential impact of the pilot program. Based on analysis of county-level population and GDP data retrieved from various sources, we identified regional differences and revealed the preferences of the central government for selecting high GDP county units for various stages of the pilot program. The results confirm a policy bias in favor of localities already at a development advantage with higher GDPs. Although these preferences have not been explicitly articulated by the designers of the plan, data reveal that policy supporters favored participation of more developed localities in the pilot program in order to maximize the odds that the experiment would succeed. As a result, the additional funding and greater land quotas associated with inclusion in the pilot program will further deepen spatial and social disparities in the already highly uneven urbanization process in China (Chen et al. 2014; Zhu, Breitung, and Li 2012).

Determining whether these spatial and social divisions will cause new challenges in local governance is an important area of research. There has been a concern that the process of urbanization already contributes to greater spatial and social differentiation (Zhu, Breitung, and Li 2012). With additional resources provided through the pilot program, urbanization in the already more developed localities is likely to be expedited, while in less developed areas, particularly those with large migrant populations, local governments will face greater challenges in both building and renewing their urban centers as well as in expanding welfare benefits to more residents. The spatial and social disparities among Chinese citizens will widen further.

The Chinese government has treated sustainable urbanization as an engine of modernization and economic growth (Guan et al. 2018), and the central state continues to support highly interventionist local initiatives (Li, Chen, and Hu 2016). Yet based on our analysis of selection into the pilot program, we are concerned that opportunistic local governments may take advantage of the National New Urbanization Comprehensive Pilot Program's opportunities to extract additional funding and land quotas for urban construction, rather than focusing on improving the quality of life of their citizens. Unless the priorities of local governments shift from attracting investments and using land sales to boost government coffers, inclusion in the pilot program will do little to improve the quality of life for new urban residents or stem urban sprawl.

To address these concerns, further research is urgently needed to determine the historical, economic, social, and political considerations that motivate local governments participating in the pilot program to reform their urban development strategies to serve the needs of their citizens. Particular attention should be paid to the effects of this process on formerly rural residents—the changes in their living environments and lifestyle, the extent to which they are entitled to urban welfare and benefits, and their success in fully integrating into urban life. While China's urbanization has made impressive progress, traditional place-centered urbanization is now threatening the likelihood of future improvement. A more human-centered approach should be adopted in order to realize the promises outlined in the National New-Type Urbanization Plan for more people-oriented urbanization.

Acknowledgments

The 2018 Urbanization and Quality of Life Survey was funded by the General Research Fund of the Research Grants Council of Hong Kong (PolyU 156637/16H) and the Li & Fung China Social Policy Research Fund. The authors thank Wu Puzhou, who created the pilot map, and Yau Chun To, who compiled the county GDP data.

Note

1. Xu et al. (2016) estimate even higher per annum land expansion of 8.1% for 1992–2015.

References

Central Committee of the Communist Party and State Council of China. 2014. National New-Type Urbanization Plan (2014–2020).

Chan, Kam Wing. 2013. "China, Internal Migration." In *The Encyclopedia of Global Human Migration*, edited by Immanuel Ness and Peter Bellwood. Hoboken, NJ: Wiley-Blackwell.

Chan, Kam Wing, and Li Zhang. 1999. "The Hukou System and Rural-Urban Migration: Processes and Changes." *China Quarterly* 160 (December): 818–55.

Chen, Juan, Shuo Chen, Pierre F. Landry, and Deborah S. Davis. 2014. "How Dynamics of Urbanization Affect Physical and Mental Health in Urban China." *China Quarterly* 220 (December): 988–1011.

Chen, Juan, Deborah S. Davis, and Pierre F. Landry. 2017. "Beyond *Hukou* Reform: Enhancing Human-Centered Urbanization in China." Paulson Policy Memoranda, Paulson Institute, 23 February.

Chen, Juan, Deborah S. Davis, Kaming Wu, and Haijing Dai. 2015. "Life Satisfaction in Urbanizing China: The Effect of City Size and Pathways to Urban Residency." *Cities* 49 (December): 88–97.

Friedmann, John. 2005. *China's Urban Transition*. Minneapolis: University of Minnesota Press.

Guan, Xingliang, Houkai Wei, Shasha Lu, Qi Dai, and Hongjian Su. 2018. "Assessment on the Urbanization Strategy in China: Achievements, Challenges and Reflections." *Habitat International* 71 (January): 97–109.

Han, Baolong, Rusong Wang, Yu Tao, and Hui Gao. 2014. "Urban Population Agglomeration in View of Complex Economical Niche: A Case Study on Chinese Prefecture Cities." *Ecological Indicators* 47 (December): 128–36.

Heilmann, Sebastian. 2008. "From Local Experiments to National Policy: The Origins of China's Distinctive Policy Process." *China Journal* 59 (January): 1–30.

Hu, Biliang, and Kunling Zhang. 2018. "New Urbanization in China." In *China: 40 Years of Reform and Development: 1978–2018*, edited by Ross Garnaut, Ligang Song, and Fang Cai, 455–86. Canberra: Australia National University Press.

Landry, Pierre F. 2008. *Decentralized Authoritarianism in China*. New York: Cambridge University Press.

Landry, Pierre F., Xiaobo Lü, and Haiyan Duan. 2018. "Does Performance Matter? Evaluating Political Selection Along the Chinese Administrative Ladder." *Comparative Political Studies* 51 (8): 1074–1105.

Li, Bingqin, Chunlai Chen, and Biliang Hu. 2016. "Governing Urbanization and the New Urbanization Plan in China." *Environment and Urbanization* 28 (2): 515–34.

Li, Han, Yehua Dennis Wei, Felix Haifeng Liao, and Zhiji Huang. 2015. "Administrative Hierarchy and Urban Land Expansion in Transitional China." *Applied Geography* 56 (January): 177–86.

Li, Tie, and Yi Fan. 2013. "Investigation and Reflection on the Construction of New Cities and New Districts." [In Chinese.] *Urban and Rural Research Trends* 229. http://ccud.org.cn /phone/article/2955.html.

Lin, George C. S. 2007. "Reproducing Spaces of Chinese Urbanisation: New City-Based and Land-Centred Urban Transformation." *Urban Studies* 44 (9): 1827–55.

Liu, Yuting, Shenjing He, Fulong Wu, and Chris Webster. 2010. "Urban Villages Under China's Rapid Urbanization: Unregulated Assets and Transitional Neighbourhoods." *Habitat International* 34 (2): 135–44.

Ministry of Housing and Urban-Rural Development of China. 2019. *China Urban Construction Statistical Yearbook 2018*. Beijing: China Planning Press.

National Bureau of Statistics of China. 2020. *China Statistical Yearbook 2020*. Beijing: China Statistics Press. www.stats.gov.cn/tjsj/ndsj/2020/indexch.htm.

NDRC (National Development and Reform Commission of China). 2014. National New Urbanization Comprehensive Pilot Program. No. 1229, National Development and Reform Commission.

———. 2015. National New Urbanization Comprehensive Pilot Program, Second Batch. No. 2665, National Development and Reform Commission.

———. 2016. National New Urbanization Comprehensive Pilot Program, Third Batch. No. 2489, National Development and Reform Commission.

Ong, Lynette H. 2014. "State-Led Urbanization in China: Skyscrapers, Land Revenue and 'Concentrated Villages.'" *China Quarterly* 217 (February): 162–79.

Shen, Jianfa. 2018. *Urbanization, Regional Development, and Governance in China*. London and New York: Routledge.

Shih, Mi, and Carolyn Cartier. 2011. "Particularities and Complexities: Unpacking State Policy in Local China." *Provincial China* 3 (1): 1–8.

Solinger, Dorothy J. 1999. *Contesting Citizenship in Urban China: Peasant Migrants, the State, and the Logic of the Market*. Berkeley: University of California Press.

Wang, Fei-Ling. 2005. *Organizing Through Division and Exclusion: China's Hukou System*. Palo Alto: Stanford University Press.

Wang, Xin-Rui, Eddie Chi-Man Hui, Charles Choguill, and Sheng-Hua Jia. 2015. "The New Urbanization Policy in China: Which Way Forward?" *Habitat International* 47 (June): 279–84.

Xu, Min, Chunyang He, Zhifeng Liu, and Yinyin Dou. 2016. "How Did Urban Land Expand in China Between 1992 and 2015? A Multi-Scale Landscape Analysis." *PLoS ONE* 11 (5): e0154839.

Yang, Hongshan. 2013. "Dual-Track Approach to Policy Experiment: The Experience of Policy Innovation in China." [In Chinese.] *Chinese Public Administration* 336 (6): 12–15.

Yeh, Anthony G. O., Jiang Xu, and Kaizhi Liu. 2011. *China's Post-Reform Urbanization: Retrospect, Policies and Trends*. London: International Institute for Environment and Development and United Nations Population Fund.

Zhou, Wang. 2013. *Shidian in Chinese Policy Process*. Tianjin: Tianjin People's Publishing House.

Zhu, Yushu, Werner Breitung, and Si-ming Li. 2012. "The Changing Meaning of Neighbourhood Attachment in Chinese Commodity Housing Estates: Evidence from Guangzhou." *Urban Studies* 49 (11): 2439–57.

CHAPTER 7

Dementia or Anomie: What Explains the Missing Older Adults Phenomenon in China?

Guibin Xiong

Introduction

In 2016, the Zhongmin Social Assistance Institute and news platform *Jinri Toutiao* (TopBuzz) jointly released "The Investigation Report of the Missing Older Adults in China." The report showed that there were about five hundred thousand older men and women reported missing across the country in 2015 (Ren and Xia 2016). Descriptive statistics from the report show that dementia or mental illness is often a significant contributing factor to older adults getting lost, a finding supported by other research (Chen and Zhang 2013; Rowe and Bennett 2003; Koester and Stooksbury 1995). However, it is worth examining whether there are also social factors contributing to the high rate of reported missing older adults (Wu 2010).

In this chapter, I hypothesize that social anomie has been a major factor leading to the high rate of missing older adults. Robert K. Merton (2006) developed the concept of anomie, which he operationalized as a type of retreatism in response to mainstream cultural and institutional goals. Under Merton's theory, missing older adults can be considered retreatists to some degree. As Sun (2003) stated, the rapid development of Chinese society leaves behind those who cannot keep up, inevitably excluding them from the evolving social structure.

For the purposes of this chapter, anomie can be understood as a product of China's transition from "mechanical solidarity" to "organic solidarity."[1] Anomie exists because old societal norms were disrupted and new norms are not yet established (Durkheim 2016, 269). As continuous market expansions stimulates the rapid rise of big cities across China, the demand for workers also increases. People from across rural China migrate to cities for employment opportunities, often moving far from their hometowns. In China, especially in poverty-stricken rural areas, older adults rely predominantly on their family for care. As many family members move to cities for work, older adults are left behind with fewer caregivers, making them particularly vulnerable.

In this chapter, I use recent data collected through mixed methods to investigate whether dementia at the individual level or anomie at the societal level is the major cause behind the phenomenon of missing older adults in China. I first present the background and trends of the missing older adult population in China, and then construct a two-dimensional typology of the causes for the phenomenon. Next, I introduce the data and methods used in this study, followed by an analysis of the quantitative and qualitative data describing the various causes for the missing older adults in China. The final section concludes the chapter and discusses policy implications.

This chapter makes several contributions. First, it places the missing older adults phenomenon against the backdrop of China's rapid urbanization, examining its causes from both individual and societal perspectives. Second, adopting the paradigm of Durkheim, it draws from sociological theory to build a conceptual framework to examine how the two causes interact with each other in explaining this relatively new but growing issue in China. Third, it combines the strengths of quantitative and qualitative research methods to provide a dynamic and in-depth analysis and offer policy and social service implications for the future.

Dementia versus Anomie

In the era of the planned economy and at the early stages of market economy reforms at the end of the last century, Chinese society's rural collective system and the urban work-unit system allowed for very little population mobility. As a result, China saw very few reports of missing older adults. After entering the new century, marketization and industrialization gave rise to continuous city expansion and urbanization. Along with it, reports of missing older adults gradually began to surface in the media. Nevertheless, there were no national statistics or surveys published on the issue until the 2016 joint report by the Zhongmin Social Assistance Institute and *Jinri Toutiao*.

The growing number of older adults reported missing are a consequence of fast-paced urbanization and social change. To a large extent, the missing older adults can be seen as an embodiment of those who have suffered the consequences of China's rapid urbanization and reform. It is necessary to conduct an in-depth study of this issue, reveal the social conditions that have led to these outcomes, and put forward policy suggestions accordingly.

Around the world, dementia has been cited as the main reason that older adults become disoriented, cannot find their way home, and are later reported missing. An annual report by Japan's National Police Agency noted that about twelve thousand people with dementia were reported missing in that country in 2015.[2] According to Chen and Zhang (2013), approximately 71 percent of dementia patients in Taiwan had been reported missing since their diagnoses. As of 2015, there were more than ten million people diagnosed with dementia in China, the largest number in a single country worldwide (Sohu Health 2016).

However, dementia alone does not fully explain the phenomenon of missing older adults in China. The situation is complicated by the large aging population and mass rural-to-urban migration. A 2016 telephone survey of guardians who reported older adults missing that year found that 25 percent of the older adults had been diagnosed with dementia. Using this rate and the known number of missing older adults in China, we can reach estimations through a comparison with Japan. The total population of China is about 10.77 times that of Japan (China's 1.37 billion in 2016 compared to Japan's 127 million in 2015). Proportionately, the ratio of 12,000 missing older adults with dementia in Japan predicts about 129,000 missing older adults with dementia in China. The aforementioned report by the Zhongmin Social Assistance Institute and *Jinri Toutiao* put the number of missing older adults in 2015 at 500,000. Multiplying this number by the estimated 25 percent of older adults diagnosed with dementia approximates that 125,000 of the total number of missing older adults have been diagnosed with dementia. In absolute terms, there is little difference between the number of missing older adults diagnosed with dementia in China and Japan. However, in China, the remaining 75 percent of missing older adults may not be due to dementia but rather to social disconnect, or anomie. It is worth noting that this is only a rough estimate because dementia is often mistaken for other symptoms of aging and is therefore difficult to diagnose (H. Li 2005).

While dementia is still a significant factor contributing to older adults missing in China, the lack of care and family support caused by the younger generation's departure from home in pursuit of employment greatly exacerbates the risk. This leads to social anomie and to the further impoverishment and neglect of the older adults left behind. In recent years, the total number of migrant workers in China has been growing steadily, reaching nearly three hundred million in 2017 (Baidu 2019). This migration should also be understood in the context of the years immediately preceding it. From 2002 to 2012, China lost nine hundred thousand natural villages, or an average of eighty natural villages per day (Yihao Guquan 2020). Taken together, it is clear that the Chinese population is becoming more concentrated in urban areas. However, there is still a substantial proportion of people who have remained in their rural hometowns, and for vulnerable populations like the older adults, these trends have serious implications for their safety and care.

Conceptual Framework: A Typology

To understand dementia and anomie as contributing factors to the missing older adults phenomenon, I construct a typology as a conceptual framework, as shown in Figure 7.1. For the purposes of this chapter, "integration" is defined as conditions under which older adults can access basic economic support, health care, emergency protection, and other social support. The framework is structured around four contributing factors that lead to reports of missing older adults.

In this conceptual framework, type I populations (socially integrated, full cognitive health) refer to the missing older adults who do not have dementia and have access to basic economic and social support systems (those who get lost despite social protections). These are the older adults who follow their adult children to new cities, often helping to take care of their grandchildren. Moving to a new urban environment presents its own set of risks. These older adults are often unfamiliar with their surroundings and may be inexperienced in using various urban transportation systems. Moreover, many people from older generations do not speak Mandarin but speak only their hometown dialects; they may also be illiterate. Many are also unfamiliar with or unable to use mobile phones. Taken together, these factors

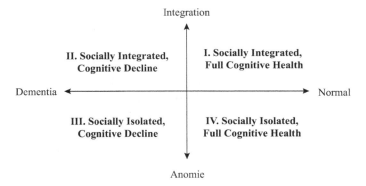

Figure 7.1. Four conditions of missing older adults in China.

create conditions that make this type of older adult vulnerable to getting lost in the city.

Type II populations (socially integrated, cognitive decline) refer to the missing older adults with dementia who have access to basic economic and social support (those with dementia who get lost despite social protections). As China's population ages, the number of people with dementia is also on the rise. According to a survey in China, over 5 percent of patients over the age of sixty-five have been diagnosed with severe Alzheimer's, and there are a growing number of cases in adults aged forty to fifty (Zhao 2010, 75). Although under the guardianship of family, older adults with dementia can be particularly difficult to look after (Liu 2000, 190).

Type III populations (socially isolated, cognitive decline) refer to the missing older adults with dementia who lack a basic economic and social support system and mainly live in poor rural areas (those with dementia who get lost without social protections). This group of missing older adults is the most vulnerable due to three main reasons. First, they do not have the ability to care for themselves due to dementia, especially at the condition's middle and late stages. Second, they lack adequate care and supervision from family or social services. Third, they lack the social support mechanisms that ensure search and rescue. With fewer family members around, it is less likely that anyone will notice if an older person is missing and call the police. Furthermore, there are fewer basic resources for survival in remote western rural areas, greatly increasing the risk and lowering the chance of survival for older adults in this group. Rowe and colleagues (2011) found that patients with dementia who wandered into populated public areas were more likely to survive than those who wandered in less populated remote areas.

Type IV populations (socially isolated, full cognitive health) refer to the missing older adults who do not have dementia but lack access to basic economic and social support systems (those who get lost without social protections). In recent years, many cities have implemented education and social policies to allow for the enrollment of migrant children in urban schools. Consequently, more and more migrant workers are moving to jobs with their spouses and children, leaving the older adults behind in their home villages. After both their children and grandchildren have departed, the older adults are less likely to receive financial support from their children, whose savings are spent raising their own children in the city. They are also less likely to receive family care or connect with social support and emergency protection.

Constructed to capture the effects of both dementia and anomie, this conceptual framework serves as the theoretical foundation for the empirical analysis carried out in the rest of this chapter. It is important to note that the typology simplifies the scenarios and only serves as a framework. The reality, shown in the sections that follow, is often more complicated and less clear-cut than the conceptualization.

Data and Methods

The study used statistical data, agency interviews, and survey data to examine the missing older adults phenomenon in China.

Statistical Data from Social Assistance Shelters

Because there are no national statistics on missing older adults, I collected statistical data from social assistance shelters in different cities across China through stratified random sampling. Even though most missing older adults receive help returning home from police, passersby, community members, local government officials, or other channels, the data related to this are hard to collect.[3] When these social forces are not present, the missing older adults are often referred to a local assistance shelter. Social assistance shelters can be considered the last formal resort. The national social assistance shelter system has set up comprehensive record-keeping and data, which allowed for a random sampling survey and comparative analysis across China.

During the stratified random sampling process, I first randomly selected one or two provinces from each of the six regions in China (North, Northeast, East, Central South, Northwest, and Southwest). At this level, eight provinces were selected: Beijing, Liaoning, Shandong, Jiangsu, Henan, Guangxi, Sichuan, and Gansu. Next, with the help of the Zhongmin Social Assistance Institute, I sent formal inquiry letters asking the selected provinces to provide three shelters' intake records on missing older adults from 1 January 2015 to 30 June 2016. The number of shelters from each province that were willing to provide records varied from one to four. In total, my team reviewed data from nineteen social assistance shelters. Taken together, the communities served by these shelters had a total population of nearly one hundred million residents. The data are presented in Table 7.1 and can be considered nationally representative.

Agency Interviews

To gain more in-depth qualitative information on missing older adults across different shelters, I interviewed representatives from one shelter in each of the eight selected provinces in July and August 2016. Each interview lasted about a day.

Telephone Questionnaire Survey

I used questionnaire surveys to understand the personal, family, and community living conditions of the missing older adults. Two social work graduate students conducted the surveys by telephone in August and September 2016, and the respondents were family members or other guardians of the missing older adults helped by the shelters. Contact information for these family members or other guardians was obtained from the records offered by the nineteen shelters. Most of the missing older adults in shelters were reunited with their families or communities, and the few for whom family could not

Table 7.1. Location distribution of social assistance shelters

Social assistance shelter	Number of missing older adults helped (persons)	Permanent resident population (millions)	Share of total population helped (person/10,000 people)
Chaoyang, Beijing	97	4	0.243
Fengtai, Beijing	17	2.3	0.074
Xicheng, Beijing	16	1.3	0.123
Nanjing	319	8.2	0.389
Qingdao	120	9	0.133
Shenyang	56	8.3	0.067
Dashiqiao	26	0.73	0.356
Kaiyuan	10	0.61	0.164
Xinmin	37	0.67	0.552
Zhengzhou	25	9.6	0.026
Nanning	19	7	0.027
Liuzhou	72	3.92	0.184
Guilin	52	4.96	0.105
Chengdu	321	15	0.214
Zigong	197	2.8	0.704
Bazhong	99	3.3	0.300
Suining	142	3.3	0.430
Qingyang	32	2.2	0.145
Zhangye	6	1.2	0.050
All locations	1,663	88.39	0.188

Note: Data for Fengtai, Xicheng, Qingdao, and Shenyang are from local official statistical 2015 year-book websites; data for Nanjing, Chaoyang, Nanning, Liuzhou, Bazhong, and Zhangye are from a 1 percent population sample survey in 2015; data for Chengdu, Zhengzhou, Guilin, Zigong, Suining, and Qingyang are from a 2015 statistical bulletin of national economic and social development; and data for Dashiqiao, Kaiyuan, and Xinmin are from respective local government websites.

be reached were transferred to the welfare agencies for long-term resettlement. In the end, we completed ninety-seven telephone surveys.

Key Indicator

The key indicator analyzed in this study was the rate of reported missing older adults, which is equal to the proportion of missing older adults at the social assistance shelters among the total local resident population. Differences across regions were examined and compared. I combined this quantitative analysis with qualitative data to reach conclusions and draw implications.

Regional Variations in Missing Older Adults: Dementia versus Anomie as Causes

In this section, I present descriptive quantitative data to show the regional variations in the missing older adults, with a focus on comparing dementia and anomie as causes. Two aspects of the regional variations are considered. The first is the location—whether the missing older adults were in the eastern, central, or western regions of China. The second is directional—whether the missing older adults were in a migration inflow, a migration outflow, or a stagnant region.

I first examine whether there are significant differences in the rates of reported missing older adults among the eastern, central, and western regions. According to mainstream interpretations in academia and media, dementia is a leading contributing factor to older adults being unable to find their way home. If this is the case, the rates of the missing elderly across different regions should not be significantly different. No existing research has shown that there is a correlation between dementia and geographic regions (Coste 2015; Hu and Wu 2015; Tian and Deng 2014).

Table 7.2 presents the average rates of reported missing older adults in the three respective regions. The western region's rate (0.307 person/10,000 people) and the eastern region's rate (0.234) are much higher than the central region's rate (0.085). However, these differences do not reach a level of statistical significance in the chi-square test, indicating no significant difference among the rates of missing older adults across the eastern, central, and western regions. In other words, dementia is one of the main factors that contribute to older adults getting lost and ultimately reaching the social assistance shelters.

The western region has the highest rate of missing older adults. It is also the origin of a significant number of migrant workers and has the highest poverty rate among the regions. With a significant proportion of the working population leaving their hometowns and having difficulties sending money home, older adults' quality of care declines and poverty becomes even more pervasive for them (Q. Li 2015). These facts are in line with Durkheim's theory of anomie brought about by rapid social change.

To investigate differences in population flow, I regrouped the data of the social assistance shelters into three regional migration types: inflow, outflow, and stagnant. Those with a residential population of more than four million are considered inflow regions, including not only the eastern region

Table 7.2. Rates of missing older adults among eastern, central, and western regions (person/10,000 people)

Region	Mean	Standard deviation	Minimum	Maximum	Number of social assistance shelters
Eastern	0.234	0.166	0.067	0.552	9
Central	0.085	0.076	0.024	0.184	4
Western	0.307	0.234	0.050	0.704	6

Pearson $\chi^2(36) = 38.0000$, Prob $= 0.378$

cities but also some large cities in the central and western provinces. Cities with a residential population under four million and with more than 25 percent of the workforce working elsewhere are considered outflow regions. Those with a residential population under four million and less than 25 percent of the workforce working elsewhere are considered stagnant regions. Conceptually, the older adults living in the outflow regions are perhaps at the highest risk due to their lack of caregivers. Those in the inflow regions are slightly better positioned because their children can still provide some care and guardianship while holding a job locally. In stagnant regions, the family structure is mostly intact.

If dementia is the predominant cause of older adults going missing, there should be no significant difference in the rates of reported missing older adults across regions with different population flows. If, however, the rates of reported missing older adults correlate with the conceptual levels of risk, we can conclude that social anomie has a significant impact. The results of descriptive statistics and this hypothesis testing are shown in Table 7.3.

Table 7.3 shows that the rates of missing older adults across the three types of regions are distinct from one another: inflow regions at 0.154 person per 10,000 people, outflow regions at 0.468, and stagnant regions at 0.111. It is important to note that the outflow regions' rate is about three and four times that of the other two regions. The statistically significant Spearman's correlation test (coefficient $= 0.6490$, p $= 0.0026$) indicates that there is a high correlation between the rates of missing older adults and risk levels of the three regions. Consequently, we can draw two conclusions: first, dementia does not account for all the reported missing older adults; second, social anomie has a significant impact on the rate of reported missing older adults.

Table 7.3. Rates of missing older adults among inflow, outflow, and stagnant regions (person/10,000 people)

Regions	Mean	Standard deviation	Minimum	Maximum	Number of social assistance shelters
Inflow	0.154	0.118	0.024	0.389	9
Outflow	0.468	0.162	0.300	0.704	5
Stagnant	0.111	0.048	0.050	0.164	5

Spearman's Rho = 0.6490, Prob>|t| = 0.0026

Notes: 1) The permanent population of Liuzhou is 3.92 million. Though it falls below the 4 million population threshold, it is an important industrial city in Guangxi Province and home to many migrant workers, so it is classified as an inflow region. 2) Though the Xicheng District and Fengtai District are located at the center of Beijing, the permanent population is relatively small. As such, these districts are classified as stagnant regions. Meanwhile, the Chaoyang District located at the urban-rural fringe of Beijing is classified as an inflow region due to its large population size.

Our telephone survey results further confirmed these conclusions. Of the ninety-seven surveyed families, 46 percent were from small and medium-sized cities, 30 percent were from western rural areas, 18 percent were from big cities or adjacent areas, 5 percent were from central rural areas, and 1 percent were from eastern rural areas. Based on the statistical test and survey results, we can conclude that most missing older adults are concentrated in small and medium-sized cities as well as in western rural areas—in other words, in places with high population outflow.

Four Types of Missing Older Adults

Our qualitative interview data confirm the conceptual typology presented earlier about the four types of missing older adults. Type I (socially integrated adults who are in full cognitive health) are seldom sent to shelters. Without dementia and with the social support of family and others, they simply do not reach the point of being directed to a shelter. Usually with help from passersby and police, most of them can return home soon after becoming disoriented or lost.

Type II—those who are socially integrated but diagnosed with dementia—are mainly found in the inflow and stagnant regions. In interviews, social assistance shelter workers said that they were able to easily identify symptoms of dementia, such as short-term memory loss, unwillingness to stay, and irritability. One staff member from a social assistance shelter in Lanzhou commented, "Older clients could remember very little information about their families, communities, even their own names." In addition, a worker from a Chaoyang social assistance shelter recalled, "Several days ago, an old lady was taken here. As soon as she came in, she started scolding others and kicking the door. But we hadn't found her home and dared not let her go, otherwise we would need to bear some responsibility."

Though older adults of this type struggle with dementia, they often have their family and support network as a protection mechanism. After realizing that older members are missing, most families do whatever they can to find them, such as posting notices on social media (WeChat and Weibo), posting flyers near their regular activity areas, and contacting the police and social assistance shelters. After one or two times of an older family member getting lost, families typically make sure that the person carries contact information when going out, using traditional methods such as putting paper strips in the person's pockets or sewing information on cloth strips to attach to clothes, and more modern solutions, such as printing QR code labels, having the person wear a GPS positioning bracelet, or tattooing a phone number on a hand or forearm. In stagnant regions where communities have not changed much over time, there are more neighbors and familiar community members who can help look for the missing older adults.

Type III older adults (socially isolated and diagnosed with dementia) are at the greatest risk of among the four types, with some extreme cases involving total abandonment of the older adults by family members. This was often confirmed by our interview data; in fact, a representative from a Lanzhou social assistance shelter reported, "The family did not accept the client when we finally found the village, although the people from the next village said that the client was from there." A worker from a shelter in Chaoyang recalled, "An old client's son said on the phone 'I am relieved knowing now that my father is in a Beijing social assistance shelter,' and then he hung up, which means he was happy because the Beijing social assistance shelter could take care of his father." And in Nanning, one staff member acknowledged, "Some families do not want to take care of older members with dementia, so they buy a long-distance bus ticket and send their elder to other cities."

The data reported by *Jinri Toutiao* show that the death rates of missing older adults in large, medium, and small cities are 6.88 percent, 12.30 percent, and 23.30 percent, respectively.[4] Given this, the missing older adults with dementia are far better off if they reach social assistance shelters than if they remain on their own.

Type IV—those who are socially isolated but in full cognitive health—accounted for a large proportion of the missing older adults in social assistance shelters in our investigation. Most older adults of this type are from outflow regions. The direct cause of these elderly going missing is the lack of economic resources or guardianship to support and protect them when their adult children leave their hometowns for work in the cities. In addition, there are a considerable number of older adults in remote rural areas who lack any kind of social security, such as social insurance or the Minimum Livelihood Guarantee (*dibao*). In our telephone survey, 29 percent of the missing older adults reported having no social security. Without a source of income in their rural hometowns, the older adults often search for jobs in nearby small and medium-sized cities to support themselves.

Conclusion and Discussion

Building on Durkheim's theory of anomie and drawing from quantitative and qualitative data collected from social assistance shelters and families, this chapter finds that the anomie caused by the urbanization process might have devastating effects on older adults in China, especially those who have cognitive declines or lack income sources or social support. The socially isolated older adults—regardless of their cognitive health status—are at greater risk of becoming missing. The population outflow regions are particularly risky for older adults, who lack social support from their adult children or other social networks.

These high risks of older adults getting lost and becoming missing reflect the effects of social breakdown or disintegration caused by the rapid expansion of cities in China (Park, Burgess, and McKenzie 1925). Social breakdown may also occur in the areas with large population outflows, especially when the population is unable to migrate freely due to *hukou* restrictions or limited social benefits for migrants in the cities. These restrictions on mobility have resulted in many family members being left behind in their home villages, including older adults.

For decades, under the urbanization strategy to strictly control the *hukou* system while accelerating labor mobility, China has avoided serious social problems, such as the disorderly expansion of large cities and the proliferation of slums that has plagued Latin America, India, and other developing countries. However, in the rural areas with a large outflow population, there have been indications of social breakdown. First, many Chinese traditional social and cultural norms have been broken. According to Fei (2013), traditional China is understood as a society regulated by cultural traditions and ruled mainly by senior elders. However, the development of modern technology and the shifts in the labor force have destroyed the traditional norms, taking a toll on principles of filial piety and the practices of family care (Zhu 2008; Yang 2012).

Second, villages have been disappearing rapidly. In 2000, the total number of natural villages in China was 3.63 million. This number dropped sharply to 2.71 million by 2010, averaging between eighty and one hundred villages disappearing per day (Luo and Dong 2015). Third, older adults who are left behind often face multiple challenges: they tend to have low income, be neglected or abused, and in poor health (Ye and He 2014), but local governments have limited resources to address these problems. In other words, the social breakdown in the outflow regions is starved of social resources (Wang 2012; Peking University Institute of Population Research 2012). The problem of missing older adults is just the tip of the iceberg. In outflow regions, there are many other social problems that need to be examined and addressed by scholars, social workers, and central and local governments.

It is important to strengthen the efforts to prevent older adults from getting lost in the first place as well as to develop search and rescue efforts once an older adult is reported missing. In inflow cities, the older person's adult children should be informed that there is some risk of their parent getting lost and that some preventive measures should be taken, especially for older adults with signs of cognitive health decline. Social work can play an active role through public outreach efforts to enhance residents' awareness. More effective collaboration between social assistance shelters and police is also needed.

It is also important to develop and expand the necessary social protection and care systems for older adults. This should include not only nationwide comprehensive pension coverage but also better quality and follow-up care services for older adults, especially those left behind in their home villages, without adult children nearby. Specifically, the local government should establish nursing homes, introduce rural social work to conduct thorough and comprehensive needs assessments within outflow regions, and match services to the older adults' specific needs. It is imperative that families, governments, and society pledge more resources to strengthen care for the older population; cover more older adults in the *dibao* system; and ensure their safety, health, and well-being.

Notes

1. Mechanical solidarity refers to the fact that most members of a traditional society are engaged in similar occupations and share common experiences and beliefs, thus forming close ties. Organic solidarity refers to what happens when the social division of labor leads to the interdependence of society's members.

2. With a rapidly aging population, Japan is facing the highest level of missing older adults (Xinhua News 2016).

3. In the investigation, we found that police reports on lost older adults mainly stayed at police station level and were seldom aggregated to county or city level. There is almost no record of help information from passersby, community members, or local governments. Besides, missing older adults should theoretically also include those who have not been found for a long time (including reported and unreported cases), but it is difficult to calculate that number accurately. So, we mainly aim at the missing older adults in social assistance shelters nationwide.

4. The death rate of missing older adults in counties and towns is over 20 percent (Ren and Xia 2016).

References

Baidu. 2019. "Total number of Migrant Workers Reaches 300 million Nationwide." [In Chinese.] 14 February. https://baijiahao.baidu.com/s?id=1625448923870179547&wfr=spider&for=pc.

Chen, Ni, and Caihua Zhang. 2013. "Research Progress on the Missing of Alzheimer's Patients." [In Chinese.] *Journal of Nursing* 1.

Coste, Joanne Koenig. 2015. *Learning to Speak Alzheimer's: A Groundbreaking Approach for Everyone Dealing with the Disease.* Translated into Chinese by Enyan Yu. Hangzhou: Zhejiang University Press.

Durkheim, Émile. 2016. *On Suicide.* Translated into Chinese by Feng Yunwen. Beijing: Commercial Press.

Fei, Xiaotong. 2013. *From the Soil: The Foundations of Chinese Society.* [In Chinese.] Shanghai: Shanghai People's Publishing House.

Hu, Huaqiong, and Ruiqin Wu. 2015. *Nursing and Health Education Guidance for Hospitalized Patients.* [In Chinese.] Wuhan: Huazhong University of Science and Technology Press.

Koester, Robert J., and David E. Stooksbury. 1995. "Behavioral Profile of Possible Alzheimer's Disease Subjects in Search and Rescue Incidents in Virginia." *Wild Environ Med* 6 (1): 34–43.

Li, Hejun. 2005. *Self-Health-Care Tutorials for the Middle and Old Aged.* [In Chinese.] Hangzhou: Zhejiang Science and Technology Press.

Li, Qiang. 2015. *Great Power and Empty Village: Rural Left Behind Children, Women and the Old Man.* [In Chinese.] Beijing: China Economic Press.

Liu, Hongkui. 2000. *Mental Health and Longevity for the Middle and Old Aged: Psychotherapy of Aging Disease.* [In Chinese.] Beijing: China Social Press.

Luo, Changzhi, and Zeping Dong. 2015. *Research Report on Creative Economy on Both Sides of the Straits*. [In Chinese.] Beijing: Social Science Literature Press.

Merton, Robert K. 2006. *Social Theory and Social Structure*. Translated into Chinese by Hepeng Jia. Beijing: Translation Press.

Park, Robert E., Ernest W. Burgess, and Roderick Duncan McKenzie. 1925. *The City*. Chicago: University of Chicago Press.

Peking University Institute of Population Research. 2012. "The Predicament and the Way Out of the Fund Guarantee for Rural Old-Age Service." [In Chinese.] *Social Welfare* 3.

Ren, Huan, and Jin Xia. 2016. "The Investigation Report of the Missing Older Adults in China." [In Chinese.] *Guangming Daily*, 8 October. https://epaper.gmw.cn/gmrb/html/2016-10/12/nw.D110000gmrb_20161012_4-08.htm.

Rowe, Meredeth A., and Vikki Bennett. 2003. "A Look at Deaths Occurring in Persons with Dementia Lost in the Community." *American Journal of Alzheimer's Disease and Other Dementias* 18 (6): 343–48.

Rowe, Meredeth A., Sydney S. Vandeveer, Catherine A. Greenblum, Cassandra N. List, Rachael M. Fernandez, Natalie E. Mixson, and Hyo C. Ahn. 2011. "Persons with Dementia Missing in the Community: Is It Wandering or Something Unique?" *BMC Geriatrics* 11 (1): 28–36.

Sohu Health. 2016. "World Alzheimer's Day." [In Chinese.] 23 September. http://health.sohu.com/20160923/n469019969.shtml.

Sun, Liping. 2003. *The Fracture: Chinese Society since 1990s*. [In Chinese.] Beijing: Social Science Literature Press.

Tian, Yan, and Sa Deng. 2014. *Medication by Looking at Pictures*. [In Chinese.] Beijing: Jindun Publishing House.

Wang, Lihua. 2012. *Research on the Construction of Special System for Rural Anti-poverty Employment Assistance*. [In Chinese.] Beijing: Ethnic Publishing House.

Wu, Zongxian. 2010. *The History of Western Criminology*. [In Chinese.] Beijing: Chinese People's Public Security University Press.

Xinhua News. 2016. "Japanese Population Ages Rapidly, the Number of Missing Older Adults Reaches Historically High Level." [In Chinese.] 19 June. http://news.xinhuanet.com/world/2016-06/18/c_129071449.htm.

Yang, Peiying. 2012. *Innovative Rural Social Management*. [In Chinese.] Beijing: Social Science Literature Press.

Ye, Jingzhong, and Congzhi He. 2014. *The China Population of Rural Left Behind Elderly: Lonely Sunsets*. [In Chinese.] Beijing: Social Science Literature Press.

Yihao Guquan. 2020. "Eighty Villages Vanish Every Day, Over One Million Villages Disappeared in Twenty Years, This Trend Will Continue!" [In Chinese.] 20 March. https://3g.163.com/dy/article_cambrian/F86K5H4U0535AW45.html.

Zhao, Huimin. 2010. *Aging Psychology*. [In Chinese.] Tianjin: Tianjin University Press.

Zhu, Lan. 2008. *Seven Lectures of Chinese Traditional Filial Piety*. [In Chinese.] Beijing: Chinese Social Press.

CHAPTER 8

Environmental Impact of Urbanization in Post-Reform China

Peilei Fan

Introduction

In December 2016, more than seventy Chinese cities issued warnings to their citizens that air pollution had reached dangerous levels. The government shut down schools temporarily and ordered some factories and power plants to close (Voice of America 2016). In Beijing, where the $PM_{2.5}$ concentration level reached over 400 ug/m^3—sixteen times higher than the safe level of 10–25 ug/m^3 set by the World Health Organization (WHO)—hundreds of flights were delayed or canceled due to poor visibility. Though this was one of the worst episodes of toxic air pollution for urban China, it was by no means the only one. Travelers to Beijing and other cities in China have been advised to avoid traveling in winter months, when pollution-related health risks are highest. Beijing cough—a new term coined to describe "the symptoms of dry cough and throat itching suffered by foreigners when they arrive in Beijing"—is used by the official newspaper *People's Daily* to describe foreigners' inability to adapt to Beijing's climate (Bruno 2013).

Air pollution is just one of the urban environmental problems that is a symptom of China's rapid urbanization and economic development. Other urban environmental problems include water and soil pollution, noise and light pollution, urban heat islands, and insufficient urban green spaces.

This chapter constitutes a critical review of existing data and literature on urban environmental problems in Chinese cities. In addition, I present new data extracted by satellite images on air pollution of cities in China (Figure 8.1).

Using global satellite imagery as a data source for air pollution, this chapter corroborates the third goal of this volume on the utility of new data sources. New findings are presented on the coevolved relationship among urbanization, economic development, and urban environmental conditions (Figure 8.2). The chapter focuses on two major issues of urban environmental problems: air pollution and urban heat islands. Assessing the current status of these two problems reveals their spatial patterns and temporal trends. Rapid urbanization has often been associated with changing patterns of urban environmental impacts. Urban environmental transition (UET) (McGranahan et al. 2001) can provide useful insights on how economic development and population change associated with urbanization can lead to various environmental impacts within cities. In this chapter, the relationship between urbanization and environmental impact will be explored through analyzing the interrelatedness of urbanization, economic development, and urban environmental conditions. The chapter also includes reflection and discussion on China's emerging socioeconomic trends and their associated environmental impacts. Finally, the chapter discusses satellite data sources to derive information on air pollution, illustrating how new data sources can be explored for urban research in China.

Air Pollution

Air pollution is one of the most severe urban environmental problems in the developing world. In 2016, while the world's average concentration of fine particulate matter ($PM_{2.5}$) was 39.6 ug/m^3 for urban areas, that of the developed region was at a low 11.9 ug/m^3 and that of developing regions was at a high 45.3 ug/m^3, with particularly high levels in western Asia (50.7 ug/m^3) and eastern Asia (49.7 ug/m^3) (WHO 2019). Analysis of global trends suggests that while air pollution has been continuously declining for developed countries since the 1960s, developing countries have been confronted with challenges, impeding their progress in mitigating air pollution (McGranahan and Murray 2012; Romieu and Hernandez-Avila 2012). As Chinese urbanization has proceeded at an unprecedented speed and scale, urban air pollution has also one of the most hotly debated topics in China by citizens and popular media. In 2016, $PM_{2.5}$ in Chinese cities averaged 51 ug/m^3 (35.7 ug/m^3 for rural areas and 49.2 ug/m^3 overall) (WHO 2019). The World Health

Organization collects and compiles data on annual mean concentrations of particulate matter (PM_{10} and $PM_{2.5}$) in 2,700 towns and cities across 91 countries. In 2016, 283 of the 500 most polluted cities were in China. Of these, 56 Chinese cities were ranked in the top 100 of the most polluted cities (WHO 2019).

Studies from across the world, including Shanghai, show that urban air pollution is linked to negative public health outcomes (Nel 2005; Pascal et al. 2013; Seaton et al. 1995; Bernstein et al. 2004; Kan and Chen 2004). According to the WHO, air pollution contributes to an estimated three to seven million deaths per year worldwide (WHO 2018), killing more people than AIDS, malaria, breast cancer, or tuberculosis (Rohde and Muller 2015). In China alone, air pollution causes an estimated 1.2 to 2 million deaths per year (Rohde and Muller 2015).

Air pollution in Chinese cities is measured by the air quality index (AQI), which is calculated using a combined measurement of all air pollutants detected. Before 2013, the overall AQI was calculated using SO_2, NO_2, and PM_{10}. As of 2013, CO, $PM_{2.5}$, and O_3 are also included in the calculations. The index is categorized into one of five grades: Grades I and II indicate excellent and fine air quality, respectively. Grades III, IV, and V refer to light, medium, and heavy degrees of air pollution. In February 2012, China released new ambient air quality standards (GB3095-2012), with a target implementation date of 1 January 2016 (Ministry of Ecology and Environment 2019). The new standards are comparable to the interim targets (ITs) set by the WHO. For example, the limits set for the annual and twenty-four-hour averages of $PM_{2.5}$ are 35 ug/m^3 and 75 ug/m^3 for Grade II of China's AQI index, which are the same as the WHO's interim target-1 (IT-1).

Geographically, the most polluted areas are in China's densely populated eastern and industrializing central regions, with the northeast corridor from Shanghai to north of Beijing particularly concentrated (Liu et al. 2010; Rohde and Muller 2015; Wang et al. 2010). One of the most recent ambient air pollution studies in China is by Song et al. (2017), which uses data on six air pollutants ($PM_{2.5}$, PM_{10}, O_3–8 h, NO_2, SO_2, and CO), measured from 2014 to 2016 across thirteen hundred national air quality monitoring stations. Overall, the study confirmed that air pollution in northern China is more severe than in southern China (He et al. 2017; Song et al. 2017).

The black smoke from stacks characterized industrial Chinese cities in the 1970s. In the 1980s, many southern cities suffered from serious acid rain pollution. Since the 1990s, air pollution made up of nitrous oxides (NO_x), carbon monoxide (CO), and photochemical smog has become more prevalent across China (He, Huo, and Zhang 2002; Chan and Yao 2008). As the severe health impacts of $PM_{2.5}$ have garnered more attention, real-time monitoring of $PM_{2.5}$—first made available by the U.S. embassy in Beijing—has become widely accessible to the public through an hourly update online. Sources of air pollution can be complex. Studies have shown that several haze events in Beijing were largely driven by meteorological conditions, pollution from industrial facilities and agricultural facilities, and biogenic emissions—factors that constitute the dominant sources of $PM_{2.5}$ at the regional level (Guo et al. 2014). Secondary aerosol—formed through gas-to-particle conversion in the atmosphere rather than through primary emission (being emitted directly from the biosphere)—and regional transportation contributed to particulate pollution during severe haze events (Guo et al. 2014; Huang et al. 2014).

For this chapter, the mean values of $PM_{2.5}$ (1999–2013) and NO_2 (1998–2011) surface air pollution were extracted from remote sensing imageries, both at 0.01×0.01 degrees resolution, in nine Chinese cities to examine the temporal trends of air pollution. The selected cities represent different geographic regions and economic development levels. While cities such as Beijing and Shanghai are included as significant economic centers, second-tier cities such as Nanjing, Hangzhou, and Shenzhen are also included. In addition, cities located in central and western China, such as Chongqing, Urumqi, Lanzhou, and Hohhot, are also included to present a geographically and economically balanced view. $PM_{2.5}$ concentration levels are estimated by combining aerosol optical depth retrievals from MODIS, MISR, and SeaWiFS instruments with the GEOS-Chem global chemical transport model. They were then calibrated to the ground-based observations of $PM_{2.5}$ using a geographically weighted regression (Van Donkelaar et al. 2016). The NO_2 concentration level was estimated based on the satellite instruments of GOME, SCIAMACHY, and GOME-2 (Lamsal et al. 2008).

All nine Chinese cities have generally experienced an increase in air pollution, as measured by $PM_{2.5}$ and NO_2 (Figure 8.1). It is interesting to note that Beijing has experienced a significantly higher concentration of $PM_{2.5}$ than the other eight cities, a gap that has been growing over the past ten to twenty years. Still, the concentration of $PM_{2.5}$ has been gradually increasing in Nanjing, Hangzhou, Chongqing, and Shanghai and can be considered in the middle range of these groups. Three cities in arid and semi-arid regions of

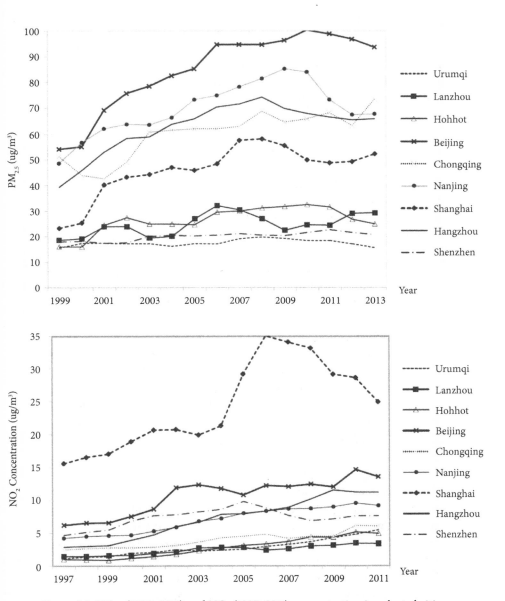

Figure 8.1. PM$_{2.5}$ (1999–2013) and NO$_2$ (1997–2011) concentration in selected cities in China.

China—Hohhot, Lanzhou, and Urumqi—as well as Shenzhen demonstrated an overall stable trend except that Lanzhou also experienced an increase of $PM_{2.5}$ concentration level beginning in 2009. NO_2 levels ranked similarly across cities except in the major economic centers, where the concentration in Shanghai surpassed that in Beijing.

Urban Heat Island

The urban heat island (UHI) effect refers to observed higher atmospheric and surface temperatures in urban areas than in surrounding suburban and rural areas. UHIs are well recognized as one of the most conspicuous impacts of urbanization (Kalnay and Cai 2003; Peng et al. 2012; Voogt and Oke 1998). UHIs are associated with a number of lifestyle changes and negative health outcomes for city dwellers, including an increase in energy consumption used for cooling as well as higher rates of heat exhaustion and premature death (Heaviside, Vardoulakis, and Cai 2016; Lowe 2016; Taylor et al. 2015).

The UHI effect can be calculated by the difference between weather station air temperature measurements in urban and rural areas (Carlson and Arthur 2000; Wilson et al. 2003; Fujibe 2009; Stone 2007). As remote sensing imaginaries become available, more researchers have used land surface temperature (LST) derived from satellite technologies, like the 1 kilometer resolution Moderate Resolution Imaging Spectroradiometer (MODIS) (Tran et al. 2006; Imhoff et al. 2010; Peng et al. 2012; Voogt and Oke 2003; Wan 2008), or the finer resolution Landsat Thematic Mapper (TM), Landsat Enhanced Thematic Mapper Plus (ETM+) and Advanced Spaceborne Thermal Emission and Reflection Radiometer (ASTER) (Kato and Yamaguchi 2005; Nichol 1996; Yue et al. 2012; Weng, Lu, and Schubring 2004; Weng, Lu, and Liang 2006; Stathopoulou and Cartalis 2007; Yuan and Bauer 2007). Methodologically, while correlation and regression analyses are often adopted to analyze the drivers of UHIs (see Peng et al. 2012; Cao et al. 2016), factor analysis is considered a more appropriate method for understanding the relationship among different factors (Weng et al. 2008; Xiao et al. 2008; Yue et al. 2012).

Studies on spatiotemporal patterns and major drivers of UHIs have focused on diurnal, seasonal, and cross-city differences. UHIs often develop through a combination of biophysical or anthropogenic factors. Biophysical factors include land cover characteristics, such as impervious surface coverage (Imhoff et al. 2010; Li et al. 2011; Yue et al. 2012), green coverage, and water surface area (Arnfield 2003). The ecological setting or city's climate zone is also a biophysical factor (Zhou et al. 2014). Anthropogenic factors that contribute to UHI include population size (Huang, Ooka, and Kato 2005), road density (Hart and Sailor 2009), industrial development (Li et al. 2011; Kato and Yamaguchi 2005), building energy use, automobile heat release, power plants, air-conditioning use, and overall greenhouse gas emissions. In Shanghai, for example, Yue et al. (2012) found that the variances of UHI were detected on a gradient from man-made to natural land cover, landscape configuration, and anthropogenic factors of heat release. It is worth mentioning that vegetation cover can substantially reduce land surface temperature (Inostroza 2014; Yue et al. 2012). Still, UHI-related measurements can be drastically different for individual cities depending on the season, the time of day, and general variations in climate.

At the global level, Peng et al. (2012), in the most comprehensive study so far, assessed 419 large (population over one million) global cities. Using as an indicator surface urban heat island intensity (SUHII), which measures the difference in surface temperature between urban and suburban areas from the MODIS, the study evaluated the UHI's diurnal and seasonal variations. Their results indicate that average daytime SUHII is generally higher than it is at night. The study found that daytime SUHII levels fluctuated depending on vegetation cover and human activity, whereas nighttime SUHII levels were linked to albedo and nighttime light.

A plethora of literature on UHIs in Chinese cities exists (Zhang et al. 2013; Li et al. 2009; Weng 2001; Yue et al. 2012). Zhou et al. (2014) evaluated thirty-two Chinese cities' UHIs, using MODIS data from 2003 to 2011, and found UHIs to be more prevalent in cities in the southeastern and northern regions. UHIs in summer and nighttime are more distinguished than those of winter and daytime. Daytime and nighttime UHIs differ. While vegetation cover, anthropogenic heat release, and climate are primary causes of daytime UHIs, nighttime UHIs are more closely linked to climate, built-up density, albedo, and anthropogenic heat release. Cao et al. (2016) assessed UHIs in thirty-nine Chinese cities by using MODIS data from 2003 to 2013. Their findings confirm those of Zhou et al. (2014), illustrating that in contrast to the global trend, the UHI effect at nighttime is greater than in the daytime for Chinese cities, especially those in the semi-arid climate zones. The study also found that the overall city population and nighttime UHI are not statistically significant. The researchers' most interesting finding was that the aerosol or haze pollution levels significantly worsened the nighttime UHI effect for Chinese cities. In addition to assessing multiple cities in China, UHI research has focused on individual case cities, such as Shanghai (Deng, Shu, and Li 2001; Li et al. 2011; Yue et al. 2012) and Beijing (Liu et al. 2007; Yang, Ren, and Liu 2013). Consistent with the findings of Zhou et al. (2014) and Cao et al. (2016), the UHI effect was stronger at night than during the day for these two major cities (Deng, Shu, and Li 2001; Liu et al. 2007; Yang, Ren, and Liu 2013). Still, the UHI effect was stronger in winter than in summer for both Shanghai and Beijing, differing from the findings of Zhou et al. (2014) in their study of multiple Chinese cities. This reminds us that factors contributing to UHIs are complex and that different driving mechanisms may be at work in different cities.

Urbanization, Economic Development, and Urban Environmental Problems

What has driven the urban environmental transition in Chinese cities? How has the level of economic development and the change in resident population affected certain urban environmental indicators? In this section, a simple correlation analysis was performed to reveal that urbanization, economic development, and environmental changes were interrelated in Beijing and Shanghai. This section is also concerned with how urban green space per capita evolved with urbanization and economic development, and how the amount of green space affected both urban air pollution (Chen et al. 2016) and UHI (Yue et al. 2012; Inostroza 2014). Annual data on residential population, gross domestic product per capita (GDPpc in U.S. dollars per person), green space per capita (m^2 per person, 1978 to 2017), and annual data on NO_2 (1998 to 2017) and $PM_{2.5}$ (1999 to 2017) were collected from the Beijing and Shanghai statistical yearbooks. GDPpc was converted from RMB to USD by using the official exchange rates for corresponding years.

Figure 8.2 illustrates that as the residential population in Beijing and Shanghai grew, the concentrations of NO_2 and square meters of green space per capita improved continuously, illustrated by the linear trend lines fitting with high R^2 values for NO_2 and green space per capita. $PM_{2.5}$ concentrations, however, did not follow the same trend. The reverse U shape suggests that $PM_{2.5}$ levels first increased then decreased as the residential population

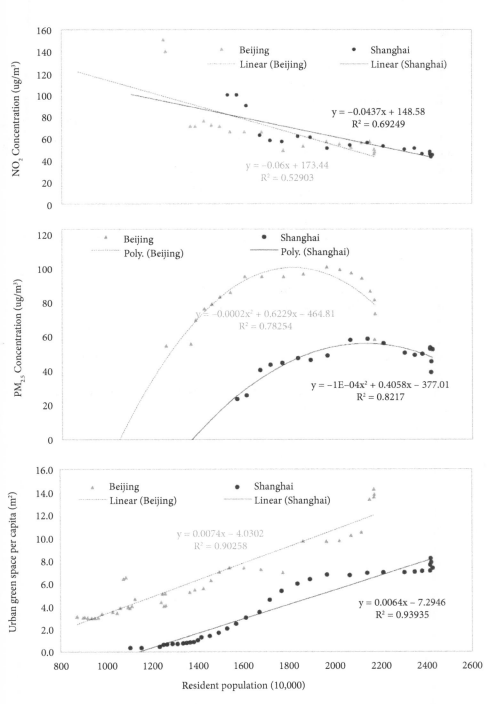

Figure 8.2. Changes in air pollution (NO_2 and $PM_{2.5}$) and green space per capita (with resident population). Source: Created by the author based on the data extracted from satellite images.

steadily increased. These results indicate that a rise in urban population does not necessarily correlate with severe environmental problems such as air pollution or insufficient urban green space.

Figure 8.3 illustrates the relationship between economic development (measured by GDPpc), concentrations of NO_2 and $PM_{2.5}$, and green space per capita. While NO_2 and green space per capita are highly correlated with the level of economic development, $PM_{2.5}$ is not. Figure 8.3 shows $PM_{2.5}$ worsening at first, then improving as the level of economic development increases. Results from Figure 8.3 imply that economic development can help to alleviate environmental problems such as air pollution and lead to more provision of urban green space; however, that trend does not hold for all air pollution types.

The dynamics of $PM_{2.5}$ vis-à-vis the economic development level for both cities can be explained by the environmental Kuznets curve (Stern 2004). The environmental Kuznets curve does not explain trends in NO_2 and green space per capita, which improved continuously. Relationships illustrated in Figures 8.2 and 8.3 suggest that in these cities, the square meters of green space per capita increased at a faster rate than did population or economic development. This can likely be attributed to planning and policy interventions that contributed significantly to overcoming an expected decline in green space per capita.

Discussion

Urban Environmental Transition and Chinese Cities

Urban environmental transition (UET) theory links a city's economic development to associated environmental burdens across local, regional, and global spatial scales (McGranahan et al. 2001). According to UET theory, poor cities or neighborhoods, common in developing countries, are more likely to have localized, immediate, and health-threatening environmental problems close to their workplaces and homes. In contrast, affluent cities in developed countries are more likely to generate longer-term environmental burdens, such as carbon emissions, with impacts at the global scale but limited local burden. Chinese cities can be mostly classified as industrial cities, lying in between the two extreme groups of poor and affluent cities. As such, Chinese cities bear the brunt of environmental burdens such as

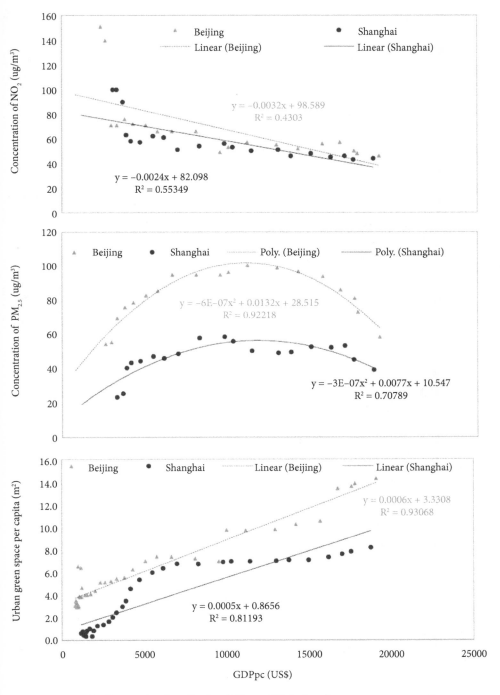

Figure 8.3. Changes in air pollution (NO_2 and $PM_{2.5}$) and green space per capita (with economic development level).

ambient air pollution at the regional level and with a moderate temporal scale (McGranahan et al. 2001).

Although applying UET theory to Chinese cities appears to be simplistic, it does characterize general urban environmental problems in China. Nevertheless, it is still worth noting that Chinese cities may also experience or contribute to the environmental problems of poor and affluent cities, although not to a prevailing extent. For example, unrepaired roads, flooding, lack of garbage collection and management, and dirty public toilets appeared in many urban villages in Chinese cities (Xinhua Net 2018). At the other end of the spectrum, high-income residents have embraced a Western lifestyle, living in single-detached houses in the suburbs with auto-based transportation for all their commuting needs. As observed in other high-income developed countries, this wealthy Chinese population contributes to the environmental problems that result from a lifestyle of high carbon emissions, which contributes to global environmental problems over a much longer time. In the middle of the two extremes, UHIs have been considered an urban environmental problem of more concern in middle- and higher-income cities.

China's carbon emissions per capita totaled 6.18 tons in 2011, generally less than the emissions in other countries and only a fraction of those in countries like the United States (17.5 tons) and Japan (9.25 tons) (United Nations Statistics Division 2015). Still, in 2018, China's carbon emissions totaled 10.1 Gt, close to 40 percent of the global 25.4 Gt that year, and almost double that of the United States (5.4 Gt) (Korsbakken et al. 2019). The sheer size of China's population means that any policies implemented in the country that have the potential to effectively alleviate environmental problems can have a significant impact on the global environment.

It is important to conduct a more nuanced analysis of UET across different Chinese cities to account for the different economic development paths and their respective environmental impacts. A Harvard study on Chinese cities' carbon emissions classified 288 cities in China into developed, developing, and less developed cities according to their respective levels of economic development (Liu and Cai 2018). The developed cities in general had lower levels of CO_2 emissions per capita than the national average, which can be attributed partially to the relocation of heavy industry to less developed neighboring regions. In contrast, cities with higher CO_2 emissions per capita than the national average tended to be the less developed and developing cities, although some may also achieve a high level of economic development (Liu and Cai 2018). These findings suggest that in China, low-carbon urbanization transitioning is both possible and critical for the global environment.

Air pollution and urban heat islands are symptoms of very different environmental factors; therefore, mitigating each will require different approaches. As shown in Figure 8.3, air pollution levels change with economic development. As cities like Beijing and Shanghai move toward postindustrialization, NO_2—mostly a result of industrial pollution—steadily declines. The trend in $PM_{2.5}$, which has a much more complex source composition, is nonlinear. Meanwhile, as global climate change spurs a growing number of extreme heat events for cities worldwide, we should expect to see UHIs become an increasingly pressing issue for planners and decision makers across Chinese cities. As Chinese cities continue to rapidly expand impervious surface coverage, they exacerbate the reach of UHIs. Still, there are changing trends in the intensity of the UHI effect. Shanghai's case actually exhibited an overall decline in UHI intensity. More research is needed to elucidate the spatial patterns and causes of UHIs. It is worth mentioning that the commitment to the provision of urban green space reflects the conscious effort by the local government to battle a wide range of environmental problems, including both air pollution and UHIs. Green space and conscientious planning are not only strategically important for building up a city's image and natural capital to attract more investment but also important for the general social welfare and health of all city residents.

Regional and Intracity Perspectives

Given China's size and diversity, it is important to take regional variations in urban environmental problems into account. For example, China's most severe air pollution occurs in the northern region and along the eastern coastal region, due to both natural and human causes, such as meteorological conditions, geographic and biophysical settings, industrial structure, mining and agricultural practices, and coal-based winter heating. While individual cities may adopt certain measures to mitigate environmental degradation, such as converting from coal-based to non-coal-based heating during the winter or limiting driving based on license plate number, a concerted effort at the regional level is still required to address issues that simply go beyond the administrative boundaries of individual cities. In addition, the improvement of air pollution at one place may come at a price to surrounding regions if sources of pollution are simply relocated elsewhere. For example, according to international environmental organization Greenpeace and IQAir—a Swiss firm that issues air quality reports worldwide—Beijing's $PM_{2.5}$ concentration level has significantly improved since 2010 and dropped to its lowest level since 2008, the year data was first collected (Shih 2019). This may ultimately lead to Beijing's fall from the top 200 most polluted cities. Beijing's improvement can be attributed to a government effort in restricting the burning of coal for heating, shutting down and relocating polluting factories, and limiting industrial trucks to outside the city's limits. However, while these regulations improved Beijing's air quality, conditions in neighboring industrial regions appear to have worsened (Shih 2019).

It is also important to consider the intracity perspective on urban environmental problems. Certain locations within a city boundary might disproportionally shoulder more of an environmental burden, or certain communities might be home to extremely vulnerable populations. For example, those who live close to sources of air pollution may suffer more immediate harm and need special attention to protect against any negative health impacts. And while per capita green space is a useful indicator, accessibility to differing degrees of quality urban green spaces should be assessed to identify locations where residents have poor access to high-quality green spaces (Fan et al. 2017). Intracity perspective on the accessibility of green space increasingly recognizes it as an environmental justice issue (Wolch, Byrne, and Newell 2014). While many cities in China, just like their Western counterparts, have been implementing strategies to provide more urban green space, the effort has paradoxically resulted in more attractive communities, thus leading to the rising cost of properties, gentrification, and the ultimate exclusion of low-income communities (Wolch, Byrne, and Newell 2014; Fan et al. 2017). This effect has been labeled variously as ecological gentrification (Dooling 2009), eco-gentrification (Patrick 2011), environmental gentrification (Checker 2011), and green gentrification (Gould and Lewis 2012). This author echoes Wolch, Byrne, and Newell (2014), who note that "urban planners and decision makers will need to be creative and strategic in terms of urban green space provision, using strategies that lead to just green enough" so that the socially marginal population can be protected and not negatively affected by the improved provision of urban green space.

Emerging Issues

Several emerging trends in China's socioeconomic transformations deserve special attention due to their ripple effect on urban environmental changes. First, China's economic development has cultivated a rising urban middle class, whose lifestyle is characterized by property and car ownership, following a similar trajectory to their Western counterparts. This trend has considerable environmental implications. While home ownership in China seldom takes the form of single detached suburban homes (and therefore results in less of an ecological footprint per household than in the West), car ownership has become common for urban residents. The number of small passenger vehicles in China has increased dramatically, from 10.79 million in 2005 to 167 million in 2017. By 2017, Beijing and Shanghai had 4.47 million and 2.71 million small passenger cars, respectively (National Bureau of Statistics of China 2018), or one car for every five people in Beijing and one car for every nine people in Shanghai. While public transportation still prevails as the common choice for urban commuting, the increasing number of automobiles will undoubtedly have a serious impact on air quality in the urban environment.

Second, with the largest e-commerce market in the world, China may have to bear the huge environmental cost that for so long has not been factored into the price of online products. With the use of Alipay and WeChat pay as popular online payments, e-commerce platforms such as Alibaba and JD.com are extremely convenient. From 2011 to 2018, e-commerce transactions in China increased more than fourfold, from RMB 6.09 trillion to RMB 31.63 trillion. By 2018, online retail in China was valued at RMB 9.01 trillion (Ministry of Commerce 2018). Some studies have demonstrated that online shopping can have a comparatively light environmental impact. For example, in his annual letter to the shareholders of Amazon in 2020, Jeff Bezos stated that online shopping is more efficient on average, citing a study conducted by Amazon, which revealed that ordering groceries online reduces 43 percent of carbon emissions when compared to traditional shopping (Nickelsburg 2020). This translates to significantly lower emissions than traditional offline shopping, which generates an estimated 466.7g of

CO_2 (Zhou 2015). However, other studies suggest otherwise (Trade on Carbon Emission 2017). According to a report issued by Greenpeace, on 11 November 2016 alone, carbon emissions from online shopping in China reached 258,000 tons. The report suggested that the convenience of online payment, cheap production costs, and mature logistic transportation networks have made online shopping a daily habit for Chinese customers. The ease of purchase alone, the findings imply, may be resulting in excessive demand and, consequentially, a substantial burden on the environment. Online shopping is widely considered the driving cause behind a dramatic increase in clothing production. From 2000 to 2014, clothing production doubled and per capita purchasing increased 60 percent. On 11 November 2016, 657 million transactions generated 52,400 tons of carbon emissions from the delivery segment alone. Packaging is another huge source of waste. According to the National Bureau of Posts in China, in 2015 its delivery section used 16.985 billion meters of tape. The bureau also estimated that by 2018 there would be fifty billion packages circulating around in China annually, or thirty-eight packages per capita per year (Trade on Carbon Emission 2017). Additionally, the rate of cardboard and plastic recycling is at less than 10 percent (Trade on Carbon Emission 2017).

Nevertheless, the 3Rs—recycle, reuse, and reduce—exist as rays of hope that China's urban environmental problems can be improved. First, the garbage and recycling campaign, initially piloted in Shanghai and soon implemented in other major cities in China, has spurred interesting discussions among citizens on sustainable development and recycling on online platforms. The experiences of Japan and European countries have reached China and have helped to raise awareness. Public education on this matter can be beneficial in improving awareness about the benefits of recycling. Second, secondhand markets have gradually emerged on China's online platforms and become particularly popular among a millennial population seeking both brand names and affordability. This has given rise to a new appreciation for reuse. Third, Chinese urban residents' renewed interest in simple living may have a positive impact on the environment through a culture of reduction. For example, *duansheli* ("to not want," "to give away," or "to leave")—which means to live a simple life without unnecessary things—is a philosophy of Hideko Yamashita, a Japanese organizing guru whose popularity in China rivals Marie Kondo's in the West. Yamashita's lifestyle philosophy, along with her organizational tips, has been enthusiastically embraced by Chinese audiences. This lifestyle calls for a considerable reduction in consumerism and has the potential to significantly mitigate many environmental problems attributed to patterns of excessive consumption.

Conclusion

This chapter focuses on the environmental impacts of urbanization in post-reform China through analyzing major urban environmental problems in Chinese cities. Air pollution remains a serious challenge for China, home to over half of the world's top 500 polluted cities. In the past two decades, nine cities studied showed increasing concentrations of air pollutants such as NO_2 and $PM_{2.5}$. As Chinese cities have rapidly expanded impervious surface coverage, so too have they expanded UHIs. With regional, seasonal, and diurnal patterns distinct to individual Chinese cities, the driving mechanisms behind UHIs are difficult to isolate.

China's experience shows that urban population growth does not necessarily lead to severe environmental problems like air pollution. While economic development can generally help to alleviate environmental problems such as air pollution and can lead to more provision of urban green space, these trends do not hold across every environmental pollutant. Urban green spaces, measured by both total area coverage and per capita, have increased in Chinese cities like Beijing and Shanghai. This can be largely attributed to economic development and institutional planning. Green coverage has been found to alleviate the effect of air pollution and UHIs.

Many Chinese cities, when considered in the context of the UET theory, can be understood as industrial cities. These cities bear environmental burdens like ambient air pollution at a regional scale and at a moderate temporal scale. Many Chinese cities also suffer the same environmental problems that both poor and affluent cities do. With recent trends toward property and automobile ownership, China has contributed to larger global environmental problems through increased carbon emissions. When viewing emerging trends in China, in addition to the increase in home and car ownership by China's rising urban middle class, the rapidly developing online shopping market has also proven to exert significant negative impacts on urban environment. In contrast, garbage classification, online secondhand markets, and simple living philosophies are among the more positive trends that can alleviate China's urban environmental problems through recycling, reusing, and reducing. As we can expect that China will continue to experience a high rate of economic growth, environmental problems in its affluent cities may increase substantially. Nevertheless, the country is moving to embrace ecological civilization and environment protection as an overall future development path, emphasized by Xi Jinping in his report to the Nineteenth National Congress of the Chinese Communist Party in 2017. It remains to be seen whether or not mobilization and strong regulations by the central government are effective in transforming the regular UET path and making China shift toward a more sustainable urban future, thus benefiting the global society.

References

Arnfield, A. John. 2003. "Two Decades of Urban Climate Research: A Review of Turbulence, Exchanges of Energy and Water, and the Urban Heat Island." *International Journal of Climatology: A Journal of the Royal Meteorological Society* 23 (1): 1–26.

Bernstein, Jonathan A., Neil Alexis, Charles Barnes, Leonard Bernstein, Andre Nel, David Peden, David Diaz-Sanchez, Susan M. Tarlo, and P. Brock Williams. 2004. "Health Effects of Air Pollution." *Journal of Allergy and Clinical Immunology* 114 (5): 1116–23.

Bruno, Debra. 2013. "Living in Beijing's Polluted Air." *Washington Post*, 11 March. www .washingtonpost.com/national/health-science/living-in-beijings-polluted-air/2013/03/11 /6606e45e-7489-11e2-8f84-3e4b513b1a13_story.html.

Cao, Chang, Xuhui Lee, Shoudong Liu, Natalie Schultz, Wei Xiao, Mi Zhang, and Lei Zhao. 2016. "Urban Heat Islands in China Enhanced by Haze Pollution." *Nature Communications* 7 (1): 1–7.

Carlson, Toby N., and S. Traci Arthur. 2000. "The Impact of Land Use—Land Cover Changes Due to Urbanization on Surface Microclimate and Hydrology: A Satellite Perspective." *Global and Planetary Change* 25 (1–2): 49–65.

Chan, Chak K., and Xiaohong Yao. 2008. "Air Pollution in Mega Cities in China." *Atmospheric Environment* 42 (1): 1–42.

Checker, Melissa. 2011. "Wiped Out by the "Greenwave": Environmental Gentrification and the Paradoxical Politics of Urban Sustainability." *City and Society* 23 (2): 210–29.

Chen, Jiquan, Liuyan Zhu, Peilei Fan, Li Tian, and Raffaele Lafortezza. 2016. "Do Green Spaces Affect the Spatiotemporal Changes of $PM_{2.5}$ in Nanjing?" *Ecological Processes* 5 (1): 1–13.

Deng, Liantang, Jiong Shu, and Chaoyi Li. 2001. "Character Analysis of Shanghai Urban Heat Island." [In Chinese.] *Journal of Tropical Meteorology* 17 (3): 273–80.

Dooling, Sarah. 2009. "Ecological Gentrification: A Research Agenda Exploring Justice in the City." *International Journal of Urban and Regional Research* 33 (3): 621–39.

Fan, Peilei, Lihua Xu, Wenze Yue, and Chen, Jiquan. 2017. "Accessibility of Public Urban Green Space in an Urban Periphery: The Case of Shanghai." *Landscape and Urban Planning* 165 (September): 177–92.

Fujibe, Fumiaki. 2009. "Detection of Urban Warming in Recent Temperature Trends in Japan." *International Journal of Climatology: A Journal of the Royal Meteorological Society* 29 (12): 1811–22.

Gould, Kenneth A., and Tammy L. Lewis. 2012. "The Environmental Injustice of Green Gentrification: The Case of Brooklyn's Prospect Park." In *The World in Brooklyn: Gentrification, Immigration, and Ethnic Politics in a Global City*, edited by Judith N. DeSena and Timothy Shortell, 113–46. Lanham, MD: Lexington Books.

Guo, Song, Min Hu, Misti L. Zamora, Jianfei Peng, Dongjie Shang, Jing Zheng, Zhuofei Du, Zhijun Wu, Min Shao, Limin Zeng, Mario J. Molina, and Renyi Zhang. 2014. "Elucidating Severe Urban Haze Formation in China." *Proceedings of the National Academy of Sciences* 111 (49): 17373–78.

Hart, Melissa A., and David J. Sailor. 2009. "Quantifying the Influence of Land-Use and Surface Characteristics on Spatial Variability in the Urban Heat Island." *Theoretical and Applied Climatology* 95 (3): 397–406.

He, Jianjun, Sunling Gong, Ye Yu, Lijuan Yu, Lin Wu, Hongjun Mao, Congbo Song, Suping Zhao, Hongli Liu, Xiaoyu Li, and Ruipeng Li. 2017. "Air Pollution Characteristics and Their Relation to Meteorological Conditions During 2014–2015 in Major Chinese Cities." *Environmental Pollution* 223 (April): 484–96.

He, Kebin, Hong Huo, and Qiang Zhang. 2002. "Urban Air Pollution in China: Current Status, Characteristics, and Progress." *Annual Review of Energy and the Environment* 27 (1): 397–431.

Heaviside, Clare, Sotiris Vardoulakis, and Xiao-Ming Cai. 2016. "Attribution of Mortality to the Urban Heat Island During Heatwaves in the West Midlands, UK." *Environmental Health: A Global Access Science Source* 15 (43): S27.

Huang, Hong, Ryozo Ooka, and Shinsuke Kato. 2005. "Urban Thermal Environment Measurements and Numerical Simulation for an Actual Complex Urban Area Covering a Large District Heating and Cooling System in Summer." *Atmospheric Environment* 39 (34): 6362–75.

Huang, Ru-Jin, Yanlin Zhang, Carlo Bozzetti, Kin-Fai Ho, Jun-Ji Cao, and Yongming Han. 2014. "High Secondary Aerosol Contribution to Particulate Pollution During Haze Events in China." *Nature* 514 (7521): 218–35.

Imhoff, Marc L., Ping Zhang, Robert E. Wolfe, and Lahouari Bounoua. 2010. "Remote Sensing of the Urban Heat Island Effect Across Biomes in the Continental USA." *Remote Sensing of Environment* 114 (3): 504–13.

Inostroza, Luis. 2014. "Open Spaces and Urban Ecosystem Services: Cooling Effect Towards Urban Planning in South American Cities." In "Smart City: Planning for Energy, Transportation and Sustainability of the Urban System," special issue, *TeMA: Journal of Land Use, Mobility and Environment*, June, 523–34.

Kalnay, Eugenia, and Ming Cai. 2003. "Impact of Urbanization and Land-Use Change on Climate." *Nature* 423 (6939): 528–31.

Kan, Haidong, and Bingheng Chen. 2004. "Particulate Air Pollution in Urban Areas of Shanghai, China: Health-Based Economic Assessment." *Science of the Total Environment* 322 (1–3): 71–79.

Kato, Soushi, and Yasushi Yamaguchi. 2005. "Analysis of Urban Heat-Island Effect Using ASTER and ETM+ Data: Separation of Anthropogenic Heat Discharge and Natural Heat Radiation from Sensible Heat Flux." *Remote Sensing of Environment* 99 (1–2): 44–54.

Korsbakken, Jan Ivar, Robbie Andrew, and Glen Peters. 2019. "China's CO_2 Emissions Grew Slower Than Expected in 2018." Carbon Brief. 5 March. www.carbonbrief.org/guest-post-chinas-co2-emissions-grew-slower-than-expected-in-2018.

Lamsal, L. N., Randall V. Martin, A. van Donkelaar, Martin Steinbacher, E. A. Celarier, Eric Bucsela, Edward J. Dunlea, and Joseph P. Pinto. 2008. "Ground-Level Nitrogen Dioxide Concentrations Inferred from the Satellite-Borne Ozone Monitoring Instrument." *Journal of Geophysical Research: Atmospheres* 113 (D16): D16308.

Li, Guiying, and Qihao Weng. 2007. "Measuring the Quality of Life in City of Indianapolis by Integration of Remote Sensing and Census Data." *International Journal of Remote Sensing* 28 (2): 249–67.

Li, Juan-jua, Xiang-rong Wang, Xin-jun Wang, Wei-chun Ma, and Hao Zhang. 2009. "Remote Sensing Evaluation of Urban Heat Island and Its Spatial Pattern of the Shanghai Metropolitan Area, China." *Ecological Complexity* 6 (4): 413–20.

Li, Junxiang, Conghe Song, Lu Cao, Feige Zhu, Xianlei Meng, and Jianguo Wu. 2011. "Impacts of Landscape Structure on Surface Urban Heat Islands: A Case Study of Shanghai, China." *Remote Sensing of Environment* 115 (12): 3249–63.

Liu, Weidong, Xiaoyuan Jiang, Zuofang Zheng, Chongping Ji, and Zhaojun Zheng. 2007. "Temporal Characteristics of the Beijing Urban Heat Island." *Theoretical and Applied Climatology* 87 (1–4): 213–21.

Liu, Xiao-Huan, Yang Zhang, Shu-Hui Cheng, Jia Xing, Qiang Zhang, David G. Streets, Carey Jang, Wen-Xing Wang, and Ji-Ming Hao. 2010. "Understanding of Regional Air Pollution over China Using CMAQ, Part I: Performance Evaluation and Seasonal Variation." *Atmospheric Environment* 44 (20): 2415–26.

Liu, Zhu, and Bofeng Cai. 2018. "High-Resolution Carbon Emissions Data for Chinese Cities." Paper, Environment and Natural Resources Program, Belfer Center for Science and International Affairs, Harvard Kennedy School, August. www.belfercenter.org/sites/default /files/files/publication/Emissions%202018.pdf.

Lowe, Scott A. 2016. "An Energy and Mortality Impact Assessment of the Urban Heat Island in the US." *Environmental Impact Assessment Review* 56 (January): 139–44.

Mage, Davi, Guntis Ozolins, Peter Peterson, Anthony Webster, Rudi Orthofer, Veerle Vandeweerd, and Michael Gwynne. 1996. "Urban Air Pollution in Megacities of the World." *Atmospheric Environment* 30 (5): 681–86.

McGranahan, Gordon, Pedro Jacobi, Jacob Songsore, Charles Surjadi, and Marianne Kjellén. 2001. *The Citizens at Risk: From Urban Sanitation to Sustainable Cities*. London: Earthscan.

McGranahan, Gordon, and Frank Murray. 2012. *Air Pollution and Health in Rapidly Developing Countries*. London: Earthscan.

Ministry of Commerce. 2018. "E Commerce in China 2018 Report." Ministry of Commerce.

Ministry of Ecology and Environment (MEE). 2019. "Ambient Air Quality Standards." [In Chinese.] GB 3095–2012. http://kjs.mee.gov.cn/hjbhbz/bzwb/dqhjbh/dqhjzlbz/201203 /W020120410330232398521.pdf.

National Bureau of Statistics of China. 2018. *China Statistical Yearbook 2018*. Beijing: China Statistics Press.

Nel, André. 2005. "Air Pollution-Related Illness: Effects of Particles." *Science* 308 (5723): 804–6.

Nichol, Janet E. 1996. "High-Resolution Surface Temperature Patterns Related to Urban Morphology in a Tropical City: A Satellite-Based Study." *Journal of Applied Meteorology* 35 (1): 135–46.

Nickelsburg, Monica. 2020. "Amazon CEO Claims Grocery Delivery Cuts Carbon Emissions by 43% Compared to Traditional Shopping." GeekWire. 16 April. www.geekwire.com

/2020/amazon-ceo-claims-grocery-delivery-cuts-carbon-emissions-43-compared-traditional-shopping.

Pascal, Mathilde, Magali Corso, Olivier Chanel, Hristophe Declercq, Chiara Badaloni, Giulia Cesaroni, Susann Henschel, Kadri Meister, Daniela Haluza, Piedad Martin-Olmedo, and Sylvia Medina. 2013. "Assessing the Public Health Impacts of Urban Air Pollution in 25 European Cities: Results of the Aphekom Project." *Science of the Total Environment* 449 (April): 390–400.

Patrick, Darren J. 2011. "The Politics of Urban Sustainability: Preservation, Redevelopment, and Landscape on the High Line." Master's thesis, Central European University, Budapest.

Peng, Shushi, Shilong Piao, Philippe Ciais, Pierre Friedlingstein, Catherine Ottle, François-Marie Bréon, Huijuan Nan, Liming Zhou, and Ranga B. Myneni. 2012. "Surface Urban Heat Island Across 419 Global Big Cities." *Environmental Science and Technology* 46 (2): 696–703.

Rohde, Robert A., and Richard A. Muller. 2015. "Air Pollution in China: Mapping of Concentrations and Sources." *PLoS ONE* 10 (8): e0135749.

Romieu, Isabelle, and Mauricio Hernandez-Avila. 2012. "Air Pollution and Health in Developing Countries: A Review of Epidemiological Evidence." In *Air Pollution and Health in Rapidly Developing Countries*, edited by Gordon McGranahan and Frank Murray, 77–95. London: Earthscan.

Seaton, Anthony, David John Godden, William A. MacNee, and Kenneth Donaldson. 1995. "Particulate Air Pollution and Acute Health Effects." *Lancet* 345 (8943): 176–78.

Shih, Gerry. 2019. "Beijing Air Improves Significantly in Past Five Years, Study Finds." *Washington Post*, 12 September. www.washingtonpost.com/world/asia_pacific/beijing-air-improves-dramatically-in-last-five-years-study-finds/2019/09/12/1b64028e-d54d-11e9-ab26-e6dbebac45d3_story.html.

Song, Congbo, Lin Wua, Yaochen Xie, Jianjun He, Xi Chen, Ting Wang, Yingchao Lin, Taosheng Jin, Anxu Wang, Yan Liu, Qili Dai, Baoshuang Liu, Ya-nan Wang, and Hongjun Mao. 2017. "Air Pollution in China: Status and Spatiotemporal Variations." *Environmental Pollution* 227 (August): 334–47.

Stathopoulou, Marina, and Constantinos Cartalis. 2007. "Daytime Urban Heat Islands from Landsat ETM+ and Corine Land Cover Data: An Application to Major Cities in Greece." *Solar Energy* 81 (3): 358–68.

Stern, David I. 2004. "The Rise and Fall of the Environmental Kuznets Curve." *World Development* 32 (8): 1419–39.

Stone, Brian, Jr. 2007. "Urban and Rural Temperature Trends in Proximity to Large US Cities: 1951–2000." *International Journal of Climatology: A Journal of the Royal Meteorological Society* 27 (13): 1801–7.

Taylor, Jonathon, Paul Wilkinson, Mike Davies, Ben Armstrong, Zaid Chalabi, Anna Mavrogianni, Phil Symonds, Eleni Oikonomou, and Sylvia I. Bohnenstengel. 2015. "Mapping the Effects of Urban Heat Island, Housing, and Age on Excess Heat-Related Mortality in London." *Urban Climate* 14 (December): 517–28.

Trade on Carbon Emission (碳排放交易). 2017. "Season to Reflect on Shopping: Carbon Emission and Other Environmental Impacts of Online Shopping (购物反思季: 网购的碳排放及其他环境影响)." [In Chinese.] www.tanpaifang.com/ditanhuanbao/2017/1113/60843.html.

Tran, Hung, Daisuke Uchihama, Shiro Ochi, and Yoshifumi Yasuoka. 2006. "Assessment with Satellite Data of the Urban Heat Island Effects in Asian Mega Cities." *International Journal of Applied Earth Observation and Geoinformation* 8 (1): 34–48.

United Nations Statistics Division. 2015. "Millennium Development Goals Indicators." http://mdgs.un.org/unsd/mdg/SeriesDetail.aspx?srid=751.

Van Donkelaar, Aaron, Randall V. Martin, Michael Brauer, N. Christina Hsu, Ralph A. Kahn, Robert C. Levy, Alexei Lyapustin, Andrew M. Sayer, and David M. Winker. 2016. "Global Estimates of Fine Particulate Matter Using a Combined Geophysical-Statistical Method with Information from Satellites, Models, and Monitors." *Environmental Science and Technology* 50 (7): 3762–72.

Voice of America. 2016. "China Battles Worst Air Pollution of the Year." 21 December. https://learningenglish.voanews.com/a/china-battles-smog-as-worst-air-pollution-of-the-year-hits-beijing-and-other-cities/3645519.html.

Voogt, James, and Timothy Richard Oke. 1998. "Effects of Urban Surface Geometry on Remotely-Sensed Surface Temperature." *International Journal of Remote Sensing* 19 (5): 895–920.

———. 2003. "Thermal Remote Sensing of Urban Climates." *Remote Sensing of Environment* 86 (3): 370–84.

Wan, Zhengming. 2008. "New Refinements and Validation of the MODIS Land-Surface Temperature/Emissivity Products." *Remote Sensing of Environment* 112 (1): 59–74.

Wang, Jun, Xiaoguang Xu, Robert Spurr, Yuxuang Wang, and Easan Drury. 2010. "Improved Algorithm for MODIS Satellite Retrievals of Aerosol Optical Thickness over Land in Dusty Atmosphere: Implications for Air Quality Monitoring in China." *Remote Sensing of Environment* 114 (11): 2575–83.

Weng, Qihao. 2001. "A Remote Sensing? GIS Evaluation of Urban Expansion and Its Impact on Surface Temperature in the Zhujiang Delta, China." *International Journal of Remote Sensing* 22 (10): 1999–2014.

Weng, Qihao, Hua Liu, Bingqing Liang, and Dengsheng Lu. 2008. "The Spatial Variations of Urban Land Surface Temperatures: Pertinent Factors, Zoning Effect, and Seasonal Variability." *IEEE Journal of Selected Topics in Applied Earth Observations and Remote Sensing* 1 (2): 154–66.

Weng, Qihao, Dengsheng Lu, and Bingqing Liang. 2006. "Urban Surface Biophysical Descriptors and Land Surface Temperature Variations." *Photogrammetric Engineering and Remote Sensing* 72 (11): 1275–86.

Weng, Qihao, Dengsheng Lu, and Jacquelyn Schubring. 2004. "Estimation of Land Surface Temperature–Vegetation Abundance Relationship for Urban Heat Island Studies." *Remote Sensing of Environment* 89 (4): 467–83.

WHO (World Health Organization). 2018. "Global Health Observatory Data Repository: Deaths by Country." Last updated 6 July. http://apps.who.int/gho/data/node.main.BODAMBIENTAIRDTHS?lang=en.

———. 2019. "Air Quality Database: Update 2018." www.who.int/data/gho/data/themes/air-pollution/who-air-quality-database.

Wilson, Jeffrey S., Michaun Clay, Emily Martin, Denise Stuckey, and Kim Vedder-Risch. 2003. "Evaluating Environmental Influences of Zoning in Urban Ecosystems with Remote Sensing." *Remote Sensing of Environment* 86 (3): 303–21.

Wolch, Jennifer R., Jason Byrne, and Joshua P. Newell. 2014. "Urban Green Space, Public Health, and Environmental Justice: The Challenge of Making Cities 'Just Green Enough.'" *Landscape and Urban Planning* 125 (May): 234–44.

Xiao, Rongbo, Qihao Weng, Zhiyun Ouyang, Weifeng Li, Erich W. Schienke, and Zhaoming Zhang. 2008. "Land Surface Temperature Variation and Major Factors in Beijing, China." *American Society for Photogrammetry and Remote Sensing* 74 (4): 451–61.

Xinhua Net. 2018. "New Era: How to Manage Urban Villages." [In Chinese.] www.xinhuanet.com/2018-01/16/c_1122264973.htm.

Yang, Ping, Guoyu Ren, and Weidong Liu. 2013. "Spatial and Temporal Characteristics of Beijing Urban Heat Island Intensity. *Journal of Applied Meteorology and Climatology* 52 (8): 1803–16.

Yuan, Fei, and Marvin E. Bauer. 2007. "Comparison of Impervious Surface Area and Normalized Difference Vegetation Index as Indicators of Surface Urban Heat Island Effects in Landsat Imagery." *Remote Sensing of Environment* 106 (3): 375–86.

Yue, Wenze, Yong Liu, Peilei Fan, Xinyue Ye, and Cifang Wu. 2012. "Assessing Spatial Pattern of Urban Thermal Environment in Shanghai, China." *Stochastic Environmental Research and Risk Assessment* 26 (7): 899–911.

Zhang, Hao, Zhi-fang Qi, Xin-yue Ye, Yuan-bin Cai, Wei-chun Ma, and Ming-nan Chen. 2013. "Analysis of Land Use/Land Cover Change, Population Shift, and Their Effects on Spatiotemporal Patterns of Urban Heat Islands in Metropolitan Shanghai, China." *Applied Geography* 44 (October): 121–33.

Zhou, Decheng, Shuqing Zhao, Shuguang Liu, Liangxia Zhang, and Chao Zhu. 2014. "Surface Urban Heat Island in China's 32 Major Cities: Spatial Patterns and Drivers." *Remote Sensing of Environment* 152 (September): 51–61.

Zhou, Wei. 2015. "Environmental Impact Assessment of On-Line Shopping." Master's Thesis, Beijing University of Posts and Telecommunications.

CHAPTER 9

Shifting Exposures in China's Urbanization Experience: Implications for Health

Justin Remais

Introduction

Urbanization in low- and middle-income countries (LMICs) is frequently characterized as essential to future prosperity, even as it is accompanied by threats to health, the environment, and global sustainability, particularly when there is a failure to effectively plan for urban growth. China's cities exemplify the profound population impacts—both beneficial and adverse—of urban expansion and growth on health (Yang et al. 2018). Among the adverse health impacts of concern in rapidly growing cities are the transmission of infectious diseases facilitated by increased density and mobility of populations, such as tuberculosis and HIV; obesity and diabetes linked to sedentary urban lifestyles and greater access to fatty and sweetened processed foods in urban areas; cardiovascular and respiratory diseases associated with particulate and other air pollutants; and dengue, Zika, COVID-19, and other diseases that capitalize on disease vectors and high host-population densities in urban environments (Corburn and Riley 2016; Gong et al. 2012; Yang et al. 2018). For many of these health impacts, complex causal pathways have been delineated linking specific socio-environmental features of urbanization to health outcomes. As just one example, the rural-to-urban migration experience in China, as in many LMICs, has been accompanied by challenges maintaining traditional support networks among migrants, which decreases social capital and increases migrant susceptibility to stress, mental health concerns, and interpersonal violence in some settings (Corburn and Riley 2016).

At the same time, key health benefits can accrue to urban populations. For instance, cities are experiencing rapid increases in social influence and political-economic power while achieving stunning milestones with regard to infrastructure (Yang et al. 2018). There is evidence that in many instances, cities have outperformed rural areas in the provision of clean water, sanitation, public transit, health care, and other public services (Satterthwaite and Mitlin 2011; Yang et al. 2018), and are able to offer greater economic and educational opportunities, stronger protections of political and gender rights, and increased opportunity for cultural, political, and religious expression (Corburn and Riley 2016). Yet the balance of health gains and losses from urbanization have been found to vary substantially among cities even within the same country, as well as between districts within cities themselves, and the urban poor are known to disproportionately experience the burden of ill effects (Yang et al. 2018). In fact, some studies indicate that the urban poor can in fact suffer greater morbidity and mortality from a range of stressors than their rural counterparts, an indication of the significant risk and barriers to critical services in certain urban areas among the most vulnerable (African Population and Health Research Center 2014).

China has experienced an immense transformation of its cities and population, with urbanization proceeding at an unprecedented pace and decades of urban growth lying ahead. Thus, the health consequences of urbanization will define, in part, population health in the country for many years to come (Gong et al. 2012). A range of health-relevant exposures shift as towns and cities in China have further urbanized, and as populations have migrated from rural to urban areas. These include shifts in distal determinants of urban health, such as factors related to the political power, human and economic resources, and institutional structures necessary to enact and sustain health-protective policies and deliver health care (Yang et al. 2018). Proximal determinants of health have also shifted, including changes in factors related to the physical, social, and personal environments that affect health status, such as traffic and pollution, greenspace and open space, pathogens and antimicrobial resistance genes, and quality of and access to health care (Yang et al. 2018).

This chapter engages with two primary themes of this book, addressing questions surrounding key interactions between health and urbanization.

First, it empirically explores how the process of urbanization is shaping—and has been shaped by—the health of China's population, including the nature of evidence for urbanization-health relationships where definitions and methodologies are highly scrutinized and contested. Second, it examines the shifts and transitions emerging in urban China as they relate to health, focusing on key trends in health-relevant exposures associated with urbanization and examining the degree to which urban environments are leading to health deficits or gains. The chapter begins with a definition of urbanization, with a particular focus on the magnitude, demography, and geography of the changes in urban areas that relate to environmental exposures. The following sections highlight key shifting exposures and discuss possible mechanisms by which these changes are linked to changes in population health among residents of urban areas. Examples are used to illustrate how these mechanisms operate, including for air pollution and infectious diseases. Finally, the chapter concludes with a discussion of challenges in establishing causal links between urbanization trends and population health, and discusses research needs in this field.

Definitions and Dimensions of Urbanization's Impact on Health in China

Clearly there are no universal indicators or measures of the many phenomena that comprise urbanization and urban growth in China. The many dimensions of the country's urbanization experience all point to its overwhelming transformation from a largely agrarian to a largely urban society, yet epidemiologic analyses of attendant health impacts require well-specified, quantitative expressions of the time course, sequence, and intensity of these changes. Epidemiological analyses seeking to understand the determinants of health linked to urbanization often consider the concepts of urbanization rate, urban population, and urban growth, but these have been highly scrutinized and pose challenges for epidemiological analysis (Farrell and Westlund 2018; Gong et al. 2012).

Urbanization rate is recognized as a measure of the proportion of the population residing in urban areas as opposed to rural areas, whereas urban population and growth are measures of the number and rate of increase in urban inhabitants. Where the mechanisms by which urbanization influences health involve density-dependent processes (such as close contact) or socio-environmental phenomena (such as traffic accidents and injuries), these simple urbanization measures are clearly insufficient, as they neglect key dimensions that relate to the presence of urban features or urban character-istics (often termed "urbanicity"), the number and configuration of cities, the associated built areas and population densities, the morphological pro-cesses of urbanization, and the urban activities that give rise to environ-mental and social stressors, as well as the rates of change in these variables (Yang et al. 2018). There is as of yet no consensus on the suitability of partic-ular urbanization measures for epidemiologic analysis, even as there is wide-spread acknowledgment that each of these measures, and their trajectories, provide a starting point for capturing the scope and scale of urban develop-ment in China.

China has experienced rapid rural-to-urban migration: between 1978 and 2015 the rate of urbanization increased from 18 percent to 56 percent, a change that took nearly a century in Western countries (National Bureau of Statistics of China 2016; Yang et al. 2018). The urban population in China now stands at more than eight hundred million—up from under two hundred million in 1978—and is expected to exceed one billion by 2030 (National Bu-reau of Statistics of China 2016; Yang et al. 2018). Meanwhile, the areal reach of built landscapes in China has expanded to more than 50,000 square kilo-meters, from less than 10,000 square kilometers in 1978 (Ministry of Housing and Urban-Rural Development of China 2016; Yang et al. 2018). Accompanying these immense changes have been shifts in political, economic, and social sys-tems, as well as changes to the physical and natural environment, all of which have important consequences for health.

Urban Drinking Water Exposures Associated with Urbanization

As China's urban population increases at an unprecedented pace, major infrastructure initiatives necessary to sustain access to safe drinking water are straining to keep up. A mix of primary municipal and private drinking water plants supply drinking water to China's cities, and these are comple-mented by secondary sources such as water storage tanks, particularly at periods of peak consumption. While access to piped water had reached an estimated 94 percent of the urban population by 2007 (up from 48 percent in 1990 [National Bureau of Statistics of China 2010]), the microbiological and chemical safety of urban water supplies has been mixed, as indicated by the varying degree of compliance with drinking water quality standards across cities (Ministry of Environmental Protection 2017; Zhang 2007; SEPA 2006). Water scarcity has contributed significantly to poor drinking water quality, and changes in China's climate are expected to exacerbate these concerns (Hodges et al. 2014). While the urban water supply across China's cities has remained relatively constant, the number of users of these systems has soared (Browder et al. 2007), driving populations to rely on more contaminated sources. At the same time that water shortages are widespread—with two-thirds of cities facing shortages—water pollution is exacerbating shortages by limiting supplies suitable for drinking water treatment and use (Yang et al. 2018).

Efforts to limit urban water demand have been vigorously pursued through a mix of policies aimed at reducing industrial use (for example, by moving industrial enterprises out of cities) and dampening domestic use (for example, by instituting pricing schemes that encourage efficiency and conservation) (Browder et al. 2007). As a result, per capita domestic water use has risen only modestly despite rapid increases in urban incomes. But rising urban populations have meant that cities in China have had to rely heavily on the industrial retreat from the urban water market to stabilize supplies (Gong et al. 2012). Some cities have been forced to limit water consumption on certain days or at certain times and to switch to lower-quality supplies to meet demand in the face of supply shortages (Yang et al. 2018). Future growth in areas that are water scarce, as well as the encroachment of urban areas into rural areas with less-developed water systems, is expected to place increasing pressures on municipal suppliers in the years to come (Zhang et al. 2010; Gong et al. 2012).

Demand management, which has been a major focus of Chinese planners and policy makers, will not be a sufficient strategy as urbanization continues; improving urban health will require a major investment in water quality improvements at multiple levels. Surface and groundwater supplies serving urban populations exhibit widespread contamination with health-damaging pollutants, including heavy metals, petroleum hydrocarbons, pesticides, arsenic, disinfection by-products, and organic chemicals. Industrial sources are major contributors, and these traditional sources overlap with emerging contaminants of urban water systems, including pharmaceuticals, hormones, endocrine disruptors, and antibiotics (Peters et al. 2015; Gan et al. 2013; Yang 2016; Pal et al. 2014). The country's most recent action plan for water pollution control (Ministry of Environmental Protection 2015) calls for urgent measures to achieve compliance with strict water quality standards in major metropolitan areas that would allow safe use of supplies for drinking, fishing, and swimming (Yang et al. 2018). At present, however, tens of millions of people across hundreds of cities and towns are reliant on water supplies that do not meet health-protective drinking water standards (Zhu et al. 2010; Ministry of Environmental Protection 2017), and further investments in source protection, efficiency, and conservation will be essential to protecting public health in China's growing cities (Yang et al. 2018).

Urban Air Quality Exposures Associated with Urbanization

China's ambient air quality standards—first released in 1996 and updated in 2012—represent an ambitious commitment to public health, yet rapid urbanization of China's cities has made achievement of these standards very challenging (Yang et al. 2018; Gong et al. 2012; Jiang et al. 2017). Ambient air pollution is a major source of ill health in the country, leading to approximately 1.1 million premature deaths in 2015 alone (Cohen et al. 2017). Both short- and long-term exposures to air pollutants across urban centers in China are associated with increased total, cardiovascular, and respiratory mortality; adverse pregnancy outcomes; and other significant health effects (Shang et al. 2013; Jiang et al. 2017; Rich et al. 2015; Qian et al. 2016; Jacobs et al. 2017). In 2013, the State Council of China issued a major policy action—the Air Pollution Prevention and Control Action Plan—that targeted specific reductions in pollutant concentrations for 2017 (Huang et al. 2018). Even as considerable progress was made under this plan, the profound transformations of transportation and energy use in China's cities have slowed progress on ambient air pollution reductions, including for particulate matter, ozone, nitrogen oxides, and mixtures of these and other pollutants.

Vehicle emissions, in particular, constitute a major and growing source of air pollution in urban areas as the nation has embraced motorization (Jiang et al. 2017; Zhang et al. 2010; Yang et al. 2018). More than 27.5 million new automobiles were registered in the country in 2016 alone, and dozens of major metropolitan areas have surpassed one million registered vehicles

(Bureau of Transportation Management 2017). China's rapid societal motorization—reaching >36 per 100 households nationwide—largely occurred over just ten years, contributing a major new source of ambient air pollution and associated adverse health effects over a very short period of time (Bureau of Transportation Management 2017; Jiang et al. 2017). On-road vehicle emissions dominate the emission of air pollutants from the transportation sector in China's cities (Wu et al. 2016; Yang et al. 2018; Gong et al. 2012; Jiang et al. 2017). Passenger cars and motorcycles are the main contributors, particularly to carbon monoxide and volatile organic compound emissions, while heavy-duty diesel trucks are major contributors to nitrogen oxides and particulate matter (Lang et al. 2014; Gong et al. 2012; Jiang et al. 2017; Yang et al. 2018). Moreover, because air pollutants emitted in urban areas are transported to surrounding rural environments, the effect of China's rapid urbanization on health has not been limited to China's large cities (Zhang et al. 2010; Jiang et al. 2017).

A second major implication of China's urbanization for ambient air pollution has been shifts in energy use and associated emissions. The indoor burning of coal in urban areas continues despite attempts to reduce this highly polluting fuel (Zhang et al. 2010). Urban residents in most northern cities continue to rely on coal for heating (Cao, Ho, and Liang 2016), and even as the supply of electricity and liquefied petroleum gas is increasing (Huang et al. 2018), these cleaner energy sources can be unreliable in rapidly urbanizing areas (Zhang et al. 2010). It will be critical that the number of households relying on coal and other solid fuels be further reduced, and that systems supplying energy from cleaner fuels be stabilized. This may include increasing the availability of natural gas in particular, to ease the transition toward cleaner household fuels in urban areas (Cao, Ho, and Liang 2016).

It is clear that the nation's policy makers can act affirmatively to improve air quality and achieve population health benefits. An evaluation of the benefits that accrued between 2013 and 2017 from the Air Pollution Prevention and Control Action Plan found that more than 47,000 deaths and 710,000 lost life years were averted in the seventy-four major cities included in the study (Huang et al. 2018). Continued progress will only be achieved with ambitious changes to urban energy infrastructure, including further shifts from coal to natural gas or electricity, as well as promotion of alternative energy vehicles in urban areas (Huang et al. 2018).

Urban Infectious Disease Exposures Associated with Urbanization

A move from rural to urban life in China is accompanied by a substantial shift in the risk of infectious diseases. While China's rural populations remain at risk of traditional infectious diseases of poverty, including certain waterborne and soil-transmitted infections, its urban populations are at risk of infectious diseases associated with crowded, urban environments, such as certain respiratory infections. This can lead many rural-to-urban migrants to experience a dual infectious disease burden, harboring infections acquired in rural areas while being at risk of the communicable diseases they are exposed to in their new urban environment (Gong et al. 2012; Yang et al. 2018). As one example, the parasitic disease schistosomiasis is caused by parasites common in rural areas of southwestern and central China, which are home to more than half of the country's migrant workers (Carlton et al. 2012; Gong et al. 2012). While rural residents can readily obtain diagnosis and treatment, migrant workers often experience gaps in health-care access in their new urban homes, leading to unrecognized, untreated chronic infections (Gong et al. 2012). These same migrants often experience poor working and living conditions, which can put them at increased risk of tuberculosis and other infections prevalent in crowded urban environments (Gong et al. 2012).

Because China's urbanization experience has been accompanied by improved living environments, increased infrastructural investments, and a robust political commitment—especially post-SARS—to infectious disease control (Zhu et al. 2011; Yang et al. 2018), infectious disease incidence is generally dropping (Yang et al. 2018; Zhang et al. 2010). This is especially true for diseases caused by environmental pathogens or carried by environmental vectors in urban areas (Yang et al. 2018; Zhang et al. 2010). At the same time, however, mass movement of people, highly connected transit networks, inaccessibility of high-quality housing among the urban poor, and other features of China's rapidly growing cities are slowing progress toward infectious disease control (Li et al. 2012; Yang et al. 2018), and these factors will interact with and be compounded by changes to China's climate (Hodges et al. 2014).

One key example of the ways in which urbanization can influence the risk of infectious disease spread is the transmission of the respiratory disease known as COVID-19, which is caused by a novel coronavirus first detected in Wuhan, Hubei Province, in late 2019, leading to a major pandemic in the years following. The SARS-CoV-2 virus that causes COVID-19 is part of a large family of viruses that are carried by zoonotic hosts, including camels, bats, and cats. While animal coronaviruses rarely infect people, animal-to-human spillover does occur and is responsible for the previous outbreaks of SARS-CoV in 2003 and MERS-CoV in 2012, and is one leading hypothesis for the origins of SARS-CoV-2. One hypothesis is that SARS-CoV-2 originated in bats, and that the initial COVID-19 outbreak was linked to an initial animal-to-person spillover event in a live animal market in Wuhan. Even as the origins of SARS-CoV-2 remain unresolved, the intensification of animal agriculture operations to feed a growing demand for animal protein is leading to conditions that facilitate spillover events. Domesticated animals are increasingly raised and traded in close proximity to dense human populations, including through animal production facilities in peri-urban areas, with trade occurring at urban marketplaces with poor hygiene protocols and weak worker and public health protections (Lam et al. 2013). The presence of these facilities and conditions in urban areas raise the risk of the emergence of novel viruses with the potential for person-to-person spread.

At the same time, crowded urban environments and poor housing quality in rapidly growing cities can facilitate virus transmission. For one, high levels of person-to-person contact in crowded urban environments can intensify and sustain person-to-person pathogen spread in the community, and there is evidence that the SARS-CoV-2 virus spreads person-to-person through respiratory aerosols and droplets transmitted in close proximity. The massive effort required to quarantine—that is, reduce infectious contacts within—the population of Wuhan in early 2020 indicates the major challenges that crowded urban environments pose for infectious disease control. At the same time, poor housing can amplify disease spread, allowing for aerosolized virus particles to spread between building floors and residents. As just one example, SARS-CoV was believed to be spread through faulty plumbing in a building in Hong Kong in 2003. Meanwhile, the urban poor are at high risk of inhabiting poor housing, increasing their susceptibility to the spread of infectious diseases. Migrants must often rely on housing that provides little protection from pathogens and vectors, including dilapidated private housing, worker housing on construction sites, and illegal basements (Huang and Yi 2015; Yang et al. 2018).

Finally, the massive expansion of modern urban transportation systems can contribute to the speed and scale of infectious disease spread (Yang et al. 2018; Gong et al. 2012). The role of aviation and rail networks in connecting distant populations in China can complicate disease control efforts (Gong et al. 2012; Yang et al. 2018). In fact, there is evidence that air travel within China was responsible for the distant, domestic spread of SARS-CoV to Beijing in March 2003 (Mangili and Gendreau 2005; Yang et al. 2018), while ground transport further propagated the virus (Fang et al. 2009; Yang et al. 2018). Meanwhile, both business and tourist air travel was implicated in the early international spread of COVID-19 in 2020, and the impact of travel restrictions as a means of control is sharply limited by the extent and scale of international transport networks (Chinazzi et al. 2020).

China has worked to address gaps in policy, infrastructure, and services in order to limit the spread of infectious diseases as the country has rapidly urbanized. The SARS-CoV outbreak in 2003 was an important turning point, leading to a major investment in health information systems to prevent and control disease spread (Liang et al. 2014; Yang et al. 2018; Zhang et al. 2010). Key cities have established community health service centers in urban areas to provide basic services to migrants, including post-birth immunization, but their use by migrant workers has been mixed (Lin et al. 2007; Qin, Li, and Qin 2007; Yang et al. 2018). And even as policy makers have sought to close poorly regulated live animal markets, their cultural and economic significance has led to their continued presence—and even expansion by municipal governments—in China's urban centers. Addressing these challenges will be critical for improving urban health in the country, and it is particularly urgent that those who make China's health policy extend infectious disease prevention and control to fully reach China's urban populations. Doing so would close key gaps in care and disparities in health that persist, particularly between China's migrant and non-migrant urban populations.

Developmental Progress and Delay in Health as Consequence of Urbanization

China has made tremendous progress reducing the disease burden from a range of sequelae, including those associated with waterborne diseases, childhood infections, and accidents and injuries. Yet continued pressures of rapid, unplanned urbanization pose a risk of potentially slowing or even reversing some of the gains in population health that the country has achieved. This possibility necessitates counterfactual analyses in which the health and other societal outcomes associated with urbanization are subjected to comparison with the outcomes that would have been achieved had China provided greater protective measures, enforced regulations, and ensured that equity governed its urbanization experience. Such analyses can reveal the conditions under which the deceleration or reversal of health gains can be avoided or minimized, acknowledging, however, that the approach tends to rely on extrapolations of health and development trajectories based on limited theories of epidemiological and environmental risk transitions (Smith and Ezzati 2005).

One way in which the impact of urbanization can be conceptualized and expressed is as a development delay, defined as the length of time required for a country to reduce disease burden in a rapid, unplanned urbanization scenario to the level projected in a measured, planned urbanization scenario. The development delay can be interpreted as the additional years of continued investment in infrastructure and human resources required in the presence of unplanned urbanization to achieve the disease burden anticipated were urbanization undertaken with greater planning and protective measures (Figure 9.1). While the development delays induced by climate change have been investigated with respect to the impact of climate on water, sanitation, and hygiene-related diseases (Hodges et al. 2014), research is urgently needed to estimate how unplanned urbanization is expected to induce development delays in China's progress toward achieving population health, and how they can be avoided or minimized. It is cautioned, however, that such efforts should involve expansion of the approach to address key features of China's urbanization experience presently absent from the framework, including aspects that exhibit marked dynamism, sharp state changes, and key multiscale and cross-boundary characteristics (Remais and Jackson 2015).

Conclusion

There are major challenges for estimating the causal effects of urbanization on health in China, including a lack of consensus surrounding key health-relevant exposures, limited rigor in defining these exposures in the context

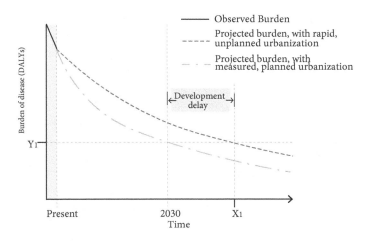

Figure 9.1. Conceptual diagram of the development delay attributable to unplanned urbanization in 2030. As the burden of disease falls in a given setting, the development delay associated with unplanned urbanization at 2030 is the time beyond 2030 (that is, X_1—2030) required to achieve the burden of disease projected for 2030 in a scenario of planned urbanization with protective measures. More generally, the development delay for a given year is calculated as the time that will pass before the burden of disease under an unplanned urbanization scenario will equal the burden of disease projected for that year in a measured, planned urbanization scenario. Source: Adapted from Hodges et al. 2014.

of urban development or urbanization processes, and limited attention paid to heterogeneity in health outcomes across diverse urban populations. Future investigations on urbanization and health should examine both proximal (for example, densification or growth of the urban extent) and distal (for example, governance factors operating at and above the city scale) determinants of health and should prioritize rigorous measurement or modeling of the morphological processes of urbanization (Batty 2008; Herold, Goldstein, and Clarke 2003). Heterogeneity in health-relevant exposures should be emphasized, including those induced by various dimensions of urbanization and urbanicity, such as rural-urban migration, endogenous population growth, densification, and increased urban complexity.

Unquestionably, cities in China have made remarkable progress, improving living conditions and investing in widespread infrastructure and services. These include improvements in drinking water and clean energy supplies, sewage and wastewater treatment, health-care quality and access, and conversion of poor-quality housing to modern high-rise residential blocks (Wong 2015; Yang et al. 2018; Gong et al. 2012). With these changes have come important health gains, including reductions in certain infectious diseases and recent progress reducing the burden of disease attributable to ambient air pollution. These gains should be subjected to counterfactual analyses, in which the health outcomes associated with urbanization are compared with the outcomes that would have been achieved had urbanization been undertaken with greater protective measures, regulation, and equity. Further progress improving population health in China will require passing and enforcing strict health protective regulations, governance models that reduce reliance on centralized authoritarian leadership and increase opportunities for multilevel policy coordination and implementation, increased investment in protective infrastructure, and expanded commitments to reducing health disparities in urban environments.

The current unprecedented pace of urbanization in China presents unique opportunities for improved health through increased access to health services, strengthening of social networks and relationships, improved infrastructure, and increased economies of scale and market access. In certain key determinants of urban ill health, China has made sufficient progress so as to exceed the average global rate of improvement with development. That is, the country has achieved greater progress than its social development position would suggest when compared to other low- and middle-income countries. This is an important means of evaluating progress in health as China's urbanization experience continues, establishing whether China's populations are achieving health before they achieve wealth. There are key areas where China's progress has outpaced the global population; for instance, compared with the global pattern of how injury rates fell with sociodemographic development in the period 1990–2017, provinces in China have shown faster decline in injury rates—including road injuries—as their development has increased (Duan et al. 2019). With respect to the health of migrants, the risks associated with air and water pollution, and the challenges of emerging infectious diseases, achieving progress greater than the global average will require not only a major recommitment to population health but the necessary policies, investments, and political dedication to achieve them (Duan et al. 2019).

Acknowledgments

The author acknowledges support from the University of California Multicampus Research Programs and Initiatives (MRP award # 17-446315), the National Science Foundation (grant no. 2032210), and the National Institute of Allergy and Infectious Diseases (NIAID awards R01AI125842 and R01AI148336).

References

African Population and Health Research Center. 2014. *Population and Health Dynamics in Nairobi's Informal Settlements: Report of the Nairobi Cross-Sectional Slums Survey (NCSS) 2012*. Nairobi: APHRC.

Batty, Michael. 2008. "The Size, Scale, and Shape of Cities." *Science* 319 (5864): 769–71.

Browder, Greg J., Shiqing Xie, Yoonhee Kim, Lixin Gu, Mingyuan Fan, and David Ehrhardt. 2007. *Stepping Up: Improving the Performance of China's Urban Water Utilities*. Washington DC: World Bank.

Bureau of Transportation Management. 2017. "Rapid Increase in Motor Vehicles and Drivers in 2016." Ministry of Public Safety. Accessed 10 March. www.mps.gov.cn/n2255040 /n4908728/c5595634/content.html.

Cao, Jing, Mun S. Ho, and Huifang Liang. 2016. "Household Energy Demand in Urban China: Accounting for Regional Prices and Rapid Income Change." In "China," special issue, *Energy Journal* 37:87–110.

Carlton, Elizabeth J., Song Liang, Julia Z. McDowell, Huazhong Li, Wei Luo, and Justin V. Remais. 2012. "Regional Disparities in the Burden of Disease Attributable to Unsafe Water and Poor Sanitation in China." *Bulletin of the World Health Organization* 90 (8): 578–87.

Chinazzi, Matteo, Jessica T. Davis, Marco Ajelli, Corrado Gioannini, Maria Litvinova, Stefano Merler, Ana Pastore y Piontti, et al. 2020. "The Effect of Travel Restrictions on the Spread of the 2019 Novel Coronavirus (COVID-19) Outbreak." *Science* 368 (6489): 395–400.

Cohen, Aron J., Michael Brauer, Richard Burnett, H. Ross Anderson, Joseph Frostad, Kara Estep, Kalpana Balakrishnan, et al. 2017. "Estimates and 25-Year Trends of the Global Burden of Disease Attributable to Ambient Air Pollution: An Analysis of Data from the Global Burden of Diseases Study 2015." *Lancet* 389 (10082): 1907–18.

Corburn, Jason, and Lee W. Riley. 2016. *Slum Health: From the Cell to the Street*. Oakland, California: University of California Press.

Duan, Leilei, Pengpeng Ye, Juanita A. Haagsma, Jin Ye, Wang Yuan, Er Yuliang, Deng Xiao, et al. 2019. "The Burden of Injury in China, 1990–2017: Findings from the Global Burden of Disease Study 2017." *Lancet Public Health* 4 (9): e449–e461.

Fang, Li-Qun, Sake J. De Vlas, Dan Feng, Song Liang, You-Fu Xu, Jie-Ping Zhou, Jan Hendrik Richardus, and Wu-Chun Cao. 2009. "Geographical Spread of SARS in Mainland China." Supplement, *Tropical Medicine and International Health* 14 (Suppl. 1): 14–20.

Farrell, Kyle, and Hans Westlund. 2018. "China's Rapid Urban Ascent: An Examination into the Components of Urban Growth." *Asian Geographer* 35 (1): 85–106.

Gan, Wenhui, Wanhong Guo, Jianming Mo, Yisen He, Yongjian Liu, Wei Liu, Yongmei Liang, and Xin Yang. 2013. "The Occurrence of Disinfection By-products in Municipal Drinking Water in China's Pearl River Delta and a Multipathway Cancer Risk Assessment." *Science of the Total Environment* 447 (March): 108–15.

Gong, Peng, Song Liang, Elizabeth J. Carlton, Qingwu Jiang, Jianyong Wu, Lei Wang, and Justin V. Remais. 2012. "Urbanisation and Health in China." *Lancet* 379 (9818): 843–52.

Herold, Martin, Noah C. Goldstein, and Keith C. Clarke. 2003. "The Spatiotemporal Form of Urban Growth: Measurement, Analysis and Modeling." *Remote Sensing of Environment* 86 (3): 286–302.

Hodges, Maggie, Jessica H. Belle, Elizabeth J. Carlton, Song Liang, Huazhong Li, Wei Luo, Matthew C. Freeman, et al. 2014. "Delays Reducing Waterborne and Water-Related Infectious Diseases in China Under Climate Change." *Nature Climate Change* 4 (12): 1109–15.

Huang, Jing, Xiaochuan Pan, Xinbiao Guo, and Guoxing Li. 2018. "Health Impact of China's Air Pollution Prevention and Control Action Plan: An Analysis of National Air Quality Monitoring and Mortality Data." *Lancet Planet Health* 2 (7): e313–e323.

Huang, Youqin, and Chengdong Yi. 2015. "Invisible Migrant Enclaves in Chinese Cities: Underground Living in Beijing, China." *Urban Studies* 52 (15): 2948–73.

Jacobs, Milena, Guicheng Zhang, Shu Chen, Ben Mullins, Michelle Bell, Lan Jin, Yuming Guo, Rachel Huxley, and Gavin Pereira. 2017. "The Association Between Ambient Air Pollution and Selected Adverse Pregnancy Outcomes in China: A Systematic Review." *Science of the Total Environment* 579 (February): 1179–92.

Jiang, Baoguo, Song Liang, Zhong-Ren Peng, Haozhe Cong, Morgan Levy, Qu Cheng, Tianbing Wang, and Justin V. Remais. 2017. "Transport and Public Health in China: The Road to A Healthy Future." *Lancet* 390 (10104): 1781–91.

Lam, Hon-Ming, Justin Remais, Ming-Chiu Fung, Liqing Xu, and Samuel Sai-Ming Sun. 2013. "Food Supply and Food Safety Issues in China." *Lancet* 381 (9882): 2044–53.

Lang, Jianlei, Shuiyuan Cheng, Ying Zhou, Yonglin Zhang, and Gang Wang. 2014. "Air Pollutant Emissions from On-Road Vehicles in China, 1999–2011." *Science of the Total Environment* 496 (October): 1–10.

Li, Xin-Hu, Ji-Lai Liu, Valerie Gibson, and Yong-Guan Zhu. 2012. "Urban Sustainability and Human Health in China, East Asia and Southeast Asia." *Current Opinion in Environmental Sustainability* 4 (4): 436–42.

Liang, Song, Changhong Yang, Bo Zhong, Jiagang Guo, Huazhong Li, Elizabeth J. Carlton, Matthew C. Freeman, and Justin V. Remais. 2014. "Surveillance Systems for Neglected Tropical Diseases: Global Lessons from China's Evolving Schistosomiasis Reporting Systems, 1949–2014." *Emerging Themes in Epidemiology* 11 (1): 19–33.

Lin, Yong-Jie, Ren-Yu Lei, Yao-Xing Luo, Xin Xie, Chen-Gang Wu, Xiao-Ping Shao, Jun Shu, and Ji-Kai Zhang. 2007. "Analysis of Immunization Coverage Rate and Its Influencing Factor of Floating Children in Zhujiang Delta River Area of Guangdong Province." *Chinese Journal of Vaccine and Immunization* (6): 87–90.

Mangili, Alexandra, and Mark A. Gendreau. 2005. "Transmission of Infectious Diseases During Commercial Air Travel." *Lancet* 365 (9463): 989–96.

Ministry of Environmental Protection. 2015. *Action Plan for Water Pollution Control.* Beijing: State Council of China.

———. 2017. *2016 Report on the State of the Environment in China.* Beijing: Ministry of Environmental Protection of China.

Ministry of Housing and Urban-Rural Development of China. 2016. *2015 Report on the Statistics of Urban and Rural Development.* Beijing: Ministry of Housing and Urban-Rural Development.

National Bureau of Statistics of China. 2010. *China Statistical Yearbook 2010*. Beijing: China Statistics Press.

———. 2016. "Census Data." Accessed 22 May. www.stats.gov.cn/tjsj/pcsj/.

Pal, Amrita, Yiliang He, Martin Jekel, Martin Reinhard, and Karina Yew-Hoong Gin. 2014. "Emerging Contaminants of Public Health Significance as Water Quality Indicator Compounds in the Urban Water Cycle." *Environment International* 71 (October): 46–62.

Peters, Marc, Qingjun Guo, Harald Strauss, and Guangxu Zhu. 2015. "Geochemical and Multiple Stable Isotope (N, O, S) Investigation on Tap and Bottled Water from Beijing, China." *Journal of Geochemical Exploration* 157 (October): 36–51.

Qian, Zhengmin, Shengwen Liang, Shaoping Yang, Edwin Trevathan, Zhen Huang, Rong Yang, Jing Wang, et al. 2016. "Ambient Air Pollution and Preterm Birth: A Prospective Birth Cohort Study in Wuhan, China." *International Journal of Hygiene and Environmental Health* 219 (2): 195–203.

Qin, Xiong-Lin, Jian-Long Li, and Cun-Wei Qin. 2007. "Immunization of Floating Children in Clustered Areas of Migrant Workers and the Influencing Factors." *Journal of Applied Preventive Medicine* (3): 31–32.

Remais, Justin V., and Richard Jackson. 2015. "Determinants of Health: Overview." In *Oxford Textbook of Global Public Health*, 6th ed., edited by Roger Detels, Martin Gulliford, Quarraisha Abdool Karim, and Chorh Chuan Tan, 81–88. Oxford, United Kingdom: Oxford University Press.

Rich, David Q., Kaibo Liu, Jinliang Zhang, Sally W. Thurston, Timothy P. Stevens, Ying Pan, Cathleen Kane, et al. 2015. "Differences in Birth Weight Associated with the 2008 Beijing Olympics Air Pollution Reduction: Results from a Natural Experiment." *Environmental Health Perspectives* 123 (9): 880–87.

Satterthwaite, David, and Diana Mitlin. 2011. "Recognising the Potential of Cities." *BMJ (Online)* 343 (7837): 1762–63.

SEPA (State Environmental Protection Administration). 2006. *State of the Environment Report*. Beijing: State Environmental Protection Administration.

Shang, Yu, Zhiwei Sun, Junji Cao, Xinming Wang, Liuju Zhong, Xinhui Bi, Hong Li, Wenxin Liu, Tong Zhu, and Wei Huang. 2013. "Systematic Review of Chinese Studies of Short-Term Exposure to Air Pollution and Daily Mortality." *Environment International* 54 (April): 100–111.

Smith, Kirk R., and Majid Ezzati. 2005. "How Environmental Health Risks Change with Development: The Epidemiologic and Environmental Risk Transitions Revisited." *Annual Review of Environment and Resources* 30 (July): 291–333.

Wong, Tai-Chee. 2015. "Developmental Idealism: Building Cities Without Slums in China." In *Population Mobility, Urban Planning and Management in China*, edited by Tai-Chee Wong, Sun Sheng Han, and Hongmei Zhang, 17–34. Switzerland: Springer.

Wu, Xiaomeng, Ye Wu, Shaojun Zhang, Huan Liu, Lixin Fu, and Jiming Hao. 2016. "Assessment of Vehicle Emission Programs in China During 1998–2013: Achievement, Challenges and Implications." *Environmental Pollution* 214 (July): 556–67.

Yang, Jun, José G. Siri, Justin V. Remais, Qu Cheng, Han Zhang, Karen K. Y. Chan, Zhe Sun, et al. 2018. "The Tsinghua-Lancet Commission on Healthy Cities in China: Unlocking the Power of Cities for A Healthy China." *Lancet* 391 (10135): 2140–84.

Yang, Junfeng. 2016. "Heterogeneity Analysis of the Relationship Between Economic Growth and Water Environmental Pollution in Beijing, Tianjin and Zhengzhou of China." *Nature Environment and Pollution Technology* 15 (1): 51–58.

Zhang, Junfeng, Denise L. Mauzerall, Tong Zhu, Song Liang, Majid Ezzati, and Justin V. Remais. 2010. "Environmental Health in China: Progress Towards Clean Air and Safe Water." *Lancet* 375 (9720): 1110–19.

Zhang, Lan. 2007. "Investigation on Drinking Water Safety in China in 2006." *Journal of Environmental Health* 24 (8): 595–97.

Zhu, Dangsheng, Jianyong Zhang, Xiaoxin Shi, and Zhuoying Liu. 2010. "Security Assessment of Urban Drinking Water Sources, II: Security Assessment for Cities in China." *Journal of Hydraulic Engineering* 41 (8): 914–20.

Zhu, Yong-Guan, John P. A. Ioannidis, Hong Li, Kevin C. Jones, and Francis L. Martin. 2011. "Understanding and Harnessing the Health Effects of Rapid Urbanization in China." *Environmental Science and Technology* 45 (12): 5099–104.

CHAPTER 10

Prospects and Social Impact of Big Data–Driven Urban Governance in China: Provincializing Smart City Research

Alan Smart and Dean Curran

We do not need to chase [after other countries]—we are the road.

—Xi Jinping, 2018

Introduction

Smart city projects have become a key focus of contemporary planning for the future of cities. This trend applies strongly to China, in some ways even more so than in North America and Europe. This chapter argues that China is at the cutting edge of smart city developments. The developing lead in smart urbanism (taken here as urban governance based on the collection and analysis of big data supported by artificial intelligence [AI]) is a new phenomenon for Chinese urban planning. Before, urban planning tended to follow, or adapt, trends from elsewhere, first from the Soviet Union and later from the West and Asian market economies like Singapore. While smart city ideas originated in the West, rapid development of AI platforms such as Alibaba's City Brain makes it likely that core technologies for smart urbanism will come from China (Lee 2018). Increasing restrictions on facial recognition in the West provide policy advantages for Chinese technology, if not for Chinese citizens. These developments indicate the need to "provincialize" smart city research, rather than continue with the assumptions of main-stream urban studies that the Global South either follows the paths set by the West or falls further behind. For data-driven urban governance, there is a new probability that China will be setting the path, making efforts in Western countries seem comparatively lacking in ambition and provincial. This probability, however, is predicated on the assumption that American attempts to counter Chinese technical advantages do not succeed in under-mining developments in Chinese AI and other core technologies for data-based governance.

China's influence on the nature of future urbanism is partly due to the sheer extent of contemporary Chinese urbanization, one aspect of the first main theme of this volume. Over six hundred million people have moved from rural areas to China's cities since 1980. Between 2000 and 2020, China's urban population increased from 670 million to 902 million (63.9 percent of the total population). Policy changes pushed real estate's share of GDP from about 5 percent in 2004 to 15 percent in 2014 (Chien and Woodworth 2018). Urbanization has been encouraged in the last three five-year plans. The massive extent of new urban habitats required for this urban transition allows rapid deployment of new smart technologies on a remarkable scale. Social fixed investments increased by 30.1 percent in 2009 in response to the global financial crisis, which China avoided through capital and other controls. This investment "led to the rapid development of infrastructure" (Wu et al. 2018, 63). Infrastructural spending facilitated the development of information and communication technologies and other precursors of smart city approaches, such as digital cities. This infrastructure spending is now being sustained by the economic impact and public health needs of the COVID-19 pandemic. China's emerging impact on future cities is also facilitated by regulatory practices that make big data analysis much more accessible to corporations for training AI.

Smart cities have become an important element of the Chinese policy agenda as a pathway to future urbanism and a way to provide solutions to various governance challenges. In 2012, the Ministry of Housing and Urban-Rural Development released the Notice on Carrying Out the National Pilot on Smart Cities. Subsequently, it issued Interim Measures for the Administration of National Smart Cities and the Pilot Index System for National Smart Cities. The 2014–2020 National New-Type Urbanization Plan promoted smart city development, emphasizing not only technology and administration but also a "meticulous social government" (Tan-Mullins et al.

2017, 2). These national programs encouraged municipal governments to apply for pilot Smart City projects. By 2015, there were 311 Chinese cities implementing smart city plans (Shi et al. 2018). Of an estimated one thousand smart city projects globally, half of them were Chinese by 2016; by 2019, over seven hundred Chinese cities proposed or claimed projects (Hu 2019). The Chinese smart city project was initially partially financed by a $16 billion infrastructure investment loan from the Asian Development Bank. By 2019, the value of Chinese smart city construction was estimated at RMB 10.5 billion, projected to reach RMB 25 billion by 2022 (Hu 2019). But these estimates count only those projects included in explicit smart city projects, omitting large investment in other forms of data-driven urban governance. In 2017, the smart city agenda was designated key to China's Belt and Road Initiative (*yidai yilu* 一带一路), which aims to build a digital infrastructure network connecting all so-called Belt and Road cities with big data, the Digital Silk Road.

Rapid expansion of smart cities has much to do with the powerful party-state regime and the centralized personnel management system in which the careers and motivations of city leaders are situated. This system requires, at minimum, compliance with state priorities and targets such as smart city plans, and rewards innovative (but politically acceptable) approaches to meeting those targets (Guo 2019). Party-state personnel reviews and growth targets create a strong impetus for rapid growth on all scales, from neighborhood to nation. Therefore, decisions by the central government to promote smart cities (and other forms of digital administration of urban areas) generate rapid creation and, sometimes, implementation of smart city plans. While explicit smart city plans are impressive in their number and apparent impact on Chinese cities, they are only part of the story of how big data is used in urban planning and management.

Despite these trends, most smart city research published in major urban journals pays little or no attention to developments in China (Browne 2020). As argued in the next section, this results in part from a continuing Eurocentric bias within urban studies, so that we need to provincialize smart city research, drawing on Dipesh Chakrabarty's celebrated work on provincializing Europe. China may be taking the lead in collecting, analyzing, and using big data to develop AI-based urban management systems that are being deployed at an unprecedented scale and extent, particularly in the form of Alibaba's City Brain. We examine these processes in the third section of the chapter.

Following that, we focus on what Chakrabarty might describe as the "History 2" (pasts opposed, though contemporaneous to, universal human history) of smart urbanism: urban informality, widely seen as the past and the opposite of "smart" despite its documented contributions to improving urban livelihoods (Breslow 2021). We examine informality as a lens on smart urbanism that helps reveal the neglect, perhaps even disdain, for ordinary people in most smart city plans. There are immense dangers in elitist plans that threaten not only social justice but also the everyday living strategies of many if not most of the population of the world's cities. Implicit in China's projected smart urban futures is an instrumentalist lens that sees certain places and people as parts of the past, to be excluded from shining futures: particularly informal urban villages, street-based commerce, and unskilled migrants.

This chapter offers contributions to the themes emphasized in this volume. First, it stresses interaction between urbanization and new technologies of governance. The scale of growth of the urban population both calls for and enables new management technologies based on the collection, analysis, and dissemination of big data, particularly given the infrastructure emphasis of the central government and its desire to selectively surpass the West in science and technology (Greenhalgh and Li 2020). These developments call out for more attention to Chinese developments in currently Eurocentric smart city research. Second, although this chapter was completed too early to include discussion of it, the heavy use of smart technologies—such as facial recognition and tracking with smartphones—in the response to COVID-19 illustrates an emerging trend in urban China toward new forms of governance of biosecurity risks. Third, by going beyond explicit smart city plans to include the broader universe of data-driven urban governance, we incorporate a variety of issues and processes that are less likely to be included in accounts of urban China.

Using Chinese Accomplishments to Provincialize and Re-Orient Smart City Research

The rapid growth of smart cities in China offers an excellent illustration of the importance of provincializing smart city research. As Chakrabarty (1992) argues, provincializing the West requires challenging explicit or implicit teleological thinking that assumes that the European present represents the future for the rest of the world, or at least it does so unless the rest fail to develop appropriately. Urban studies have been badly in need of this theoretical correction, since they have taken Western cities as the fount of urban change, with cities of the Global South relegated to parochial regional specialists whose work was thought to offer little to the cutting edge of urban theory (Robinson 2013; Datta 2018). There has been what has been described as a "Southern turn" in urban studies, attempting to correct the Eurocentric predominance of Western cities in the field (Rao 2006) and focusing particularly on informality (McFarlane and Söderström 2017), but its influence is still limited in actual practice.

The dangers of Eurocentric urbanism are clearly revealed in smart city projects. China is no longer lagging behind the West in developing cutting-edge technologies for data-driven governance and is often further ahead in actually deploying them for urban management, such as with COVID-19. Provincializing smart city research and moving beyond the still-dominant influence of Eurocentrism in mainstream urban studies shows those of us in the Global North our possible futures (Curran and Smart 2021) in a reversal of the ways that colonial and postcolonial cities have more commonly been shown their paths to their futures by the presents of their colonizers. In both situations, there is a prospect of learning before launching into mimetic duplication of others' mistakes.

There is a tendency within Western smart city research to either ignore Chinese smart city initiatives or see them as derivative of Western innovations, adding perhaps some local "color" to mainstream initiatives. This tendency is partly a result of limiting the scope of analysis to formal smart city plans rather than extending the analysis to the broader but related scope of urban governance using big data to monitor, analyze, and influence everyday activities. The centrality of surveillance using biometric ID and cutting-edge facial and gait recognition, for example, is becoming particularly apparent in the management of the COVID-19 pandemic. The role of technology in effective management has reached the point that the *Economist* (2020) has referred to the "coronopticon," referencing Foucault's panopticon. The weakness of China's limits on data privacy facilitate implementation of such tracking and controls in ways that might not be feasible (yet?) in the West and that generate massive data that is used to train rapidly improving AI.

Explicit smart city plans generally omit other projects that link closely to a core meaning of smart cities: collection of vast amounts of data about urban activities, such as commuting through high-tech sensors, and urban governance driven by such big data. Smart urbanism and data-driven (urban) governance involve three key aspects that differentiate them, at least discursively, from previous forms of governance: the collection of big data, the use of proprietary algorithms to analyze the data, and the real-time use of data to manage the urban environment (Kitchin 2014; Tang 2015). The result is a distinct configuration of actually existing smart cities, as opposed to those only virtually existent in unimplemented official plans. While this disjunction between plan and reality may result in empty stage sets or Potemkin villages (*xingxiang gongcheng*, "image projects" [Steinmüller 2013, 199]), under Chinese conditions it can also lead to smartification that goes more rapidly and in directions that those attuned only to official strategies may not be inclined to look.

Shelton, Zook, and Wiig argue that research should be focused on "actually existing smart cities" (2015). Critiques of smart cities tend to see the smart city as a "universal, rational and depoliticised project that largely plays out according to the terms of profit-maximising, multinational technology companies" (Shelton, Zook, and Wiig 2015, 14). They argue instead that the smart city interventions that exist do not look like this, nor like the iconic cases of Masdar (United Arab Emirates) or Songdo (South Korea), which have largely failed to materialize in the ways projected. As a result, they champion moving away from focusing on "new cities built from scratch in such peripheral locales . . . to examine how the smart city paradigm is becoming grounded in particular places, especially in the more mature cities and economies of the global north" (14). They assert that greenfield smart cities are the exception rather than the rule.

We agree with two aspects of their challenge: the need to pay more attention to the "ways that an increasing attention to data is affecting the tangible outcomes of urban governance," and the desirability of grounding the critique of smart cities in the "historical and geographical context from which these ideas have arisen, connecting the ways these problems are conceived to the material effects of data-driven policy initiatives" (Shelton, Zook, and Wiig 2015, 14). However, we disagree strongly with the claim that such a research program should focus on cities of the Global North and dismiss greenfield site projects. Both of these claims are Eurocentric, as is the vast majority of smart city publications in major journals. Developments in China generally receive little attention other than in papers specifically focusing on China. Political considerations are resulting in a more rapid and consequential rollout of data-driven urban governance in India (Datta 2018),

Singapore (Ho 2016), and particularly China. While many greenfield smart city projects have stalled or never moved much beyond paper or glossy video (Watson 2013; Datta 2015), the rapid growth of cities in the Global South means that there are immense opportunities for building smart city projects in the urban fringes, and that this allows bypassing the immense challenges of redeveloping the messy and largely informal landscapes of older urban centers in the cities of the Global South. The alleged unimportance of greenfield smart cities in the Global North may be related to declining population growth and urban decline, combined with an emphasis on smart city projects that target urban renewal and gentrification of central city areas.

Taylor Shelton's sequel with Thomas Lodato (2019) on "actually existing smart citizens" illustrates more of the problems in Eurocentric neglect of what is going on in places like China and India. While the recent growth in research on smart citizens is significant and useful, we see a tendency to focus on both proposals and pilot projects, and criticism and counter pilot projects by activists to demonstrate alternatives more compatible with social justice and local democracy. However, most pilot projects are likely to be ephemeral. The trends among the tech giants are clearly toward oligopoly and standardization of templates and platforms. Privileged by network effects and strong intellectual property rights, they are extracting rates of return on equity among the highest in history (for large companies). Rather than start-ups being the motive force in the tech economy, the goal of many is enough success to be bought out (*Economist* 2018a, 57). For these reasons, local pilot projects, while perhaps "actually existing," may be unlikely to be actually surviving or influential in future directions taken by data-driven urban governance. What is happening in China should not be neglected because smart cities with Chinese characteristics are being governed in ways that are producing the world's biggest data pools, allowing the training of what will likely become the most powerful forms of deep machine learning. The urban governance monopolist of the future may be Alibaba rather than Google or IBM. Besides being Eurocentric and parochial, the widespread neglect of the trends in China limits our ability to chart alternative versions of governance driven by big data.

Transferring Chakrabarty's (2008) ideas about provincializing Europe to smart city research and China requires careful consideration of his original ideas and adapting them to the requirements for understanding smart urbanism. Doing so brings the approach into closer parallel with Andre Gunder Frank's idea of "reorienting" (1998). Frank's "reorient" thesis, alongside Pomeranz's (2000) work, has highlighted the significance of Asian economic development, particularly that of China, prior to the Industrial Revolution in the nineteenth century. Rather than viewing a long period of the prominence of the West, Frank (1998) has emphasized how the period of 1800–2000, during which European and North American countries were significantly more economically developed than China, may be understood as a temporary anomaly to the longer dominance of Asia, particularly China, in terms of economic development and centrality to the global economy. Pomeranz (2000) has likewise emphasized the long-term strength of the Chinese economy and the high level of economic development of many areas in China leading up to the Industrial Revolution.

The specific timing of when European economic development overtook that of China and the respective importance of different factors have been the subject of important debates following Frank (1998) and Pomeranz (2000). Arrighi (2007) builds on their work to pursue the goal of decentering European and North American, Global North frameworks. Emphasizing the historical contingency of Western economic and technological dominance, Arrighi questions whether the turn of the century and American economic and foreign policy weaknesses signal a larger crisis of American hegemony. In this way, the rise of the Chinese digital economy, with cooperation between large companies and the state accumulating massive shared data sets, may signal the beginning of a larger crisis of the domination of Silicon Valley and of conceptions of smart cities built on American and European models (see also Lee 2018).

For Dipesh Chakrabarty (2008), the problem was the need to decenter perspectives that saw Western historical and social theory as universal rather than as belonging to particular European traditions—that is, as being provincial in ways similar to Bengali history and tradition. His project challenged Eurocentrism by revealing that key elements of Europe's "parochial histories must have lingered into concepts that otherwise seemed to be meant for all"— like modernity, individualism, and progress (Chakrabarty 2008, xiii). To provincialize Europe was "to find out how and in what sense European ideas that were universal were also . . . drawn from very particular intellectual and historical traditions that could not claim any universal validity" (xiii). The result is that Europe is presented as the sovereign subject of all histories, including Indian or Chinese history, which become variations on the European master narrative. To repair this situation, he distinguishes between History 1, a universalistic history based on the logic of capital's development and expansion, and History 2s, which insert the undertow of singular and unique histories that serve to arrest, divert, and inflect the universal logic. All concrete histories, including the Western ones, are a combination of both "the universal logic of History 1 and the heterotemporal horizons of innumerable History 2s" (xvii). However, History 2s are not pasts separate from capital but "inhere in capital and yet interrupt and punctuate the run of capital's own logic" (64). A comparable tension can be seen in Wang's (2014) interpretation of Chinese political history as a continuing struggle between what he calls the "universal principle," based on reason and science and external to history, and the "heavenly principle," based on Confucian ideas of ritual as a way of reaching harmony between society and heaven.

What is absent in Chakrabarty's provincializing efforts but very apparent in contemporary Chinese rhetoric and practice is a provincialization of Europe/the West that reverses the positions, putting the West into a teleological account of decadence as it (potentially?) slips behind a resurgent China that aspires to making roads to the future, as part of the Chinese dream. While this counterhistory is particularly apparent in the field of smart urbanism, the aspirations are clear in a variety of technological fields, from high-speed rail to self-driving cars. We can usefully echo Chakrabarty's distinction between History 1 and History 2 here. Provincialization 1 is the deconstruction of universal history based on the logic behind capitalist development and its inevitable entanglement with specific and provincial histories, while Provincialization 2 not only interrupts and punctures the equation of Europe with universalist modernization but also reverses the positions of the West and China, projecting an emerging history of the future where China creates the new roads to be followed by others.

Provincialization 2, unlike Provincialization 1, does not so much challenge the universalist teleology of Eurocentric history as reinvigorate it with a new protagonist: China and the Communist party-state, or state capitalism rather than Europe and capital. The Xi Jinping regime appears to be reviving an older counter-capital teleology in which Chinese socialism can be seen as a "counter-reaction against European modernity and capitalism" and where the "seductive and corrupting attractions of capitalism had to be fought every day and everywhere" (Steinmüller 2013, 15), although now framed more as liberal democracy rather than capitalism in general. After a period in which the rise of reform China was seen as a variant of (Western) neoliberalism (Harvey 2007), we seem to be hearing echoes of an earlier era in which, after 1949, "New China seemed to offer a new world that could teach the old one, and it caught the imagination across the globe" (Bickers 2017, xxxix–xl). In this way, our Provincialization 2 shares features with Frank's argument that the world is returning to a past world system dominated by East Asia. In the next section, we briefly lay out why we see China as coming into the lead with AI and data-driven smart urbanism.

Big Data–Driven Urban Governance

Smart cities are best seen in a broader context of data-based urban governance. Governance, as opposed to government, emphasizes the attempt to steer an organization beset by forces it does not directly control, which is more the case for cities than for other levels of government. Like a ship on the ocean, responsiveness is crucial, and smart cities promise technological solutions as long as sufficient information is made available for real-time responses to volatile problems, like traffic congestion or financial risks. Governance networks "help cities manage the risks associated with innovation, unexpected events and contextual factors" (Han and Hawken 2018, 1). The strengths and weaknesses of Chinese cities in steering, though, are quite distinct from those of Western urban centers. Western smart cities "enact a blueprint of neoliberal urbanism and promote a form of neoliberal citizenship" (Cardullo and Kitchin 2019, 813) consistent with political limits on their ability to control markets or the commands of superior governments. By contrast, China has a mode of governance that uses market instruments but at the same time maintains state planning centrality (Wu 2018, 138). Chinese (explicit) smart city projects are dominated by central state projects and preferences, and the need of urban leaders to support these in order to further their careers, much more so than by the corporate dominance seen in Western cities (Curran and Smart 2021). However, the financial problems of Chinese cities induce them to promote smart city projects that generate real estate profits to support their property development growth regimes (Lin et al. 2019).

While many explicit smart city projects are disguised property plays or more plan than completed project, governance of cities based on big data is often more influenced by alliances between urban leaders and China's tech giants. Of particular importance in this regard for China are initiatives in AI and digital money. Mobile money systems like Alipay generate incredible amounts of geolocated data about movement, consumption, and their patterning. With fifty times more digital money used in China than in the United States (prior to COVID-19, which is spurring faster adoption in the United States) and minimal data-privacy restrictions, this data provides the world's deepest and richest pools of big data, essential for training AI for machine learning and deep learning, where the algorithm does not program procedures but sets goals to be achieved. However, a recent crackdown on China's tech giants, particularly Alibaba, is reducing their control over data and increasing the government's control, as well as state control over the corporations (*Economist* 2021). The urban model for this recent shift may be Xiong'an New Area, a new city one hundred kilometers south of Beijing. It has been seen as representing the state taking back control from the market and is leading a new state-led model of innovation, including in the digital realm, and could become an official blueprint and master model for smart urbanization (Noesselt 2020) with Chinese state characteristics. However, Alibaba has so far been central to its smart urbanization. Whether this shift can succeed in replacing the vitality of the private and semiprivate tech ecologies that have emerged remains to be seen (Stokols 2021).

The most relevant project for this chapter is the City Brain (*chengshi danao* 城市大脑) urban management platform, launched by the Hangzhou government with Alibaba Group in October 2016. This smart city project uses the AI technology of Alibaba Cloud for real-time analysis of the city, to automatically deploy public resources and improve urban operations. Experiments in one district for transportation management increased traffic efficiency by 11 percent. The geographical boundary of the project was then expanded to include other parts of the city. Implementation of the City Brain is possible due to the project's connection to government databases (Revell 2017). Combined with China's myriad of highly capable video cameras (the largest array in the world), the system can index all video footage to be searched quickly when needed. China is home to eight of the top ten cities in the world for surveillance cameras per capita, with London and Atlanta ranking sixth and tenth. Although the United States has the most CCTV cameras per capita, China has the most overall, and many more of them are capable of facial recognition. The top-ranking city in this group is the southwestern Chinese city of Chongqing (Feng 2019). Over five hundred cities in China have announced that they would contract with City Brain, as well as Kuala Lumpur and Macau (Naughton 2020). The network effects of

such rapid deployment of smart urbanist AI, and its attendant data generation, is very likely to put China into the lead in this field, if tech wars between
China and the West do not hobble it. However, it may also be under threat
from its own government. Possessing an important platform in its network-
ing technology, embattled Huawei has also developed smart city projects,
adopted in 160 cities in forty countries, leveraging its lead in 5G phone networks (Hu 2019). Given its increasing pressure from the United States and
reliance on Beijing, Huawei could be a more trusted partner for digital urban governance.

While hyperbole is intense in fields like AI and data-driven governance,
with hopes and fears of pervasive disruption, some acknowledge the disrup-
tive potential of new technologies but cautiously hold that there has been less
change than appears in the rhetoric from corporate and government proponents. There may, in fact, be less change than would be desirable, probably
because of the global tech giants themselves, which are extracting rates of
return on equity that are among the highest in history (for large companies).
These average 32 percent for the seven largest tech companies, close to historical cases of corporate dominance in terms of profits as a share of GDP:
the East India Company, Standard Oil, U.S. Steel, IBM, AT&T, and Microsoft
(*Economist* 2018c).

Today's oligopolists are said to be creating kill zones: fields that venture
capitalists "will not invest in because one of the big players may squeeze the
life out of startups or buy them out at a low price" (*Economist* 2018b, 4). Rather
than start-ups being the motivating force in the tech economy, the goal of
many is to be bought out by one of the giants (*Economist* 2018a, 57). This dynamic is particularly stark in China. Three companies—Chinese Baidu, Alibaba, and Tencent—account for 50 percent of domestic venture capital.
Ambition at start-ups has shrunk, while those who get support "expect to
profit from reams of data, logistic networks, payment gateways and technological support" (*Economist* 2018c, 54). The Chinese government benefits from
the existence of such oligopolies because it "makes the whole tech industry
easier to control" (*Economist* 2018a, 55).

China is trying to boost innovation and creativity through digital networks and "mass innovation" (*wanzhong chuangxin* 万众创新) while also
developing the world's best tools for controlling the social disruptions that
may follow in their wake, such as the Great Firewall (*fanghuo changcheng*
防火长城). Meanwhile, its tech giants expand, feeding from massive data
streams of highly connected Chinese consumers to produce cutting-edge

facial recognition and other AI systems. China's Alibaba, Baidu, and Tencent are intended to become national data champions (*Economist* 2018b). More so than anywhere else but the United States, where the corporations promoting smart cities tend to operate on a global basis, in China the corporations implementing national policies promoting smart cities are seen as national champions and are often deeply entangled with state-owned enterprises, ministries, and governmental agencies. In addition, the approaches to smart cities differ from those in Europe and North America because of (even) fewer protections for data privacy and restrictions on administrative actions (such as linking household registration ID with facial recognition systems and social credit scores), which intensify the surveillance capacities of Chinese governments at all scales. The Personal Information Protection Law, which came into effect on November 1, 2021, does appear to limit corporate use of data, however. The surveillance dimension is usually not explicit in the plans, so it has to be explored through information on other forms of big data collection and data-based administration of urban populations.

Informality and Smart City Projects

There are many implications of data-driven urban governance for society and distribution of risks and advantages, such as exclusion from mobility and loans for those ranked poorly by the emerging social credit system (Curran and Smart 2021), the labor market disadvantaging those without technological skills (Browne 2020), crime prevention (Wu, Sun, and Hu 2021), and the extent of citizen participation (Dameri et al. 2019). One area receiving considerable attention is the environment (Li et al. 2020), perhaps because many projects promoted as eco-cities have been rebranded as smart city initiatives. In a study of 152 Chinese cities, Yao, Huang, and Zhao (2020) found that smart city construction significantly improves eco-efficiency, particularly in smaller cities. Rather than survey these broader issues, we use informality as an extended example because it is usually neglected in smart city projects despite its practical importance, not just for the marginalized who are most likely to be negatively affected but also for fostering urban vitality and creativity. Informality regularly mediates between people and plans (Smart 2018) but is neglected in most smart city research (Smart, forthcoming). It also has the advantage of mapping on well to Chakrabarty's idea of

History 2 and thus complements the discussion of provincializing smart city research presented earlier.

Informality involves activities that do not conform to prevailing rules and regulations, but the goods and services are not themselves illegal—housing rather than heroin, for example. We suggest seeing informality as an important form of History 2 for smart urbanism. It is widely seen as the undesirable past of the smart city projected for the future. Messy and possibly disease-spreading street markets (of even more concern after the first outbreak of COVID-19), grubby and disorganized informally developed "urban villages," often undesired (even if needed) low-skilled migrants from rural areas with low *suzhi* (population quality)—these are implicitly or explicitly narrated as vestiges of a less civilized, less modern, and less "smart" past, which need to be transformed or removed to fit the new urban vision.

Proponents of smart cities beg the question of what makes a city smart and, in doing so, neglect forms of intelligence that do not involve sophisticated technology controlled by technical and corporate elites. For example, making traffic flow more smoothly in a sprawling, auto-dependent urban region is a very limited conceptualization of smartness. Cities can be "smarter" (if we mean anything other than the quantity of information and communication technology) in a variety of ways, including (1) citizen engagement, (2) low-tech but effective architectural and urban design, and (3) high technology (distributed cognition through studding cities with sensors used with big data analytics). Eradicating or formalizing informal practices with higher technology alternatives may not make a city smarter in a broader sense.

In many smart city projects in the Global South, urban informality is treated as an obstacle to modernization. Yet many studies show that informal practices are better than formal institutions at meeting many real needs of citizens (Smart 2020). Cities are frequently not effective at meeting the needs of low-income people. Urban or national policies often make things worse, as is clearly the case for most non-*hukou* migrants in China. Elitist smart city strategies that increase inequality are far from wise, since there is clear evidence that inequality is a major factor in the social determinants of health and other social problems and costs, creating pressure for government spending to correct problems that might have been prevented with less polarizing policies.

If informality can make it possible for people to achieve goals not met by existing institutions (employment, adequate food or shelter), this would seem to have the effect of increasing the responsiveness and intelligence of urban arrangements; clearly, informal governance makes some things better. If nothing else, neglect or active antagonism toward informality in smart city projects is problematic when we realize that more than half of the jobs in the world are informal. In some regions, this rate reaches at least 80 percent (Jutting and Laiglesia 2009, 13). If smart cities are to be more than islands of privilege and connectivity, we need to consider their impact on people involved in informal activities—that is, most (if not all) of the world's population. More than simply acknowledging a need to mitigate negative consequences due to the displacement of informality, more intelligent cities require thoughtful consideration of how to work effectively with informality—to harness its capacities rather than struggle to extinguish it.

Urban informality in cities of the Global South is often seen, if not always acknowledged, as one of the problems that need to be tamed or eradicated— vestiges of the past that take up valuable space, impede traffic, and create many of the problems that the strategies are intended to overcome. In this way, smart city projects in the postcolonial world are part of a long genealogy of urban policies that see slums, street markets, and informal transport as eyesores and threats to public safety, security, and morality. Modernist urban planning in all its forms has usually been directed at replacing such inefficient and destructive "traditional" urban forms (Bhattacharya and Sanyal 2011; Hoelscher 2016).

Most published research on Chinese smart city projects focuses on the technology, with little about how people are reacting and being affected. However, it seems likely that patterns identified in urban planning are generally continuing. Demolition is massively used for redevelopment: out of 10.2 million "forced evictions" worldwide from 1995 to 2005, 4.1 million occurred in China (Advisory Group on Forced Evictions 2007). The continued ubiquity of demolition has prompted descriptions of "bulldozer urbanism," characterized by "escalated demolition and displacement under the joint forces of a socialist state and neoliberal market" (Ling 2021, 1142; see also Chapter 2 in this volume). The predominant planning tendencies center around biases against migrants, informally developed "urban villages," and "low-end" populations and built environments in general, and promoting land use that meets central government targets, looks modern, and generates as much revenue as possible for real-estate-dependent local governments.

Commerce on the street and low-rise covered markets are not only seen as targets for redevelopment for "better uses" but also as uncivilized and backward ways that need to be modernized and cleaned up (Bell and

Loukaitou-Sideris 2014). Closings or more regulation of street markets may intensify in the context of the COVID-19 crisis, but there are also indications that they are receiving some official support as part of efforts to revitalize the post-pandemic economy (Song 2020). Informal labor recruitment, often through labor brokers, is central to the economy, and practices in the informal economy are often more innovative than generally thought (Sheikh 2019). The informal, unregistered labor force in China grew from 13.6 percent of the total labor force in 1990 to 32.8 percent in 2010, a total of 114 million. A survey in Guangzhou found that 8.8 percent of migrants engaged in street vending (while 92.5 percent of vendors are migrants); extrapolation estimates that there are 19.5 million urban street vendors in China and 407,000 in Guangzhou (Xue and Huang 2015). Efforts to reduce and regulate street vending were prompted by campaigns to create a "National Sanitary City" (*guojia weisheng chengshi* 国家卫生城市) (1990) and a "National Civilized City" (*quanguo wenming chengshi*全国文明城市) (1998), under which street vending became seen as a sign of "dirt, disorder and backwardness," becoming "an obstacle to current urban development" (Xue and Huang 2015, 161). However, a national goal of a harmonious society (*hexie shehui* 和谐社会) conflicted with these dynamics, emphasizing livelihoods and the avoidance of conflict. A policy emerged to try to reconcile these goals, a combination of accommodation/authorization and prohibition/oppression. Spatially, vending should be more tolerated in peripheral and less significant places, in pursuit of a "balance between the city appearance and people's livelihoods" (Xue and Huang 2015, 161).

While restrictions and efforts against informal activities and uses of urban space have existed for decades, what is new are the technologies available to intensify control. Surveillance is not new in the PRC, nor is it dependent on digital technology; it builds on old paper technologies that took modern form in the 1950s as household registration (*hukou*) (Smart and Smart 2001). This prevented people from moving from their native place without permission. After reforms began in 1979, movement became possible, but in most cases without transfer of household registration, creating a vast population of second-class citizens (Solinger 1999). For migrants—unable to access public housing and with private housing increasingly expensive—informally developed urban villages are a major source of housing. While governments often see this as a problem, the distinctive property rights of urban villages have "enabled indigenous villagers to build inexpensive housing units in order to start small rental businesses and . . . provide low-rent housing for migrants" (Sheng, Gu, and Wu 2019, 339). Partially because of their second-class citizenship, migrants have strong attachments to their enclaves, despite the often poor housing conditions, because informal social networks help them find jobs and access other needed help and resources (Sheng, Gu, and Wu 2019, 342). Demolishing these neighborhoods can have very damaging consequences for their livelihoods. Some cities, such as Shenzhen, appear to have a greater understanding of the contributions of urban villages, probably because their explosive growth rates could hardly have been sustained without such informal expansion of the housing supply.

Without local *hukou*, migrants are easily removed when they are considered problems, but they could go underground. However, avoiding detection is becoming harder in an environment of ubiquitous cameras, links to biometric ID cards, and the world's most effective facial recognition system. While household registration reform means that conversion is becoming easier in smaller cities and more welcoming ones (like Shenzhen and Chongqing), it has become harder in Shanghai and Beijing. This combination of bureaucracy and technology allows much greater control over everyday life, as can be seen in pilot projects that might be rolled out nationally if they are seen as successful.

Some urban management staff in Shenzhen use tablets to manage rental properties. Information for each household is collected, such as room number, identity card, arrival date, length of residence, household composition, and lease conditions. Shenzhen started an information system to manage migrants and rental properties in 2004, investing forty million yuan. By 2013, 10.2 million suites were recorded. In Guangzhou, strict control over rentals was deployed in one of the main areas of concentration for Africans, pushing them into other districts.

This is just one example of a shift described by Gong (2016): "In major cities and provinces, the surveillance is shifting from [*hukou*-based police management], which targets migrants' household identities, to spatial-oriented management targeting these migrants' rental housing" (Gong 2016, 1000). Multiple local authorities combine their forces to "shape panoptic spaces of rental housing while continuously developing various surveillance techniques in order to inspect, identify, and control migrants" (1000). Four main techniques are "partitioning, monitoring, digital entrance guarding, and local registration" (1000).

Since hundreds of millions of urban Chinese are reliant on informality, either for their income or for affordable housing, food, and services, smart urbanism biased against informal (backward) practices and equipped with the world's highest density of facial recognition enabled cameras and a nearly complete biometric database of citizens could be immensely destructive. While we still know too little about the social impact of Chinese smart city projects, if they follow the existing path of bulldozer urbanism and exclusionary practices targeting migrants and informality, the consequences could be dire. There is a strong need for incorporation of concerns about social harmony into the emerging forms of smart urbanism.

Conclusion

It is difficult to offer clear conclusions on a topic like this. Insufficient solid information on the implementation of smart city projects makes it hard to state what their social impacts have been. The still-emerging nature of the technologies of data-based urban governance means that their prospects, such as for increasing efficiency, sustainability, or inequality, are even more uncertain. The global confrontation of "Anglosphere v Sinosphere" (*Economist* 2019a, 19), and America's attempts to prevent Chinese technological progress, seen to be creating cybersecurity and economic threats, raises questions about whether City Brain will be allowed to compete in the West. This in turn raises questions about our Provincialization 2 argument on smart city research. If Chinese AI falters due to tech trade conflicts, the narrative of technological overtakes will lose one of its strongest claims to emerging supremacy. China still accounts for only one-tenth of dollars spent on IT in general, compared with four-tenths for America. However, the tech trade war may spur China to become more self-reliant, producing a globally divided technosphere, with countries bound into the Belt and Road likely to adopt Chinese technologies such as Huawei's 5G networks and Safe City technology. Chinese firms hold more than a third of 5G-related patent applications, with Huawei alone holding 15 percent of the world's total. Bans on its tech are threatening to turn the Internet of things (a core part of most smart city projects) into the "splinternet of things" or a "digital Berlin Wall" that will undermine many of the productivity gains promised by 5G (*Economist* 2019b).

All of this will have major, if still murky, consequences for China's urbanization and the ways in which its cities and its citizens change in the coming years and decades. And, as we have argued, those changes will have an outsize impact on urbanization globally, if only because so many of the countries where the urban population is exploding are becoming part of the "Sinosphere" and borrowing money to contract the provision of much needed infrastructure from China and its companies. Adam Segal (2018, 18) has aptly claimed that "Whatever Washington does, the future of cyberspace will be much less American and much more Chinese." The same is also very likely to apply to the future of the world's cities.

As strong as that claim might be, it might also be too limited. While we have emphasized data-based urban governance in this chapter, there is nothing inherently urban about the emerging AI management platforms. While cities are excellent test beds for developing and testing the technologies, because of their data density, their compactness, and the high stakes of urban problems, once perfected they should be able to be deployed on any scale, from the local to the global. Indeed, global climate change management or mitigation might be an ideal domain in which AI governance could achieve the greatest gains for humans and nonhumans alike. Regional integration of transport and economic collaboration has become increasingly important in Chinese urban governance and is likely to require sophisticated technology to manage efficiently and (hopefully) equitably.

The technological governance changes we have discussed are not neutral; rather, they have the potential to intensify risk inequalities in powerful ways. The already advantaged in terms of security and social legitimacy can exercise greater control over flows of people, while the informal, the marginal, the disadvantaged, and those who fall outside socially dominant valuations can see their disadvantages multiplied as facial recognition and social credit allocate them to "risky" categories and exclude them in various ways. The potential for inequalities to be multiplied are significant in view of the emergence of this governance modality driven by big data, statistical categorization, and prediction based on algorithms rather than democratically determined characteristics.

Our sketch for a History 2 of informality demonstrates the risks, and the possible losses, not only for those displaced but also for society as a whole. Informality offers a rich vein of innovation, but in most smart urbanist projects, it is either ignored or treated as an obstacle. While in India the tendency is to bypass spatial informality, in China bulldozer urbanism and massive displacement of "backward" populations and places has been much more easily accomplished, resulting in both greenfield and redevelopment forces of informality-displacing "smart" urbanism.

References

Advisory Group on Forced Evictions. 2007. *Forced Evictions—Towards Solutions? Second Report of the Advisory Group on Forced Evictions to the Executive Director of UN-HABITAT.* Nairobi: UN-HABITAT. https://unhabitat.org/forced-evictions-towards-solutions-second-report-of-the-advisory-group-on-forced-evictions-to-the

Arrighi, Giovanni. 2007. *Adam Smith in Beijing: Lineages of the Twenty-First Century.* New York: Verso.

Bell, Jonathan S., and Anastasia Loukaitou-Sideris. 2014. "Sidewalk Informality: An Examination of Street Vending Regulation in China." *International Planning Studies* 19 (3–4): 221–43.

Bhattacharya, Rajesh, and Kalyan Sanyal. 2011. "Bypassing the Squalor: New Towns, Immaterial Labour and Exclusion in Post-Colonial Urbanization." *Economic and Political Weekly* 46 (31): 41–48.

Bickers, Robert. 2017. *Out of China: How the Chinese Ended the Era of Western Domination.* Cambridge, MA: Harvard University Press.

Breslow, Harris. 2021. "The Smart City and the Containment of Informality: The Case of Dubai." *Urban Studies* 58 (3): 471–86.

Browne, Nigel J. W. 2020. "Regarding Smart Cities in China, the North and Emerging Economies—One Size Does Not Fit All." *Smart Cities* 3 (2): 186–201.

Cardullo, Paolo, and Rob Kitchin. 2019. "Smart Urbanism and Smart Citizenship: The Neoliberal Logic of 'Citizen-Focused' Smart Cities in Europe." *Environment and Planning C: Politics and Space* 37 (5): 813–30.

Chakrabarty, Dipesh. 1992. "Provincializing Europe: Postcoloniality and the Critique of History." *Cultural Studies* 6 (3): 337–57.

———. 2008. *Provincializing Europe: Postcolonial Thought and Historical Difference.* Princeton, NJ: Princeton University Press.

Chien, Shiu-Shen, and Max D. Woodworth. 2018. "China's Urban Speed Machine: The Politics of Speed and Time in a Period of Rapid Urban Growth." *International Journal of Urban and Regional Research* 42 (4): 723–37.

Curran, Dean, and Alan Smart. 2021. "Data-Driven Governance, Smart Urbanism and Risk-Class Inequalities: Security and Social Credit in China." *Urban Studies* 58 (3): 487–506.

Dameri, Renata Paola, Clara Benevolo, Eleonora Veglianti, and Yaya Li. 2019. "Understanding Smart Cities as a Glocal Strategy: A Comparison Between Italy and China." *Technological Forecasting and Social Change* 142 (May): 26–41.

Datta, Ayona. 2015. "New Urban Utopias of Postcolonial India: 'Entrepreneurial Urbanization' in Dholera Smart City, Gujarat." *Dialogues in Human Geography* 5 (1): 3–22.

———. 2018. "The Digital Turn in Postcolonial Urbanism: Smart Citizenship in the Making of India's 100 Smart Cities." *Transactions of the Institute of British Geographers* 43 (3): 405–19.

Economist. 2018a. "Into the Danger Zone." 2 June, 55–57.

———. 2018b. "Fixing the Internet." 28 June, 1–12.

———. 2018c. "History's Biggest Companies." 7 July, 56.

———. 2019a. "Anglosphere v Sinosphere." 22 November, 19.

———. 2019b. "Splinternet of Things." 22 November, 117–18.

———. 2020. "Creating the Coronopticon: Countries Are Using Apps and Data Networks to Keep Tabs on the Pandemic." 28 March. www.economist.com/briefing/2020/03/26/countries-are-using-apps-and-data-networks-to-keep-tabs-on-the-pandemic.

———. 2021. "An Uncertain New Path." 10 April, 57–60.

Feng, Coco. 2019. "China the Most Surveilled Nation? The US Has the Largest Number of CCTV Cameras per Capita." *South China Morning Post*, 9 December. www.scmp.com/tech/gear/article/3040974/china-most-surveilled-nation-us-has-largest-number-cctv-cameras-capita.

Frank, Andre Gunder. 1998. *Reorient: Global Economy in the Asian Age.* Berkeley: University of California Press.

Gong, Yue Ray. 2016. "Rental Housing Management as Surveillance of Chinese Rural Migrants: The Case of Hillside Compound in Dongguan." *Housing Studies* 31 (8): 998–1018.

Greenhalgh, Susan, and Zhang Li, eds. 2020. *Can Science and Technology Save China?* Ithaca: Cornell University Press.

Guo, Jie. 2019. "Promotion-Driven Local States and Governing Cities in Action—Re-Reading China's Urban Entrepreneurialism from a Local Perspective." *Urban Geography* 41 (2): 225–46.

Han, Hoon, and Scott Hawken. 2018. "Introduction: Innovation and Identity in Next-Generation Smart Cities." *City, Culture and Society* 12 (March): 1–4.

Harvey, David. 2007. *A Brief History of Neoliberalism.* New York: Oxford University Press.

Ho, Ezra. 2016. "Smart Subjects for a Smart Nation? Governing (Smart) Mentalities in Singapore." *Urban Studies* 54 (13): 3101–18.

Hoelscher, Kristian. 2016. "The Evolution of the Smart Cities Agenda in India." *International Area Studies Review* 19 (1): 28–44.

Hu, Richard. 2019. "The State of Smart Cities in China: The Case of Shenzhen." *Energies* 12 (22): 4375.

Jutting, Johannes, and Juan R. De Laiglesia, eds. 2009. *Is Informal Normal? Towards More and Better Jobs in Developing Countries.* Paris: OECD.

Kitchin, Rob. 2014. "The Real-Time City? Big Data and Smart Urbanism." *GeoJournal* 79 (1): 1–14.

Lee, Kai-Fu. 2018. *AI Superpowers: China, Silicon Valley, and the New World Order.* Boston: Houghton Mifflin Harcourt.

Li, Lei, Yilin Zheng, Shiming Zheng, and Huimin Ke. 2020. "The New Smart City Programme: Evaluating the Effect of the Internet of Energy on Air Quality in China." *Science of the Total Environment* 714 (April): 136380.

Lin, George C. S., Alan Smart, Xun Li, and Zhiyong Hu. 2019. "Financializing Chinese Cities: State–Capital Nexus and the Uneven Geography of Housing Speculation." *Area Development and Policy* 4 (4): 435–53.

Ling, Minhua. 2021. "Container Housing: Formal Informality and Deterritorialised Home-Making amid Bulldozer Urbanism in Shanghai." *Urban Studies* 58 (6): 1141–57.

McFarlane, Colin, and Ola Söderström. 2017. "On Alternative Smart Cities: From a Technology-Intensive to a Knowledge-Intensive Smart Urbanism." *City: Analysis of Urban Change, Theory, Action* 21 (3–4): 312–28.

Naughton, Barry. 2020. "Chinese Industrial Policy and the Digital Silk Road: The Case of Alibaba in Malaysia." *Asia Policy* 27 (1): 23–39.

Noesselt, Nele. 2020. "City Brains and Smart Urbanization: Regulating 'Sharing Economy' Innovation in China." *Journal of Chinese Governance* 5 (4): 546–67.

Pomeranz, Kenneth. 2000. *The Great Divergence*. Princeton, NJ: Princeton University Press.

Rao, Vyjayanthi. 2006. "Slum as Theory: The South/Asian City and Globalization." *International Journal of Urban and Regional Research* 30 (1): 225–32.

Revell, Timothy. 2017. "China's Super-Smart City Tracks Your Every Move." *New Scientist* 236 (3149): 7.

Robinson, Jennifer. 2013. *Ordinary Cities: Between Modernity and Development*. New York: Routledge.

Segal, Adam. 2018. "When China Rules the Web." *Foreign Affairs*, September/October. www .foreignaffairs.com/articles/china/2018-08-13/when-china-rules-web?fa_package =1122877.

Sheikh, Fayaz Ahmad. 2019. "Undervaluation of Informal Sector Innovations: Making a Case for Revisiting Methodology." *African Journal of Science, Technology, Innovation and Development* 20 (4): 505–12.

Shelton, Taylor, and Thomas Lodato. 2019. "Actually Existing Smart Citizens: Expertise and (Non)participation in the Making of the Smart City." *City: Analysis of Urban Change, Theory, Action* 23 (1): 35–52.

Shelton, Taylor, Matthew Zook, and Alan Wiig. 2015. "The 'Actually Existing Smart City.'" *Cambridge Journal of Regions, Economy and Society* 8 (1): 13–25.

Sheng, Mingjie, Chaolin Gu, and Weiping Wu. 2019. "To Move or to Stay in a Migrant Enclave in Beijing: The Role of Neighborhood Social Bonds." *Journal of Urban Affairs* 41 (3): 338–53.

Shi, Hongbo, Sang-Bing Tsai, Xiaowei Lin, and Tianyi Zhang. 2018. "How to Evaluate Smart Cities' Construction: A Comparison of Chinese Smart City Evaluation Methods Based on PSF." *Sustainability* 10 (37): 1–17.

Smart, Alan. 2018. "Ethnographic Perspectives on the Mediation of Informality Between People and Plans in Urbanising China." *Urban Studies* 55 (7): 1477–83.

———. 2020. "Squatter Housing." In *Oxford Research Encyclopedia of Anthropology*. Oxford: Oxford University Press.

———. Forthcoming. "Does Formalization Make a City Smarter? Towards Post-Elitist Smart Cities." In *Digital (In) Justice in the Smart City*, edited by Debra Mackinnon, Victoria Fast, and Ryan Burns. Toronto: University of Toronto Press.

Smart, Alan, and Josephine Smart. 2001. "Local Citizenship: Welfare Reform Urban/Rural Status, and Exclusion in China." *Environment and Planning A* 33 (10): 1853–69.

Solinger, Dorothy J. 1999. *Contesting Citizenship in Urban China: Peasant Migrants, the State, and the Logic of the Market*. Berkeley: University of California Press.

Song, Shangcong. 2020. "Street Stall Economy in China in the Post-COVID-19 Era: Dilemmas and Regulatory Suggestions." *Research in Globalization* 2 (December): 100030.

Steinmüller, Hans. 2013. *Communities of Complicity: Everyday Ethics in Rural China*. New York: Berghahn.

Stokols, Andrew. 2021. "Xiong'an: Designing a 'Modern Socialist City.'" *The Space Between*, 24 May. https://aspacebetween.substack.com/p/xiongan-how-to-design-a-modern -socialist.

Tan-Mullins, May, Ali Cheshmehzangi, Shiuh-Shen Chien, and Linjun Xie, eds. 2017. *Smart-Eco Cities in China: Trends and City Profiles 2016*. Exeter: University of Exeter (SMART-ECO Project).

Tang, Alice. 2015. "Questioning Smart Urbanism: Is Data-Driven Governance a Panacea?" *Chicago Policy Review*, 2 November. http://chicagopolicyreview.org/2015/11/02/questioning-smart-urbanism-is-data-driven-governance-a-panacea.

Wang, Hui. 2014. China from Empire to Nation-State. Cambridge, MA: Harvard University Press.

Watson, Vanessa. 2013. "African Urban Fantasies: Dreams or Nightmares?" *Environment and Urbanization* 26 (1): 213–31.

Wu, Fulong. 2018. "Planning Centrality, Market Instruments: Governing Chinese Urban Transformation Under State Entrepreneurialism." *Urban Studies* 55 (7): 1383–99.

Wu, Yuning, Ivan Y. Sun, and Rong Hu. 2021. "Cooperation with Police in China: Surveillance Cameras, Neighborhood Efficacy and Policing." *Social Science Quarterly* 102 (1): 433–53.

Wu, Yuzhe, Weiwen Zhang, Jiahui Shen, Zhibin Mo, and Yi Peng. 2018. "Smart City with Chinese Characteristics Against the Background of Big Data: Idea, Action and Risk." *Journal of Cleaner Production* 173:60–66.

Xue, Desheng, and Gengzhi Huang. 2015. "Informality and the State's Ambivalence in the Regulation of Street Vending in Transforming Guangzhou, China." *Geoforum* 62 (June): 156–65.

Yao, Tingting, Zelin Huang, and Wei Zhao. 2020. "Are Smart Cities More Ecologically Efficient? Evidence from China." *Sustainable Cities and Society* 60 (September): 102008.

CONTRIBUTORS

JUAN CHEN is a professor in the Department of Applied Social Sciences at the Hong Kong Polytechnic University. Her research focuses on migration, urbanization, and urban governance; health, mental health, and well-being; help seeking and service use; and social policy and the social service system.

DEAN CURRAN is an associate professor of sociology at the University of Calgary. He is the author of *Risk, Power, and Inequality in the 21st Century* (Palgrave), and he has previously published papers in multiple journals.

DEBORAH DAVIS is a professor emerita of sociology at Yale University. She also serves on the editorial board of the *China Quarterly*, the *China Review*, and the SAGE Modern China handbook series, and as a member of the Advisory Committee for the Universities Service Centre for China Studies at the Chinese University of Hong Kong. Her current research focuses on the impact of urbanization and migration on family relationships.

PEILEI FAN is a professor of urban and regional planning at Michigan State University (MSU) and directs the Center for Global Change and Earth Observations at MSU. She is the associate editor for *Landscape and Urban Planning*. Dr. Fan's research focuses on urban environment, innovation, and planning.

QIN GAO is a professor at Columbia University School of Social Work and Director of the Columbia China Center for Social Policy. Her research focuses on poverty, inequality, and social policy in China, and the social protection and well-being of rural-to-urban migrants in China and Asian immigrants in the United States.

PIERRE F. LANDRY is a professor of government and public administration at the Chinese University of Hong Kong and an affiliate of the Program of Governance and Local Development at the University of Gothenburg. His research centers on the study of local governments and public administration performance as they relate to the urban process—in China as well as in other developing countries—which he conducts through survey research.

SHI LI is a professor at the School of Public Affairs at Zhejiang University. He has published numerous books and articles on China's poverty, income distribution, and public policy, and he directs the China Household Income Project surveys.

SHIQI MA is a PhD candidate in the Government Department at Cornell University. Her research focuses on Chinese urban politics seen through the lens of state control and social stability. Shiqi's writing has been published or is forthcoming in the *China Quarterly* and the *Journal of Contemporary China*.

JUSTIN REMAIS is a professor and chair of environmental health sciences at the University of California, Berkeley. He leads global partners in interdisciplinary collaborations investigating the societal implications of a range of environmental and social changes spanning global climate change, pandemic disease, unplanned urbanization, and rising social inequality.

ALAN SMART is a professor emeritus in the Department of Anthropology and Archaeology at the University of Calgary, Canada. His research interests include political economy, housing, urban anthropology, anthropology of law, borders, zoonotic diseases, smart cities, and posthumanism. He is the author of *Making Room: Squatter Clearance in Hong Kong, The Shek Kip Mei Myth*, and *Posthumanism* (coauthor Josephine Smart).

SHIN BIN TAN is a postdoctoral research fellow at the Lee Kuan Yew School of Public Policy at the National University of Singapore. She obtained her PhD from the Department of Urban Studies and Planning at the Massachusetts Institute of Technology in 2021. Her research focuses on how built environment interventions and public policy can improve social and health equity.

JEREMY WALLACE is an associate professor in the Government Department at Cornell University. His research explores authoritarian politics with a focus on China, especially cities, statistics, and climate change. His first book, *Cities and Stability: Urbanization, Redistribution, and Regime Survival in China*, was published by Oxford University Press, and his second, *Seeking Truth and Hiding Facts: Ideology, Information, and Authoritarianism in China*, is forthcoming.

SARAH WILLIAMS is an associate professor of technology and urban planning at the Massachusetts Institute of Technology, where she is also Director of the Civic Data Design Lab and the Leventhal Center for Advanced Urbanism. Williams combines her training in computation and design to create communication strategies that expose urban policy issues to broad audiences and create civic change. She calls the process *Data Action*, which is also the name of her recent book, published by MIT Press.

BINBIN WU is an assistant professor at the Business School of Yangzhou University, whose main research area is labor force participation and social protection of migrant workers in China.

WEIPING WU is a professor in the Graduate School of Architecture, Planning and Preservation and Director of Urban Planning Program at Columbia University. She is the author and editor of eight books, including the second edition of *The Chinese City* (Routledge 2020). Her research interests include migration and urbanization, comparative urban development, and urban infrastructure.

GUIBIN XIONG is an associate professor of social work in the School of Sociology at the China University of Political Science and Law. His research focuses on forensic social work, community governance, criminology, dispute mediation, and urbanization.

WENFEI XU is a recent PhD graduate from the Urban Planning Program in the Graduate School of Architecture, Planning and Preservation at Columbia University. Her work focuses on historical socio-spatial segregation, quantitative methods, and neighborhood change in the United States.

absolute poverty, 116–19, 121, 126
administrative reclassification, 131–32
Advanced Spaceborne Thermal Emission
   and Reflection (ASTER), 170
aging, 3, 151–52, 163n2
air pollution, 6–7, 12, 25, 165–68, 172–78, 181,
   190, 193–94, 200; haze pollution, 172
Alibaba, 179, 205, 207, 211, 215–17
animal agriculture, 196
anomie, 149–54, 157–58, 161; social anomie,
   149, 152, 158
anthropogenic factors, 170–71
artificial intelligence (AI), 205–7, 209,
   214–17, 222–23

bank loan, 17, 19, 22, 25, 33. *See also*
   infrastructure financing
Beijing, 18, 21, 23–25, 38–40, 42–49, 51, 53,
   55–56, 56nn7–8; Beijing cough, 165
Belt and Road Initiative, 207. See also *yidai
   yilu*
big data, 10, 12, 53, 205–11, 214–15, 217–18,
   223; housing price data, 64
borrowing, 16–17, 19–22, 32
build-operate-transfer (BOT), 23
built environment, 1, 3, 18, 219

carbon emissions, 174, 176, 179–81
census administrative units, 63
central-local relations, 8, 42, 46, 55;
   central-local fiscal relation, 18; decentralization, 18–19, 26; local public finance, 19
Chengdu, 6, 24, 66, 70, 72–80, 82–83
China Family Panel Studies (CFPS), 93–95,
   99–101, 104, 107, 112nn4–8, 121, 124–25
China Household Income Project (CHIP),
   93–97, 99–101, 104, 106–7, 112n4–8, 117,
   121–22, 124–25

climate change, 2–3, 11, 39, 177, 198, 223
counterfactual analysis, 93, 100–101;
   counterfactual estimation, 99, 103
COVID-19, 3, 5, 10, 13, 127, 188, 196–97, 206,
   208–9, 215, 218, 220

Daxing, 38, 47, 49, 53
decentralized experimentation, 134
dementia, 149–54, 157–61; dementia patients,
   151
development, 1–2, 4–7, 9–13, 17–29, 40–42,
   44–46, 49, 55, 66–68, 72–73, 75, 78–83,
   111, 116–17, 131–32, 134, 137, 140, 143–45,
   149, 156, 162, 165–66, 168, 171–72, 174–77,
   179–82, 191, 197–200, 205–8, 210, 212–14,
   219–20, 224
development delay, 10–11, 198–99
dibao, 115, 118, 120–28
Dipesh Chakrabarty, 207, 212
Duncan coefficient, 95–100, 112n2

eco-cities, 217
e-commerce, 179
employment, 115, 120, 123–24, 126–27;
   employment status, 91, 94
energy use, 6, 171, 193–94
environment, 1, 3, 6, 13, 18, 22, 33, 68, 70–71,
   73, 84–85, 146, 152, 167, 176–77, 179–81,
   188–91, 194–96, 200, 210, 217, 219, 221;
   environmental change, 172, 179; rural
   environment, 194; urban environment,
   188–90, 195–96
Eurocentrism, 209, 212
eviction, 42, 48, 55

facial recognition, 205, 208, 215, 217,
   221–23
family care, 154, 162; caregiver, 150, 158

family consumption, 115, 120, 122–23
Fang.com, 64, 67, 69, 76, 81–83, 85n1

ghost cities, 18, 28–29
governance, 4–5, 8, 10, 13, 19, 24, 42–44, 50, 145, 199–200, 205–11, 214, 216–17, 219, 222–23; urban governance, 205–11, 216–17, 222–23; data-based governance, 206, 214; data-driven governance, 208–10, 214, 216; informal governance, 219; AI governance, 223; technological governance, 223
green gentrification, 178

health, 188–200; adverse health effects/impacts, 188, 200; population health, 189–90, 194, 198, 200; public health, 193, 196; urban health, 189, 192, 197
heat-island effect, 6. See also urban heat island (UHI)
household registration, 1, 56, 91, 111, 112n1, 116, 133, 217, 220–21. See also household registration system. See also hukou
household registration system, 1, 97, 133. See also hukou
hukou, 1, 8, 41, 43, 45, 56, 91–92, 99–101, 103–5, 107, 109–12, 116–18, 127, 133–34, 161, 218, 220–21; point-based system, 43; hukou reform, 133

image projects, 210
income disparity, 92
income inequality, 117, 119–20, 126
infectious disease, 188, 190, 195–97, 200–201
informality, 208–9, 217–19, 221–24; urban informality, 208, 218–19
infrastructure financing, 16, 21, 25, 27; bank loans, 17
in situ urbanization, 2, 33, 111, 131, 136
Internet of things, 11, 222

Jing-Jin-Ji coordination, 40, 43–46

land finance, 4, 6, 16, 18, 20, 25, 27, 32, 134. See also land financialization. See also land mortgage
land financialization, 6, 17. See also land finance
land-infrastructure-leverage, 17–18, 32–33

land lease/transfer, 17–18, 22, 24–27, 33; land lease revenue, 17
land mortgage, 17, 25. See also land financialization
land surface temperature, 170–71
local governance, 145
local government, 1, 5, 8, 17–21, 25–27, 32–33, 39–41, 43, 45, 48, 50, 79–80, 125, 127, 132–36, 144–45, 154, 156, 162, 163n3, 177, 219
local government financing vehicle (LGFV), 17–20; loans, 21–22, 24–26; Beijing Capital Group (BCG), 23–24; Shanghai Chengtou, 21–22; urban development investment corporation, 17

mass innovation (wanzhong chuangxin), 216
migration, 1, 44, 131, 151–52, 157, 188, 191, 199, 229–30; migrant workers, 39, 41, 43, 45, 51, 53
missing, 149–63, 163nn2–4
Moderate Resolution Imaging Spectroradiometer (MODIS), 168, 170–71
modifiable areal unit problem, 67

National New Comprehensive Urbanization Pilot Program, 136, 144
National New-Type Urbanization Plan, 131, 133–34, 146
NO_2, 177

older adults, 149–63, 163nn3–4

penghuqu (shantytown), 40, 43–44, 55–56, 56n3
people-oriented urbanization, 135, 146
pilot program, 134–37, 140–41, 143–45
$PM_{2.5}$, 166–68, 174, 178
population mobility, 156; population outflow, 8
poverty, 115–22, 124, 126–28; relative poverty, 116–17, 119, 121–22, 126; absolute poverty, 116–19, 121, 126; anti-poverty, 115, 120–22, 126; rural poverty, 115; urban poverty, 115–20, 126; income poverty, 115, 120–21, 126
provincialization, 213–14, 222

quality of life, 133, 145–46

real estate, 64, 67–68, 81–82
real estate online listings: online housing
   listing, 67, 81; resale listing, 67
recycle, 180
redevelopment, 39, 42, 44, 46, 55
reduce, 171, 179–80
regional variation, 131, 136, 140; regional
   disparities, 134, 140
reuse, 180
rural migrants, 91–112, 112nn1–3, 112n5; rural
   migrant workers, 91–112, 112nn1–3, 112n5

satellite imagery, 3, 12, 39–40, 49–53, 56n8,
   166
segregation, 61–67, 69–73, 75–76, 78–82, 84;
   residential segregation, 62–66, 69, 78–79,
   84; spatial segregation, 61, 63, 65–66, 69,
   71–73, 75–76, 78–80, 82, 84; socioeconomic segregation, 62, 64, 84
Shanghai, 18, 21–22, 25, 66, 70, 72–80, 82–83,
   85n2
Shenyang, 66, 70, 72–80, 82–83
shrinking cities, 4
smart cities, 206–12, 214, 217–19; greenfield
   smart cities, 210–11
social assistance, 122, 127; social assistance
   shelters, 154–63, 163n3
social protection, 152–54, 162
social safety net program, 126
social security, 92–94, 105–9, 111–12, 112n4
spatial concentration of affluence, 63, 80
spatial exposure index, 70
spatial inequality: spatial differentiation, 6,
   145; spatial disparities, 145; spatial
   division, 145
spatial information theory index, 70–72, 75,
   84
spatial isolation index, 70
street vending, 220
subjective well-being, 115, 120, 124–26

tech giants, 211, 214–16
transition, 2–3, 9–10, 13, 16, 18, 61–63, 78,
   91–92, 149, 166, 172, 174, 177, 190, 194, 198,
   206

transportation, 193–94, 197
typology, 150, 152, 154, 159

urban citizenship, 2
urban demolition, 38; Beijing 2017
   demolition, 39, 46, 53, 55; urban village
   demolition, 55
urban environmental problems, 165–66, 172,
   176–78, 180–81; urban environmental
   changes, 179
urban environmental transition, 166, 172,
   174
urban form and lifestyle, 1
urban green space, 165, 172–75, 177–79,
   181
urban heat island (UHI), 170–72, 176–77,
   181; surface urban heat island intensity
   (SUHII), 171. See also heat-island
   effect
urban infrastructure, 16–17, 21, 23
urbanization, 1–11, 13, 16, 18, 27, 33, 39–40,
   45, 63, 78, 115, 117–18, 131–36, 140, 144–46,
   150–51, 161, 165–66, 170, 172, 177, 181,
   188–95, 197–200
urban-rural unification, 127
urban spatial expansion, 3
urban sprawl, 18
urban village, 40–44, 46–47, 49–53, 55–56,
   56n8, 208, 218–21; informally developed
   urban villages, 218–20
urban welfare, 106, 133, 146

wage income: wage gap, 91–93, 100–101,
   103–5, 111; wage discrimination, 92, 101,
   104–5
water pollution, 192–93, 200
WeChat, 160, 179
welfare dependency, 115, 120, 123, 127
work support program, 126–27

Xi Jinping, 39, 44–45, 56n3, 182, 205,
   213

yidai yilu, 207. See also Belt and Road
   Initiative

CPSIA information can be obtained
at www.ICGtesting.com
Printed in the USA
JSHW061430120722
27850JS00003B/3